AMERICAN STUDIES – A MONOGRAPH SERIES
Volume 220

Edited on behalf
of the German Association
for American Studies by
REINHARD R. DOERRIES
GERHARD HOFFMANN
ALFRED HORNUNG

SUSANNE ROHR
MIRIAM STRUBE (Eds.)

Revisiting Pragmatism

William James in the New Millennium

Universitätsverlag
WINTER
Heidelberg

Bibliografische Information der Deutschen Nationalbibliothek
Die Deutsche Nationalbibliothek verzeichnet diese Publikation in der Deutschen Nationalbibliografie; detaillierte bibliografische Daten sind im Internet über *http://dnb.d-nb.de* abrufbar.

COVER:
Einbandabbildung von Tanja Reiffenrath und Miriam Strube unter Verwendung eines Fotos von William James (1894), Abdruck des Fotos mit freundlicher Genehmigung der Houghton Library, Harvard University.

ISBN 978-3-8253-6026-9

Imprimé en Allemagne · Printed in Germany
Druck: Memminger MedienCentrum, 87700 Memmingen

Gedruckt auf umweltfreundlichem, chlorfrei gebleichtem und alterungsbeständigem Papier

Den Verlag erreichen Sie im Internet unter:
www.winter-verlag.de

Acknowledgments

We wish to thank the Deutsche Forschungsgemeinschaft (DFG), the German Association for American Studies and the Embassy of the United States of America for their generous support of this project. Tanja Reiffenrath put a lot of time into editing and formatting the manuscript. Her efforts are highly appreciated, as are those of Ian Copestake, who also helped put the book into final shape.

List of Contents

‘Life is in the Transitions’: Revisiting William James’s Pragmatism

Susanne Rohr and Miriam Strube

Philosophic study means the habit of always seeing an alternative, of not taking the usual for granted, of making conventionalities fluid again, of imagining foreign states of mind.

William James

William James is not only one of the most significant American thinkers but also one of the fathers of the single uniquely American contribution to the history of philosophy: pragmatism. To us, the recent hundredth anniversary of his death therefore seemed like an appropriate occasion to reflect on his impact and to honor his innovative ideas. After all, the thinking of James and his pragmatist followers have become so powerful that they pervade American culture as a whole. Indeed, as James Kloppenberg rightly claims, “the ideas of philosophical pragmatism have spread so broadly through American culture that it has become almost impossible to identify the direct lines of their influence” (62). Nevertheless, in this volume we aim to trace numerous of James’s influences, some direct, some indirect, some older, some newer, some transitioning into the new millennium.

Furthermore, in a more general perspective, this collection explores the potential of pragmatism within an international context. Due to the powerful re-thinking of some of the established paradigms in an ever increasing flow of scholarly activity, towards the end of the twentieth century the academic scene in the United States initiated pragmatism’s keen revival in the so-called “pragmatist turn.” Yet, European humanities, including American Studies, have not taken up the discussion in equal measure. This comes as a surprise, given the fact that this American philosophy, in both of its versions as classical pragmatism and neo-pragmatism, offers us a wealth of ideas and perspectives that in our understanding has not received the amount of attention it deserves on the European scene. In Europe there is still a palpable reluctance to fully engage in a pragmatist discourse that would break new grounds and further new perspectives in a theoretical debate that still seems to be largely dominated by European traditions. Thus, we cannot but suspect that pragmatism in Europe is still – and has traditionally been for a long time – tacitly stigmatized as somehow parochial and unsophisticated, and, truth be told, as somehow too American in its orientation towards "practical results."[1] A very dated yet – it seems to us – still leading prejudice.

Thus, like it or not, it may be the Americans (again) who will point us into the right direction.[2] In an important study that came out in 2010, Joseph Margolis talks about "pragmatism's advantage" when he investigates the exchanges between pragmatism and continental movements in philosophy. Explaining this advantage, Margolis holds that he endorses pragmatism's "good sense in favoring the flux of history over fixity, invariance, universalisms of every sort, cognitive privilege, abstract truths" (xii).

This volume takes pragmatism's advantage as its starting point, inquiring into the role pragmatist thinking currently plays and could play in the future – not only in philosophy but also in Literary and Cultural Studies, in medical as well as historical discourses both in the United States and in Europe. Thus, this collection is neither meant as a simple introduction nor a mere interpretation of James's work. Rather, it is a revisiting; it sees itself – in James's spirit – as part of and inspiration to pragmatism's (ongoing) experimentation at the beginning of the twenty-first century. As such, we put emphasis on James's notion of pragmatism's procedural character, being first and foremost an attitude or way of approaching problems, more a set of methods than a set of doctrines. James cautions against relying uncritically on fixed truths. Indeed, he introduces "uncertainty into to the domain of legitimate intellectual inquiry" (Croce 224). He therefore repeatedly uses expres-

1 See, for example, James's well-known celebration of "*the attitude of looking away from first things, principles, 'categories,' supposed necessities; and of looking towards last things, fruits, consequences, facts*" (James, "What Pragmatism Means" 380; emphases in original).

2 We are here speaking for the new millennium, as we are aware of the complex and dynamic exchange: "When Habermas began to identify his widely influential theory of communicative action with the writings of American pragmatists [...] young American radicals were caught off-guard. They were surprised to learn that ideas they found compelling had roots in the unlikeliest of places, the supposedly anemic American intellectual tradition, which they had been taught by the political theorist Louis Hartz was all about property holding and thus bereft of radical ideas they could use. Now that Habermas and Bourdieu, among others, were declaring themselves good pragmatists and social democrats in the Deweyan tradition, more Americans decided it was time to begin investigating their forgotten heritage." (Kloppenberg 130)

sions such as "ongoing," "interaction" and "process." Focusing on activities rather than products, meaning, according to James, is located in the ongoing fabric of relations: "Any attempts to extrapolate a fixed meaning for other than functional purposes are denials of this process" (McDermott 36).

In this course of events, as James repeatedly points out in *Pragmatism*, man is creative, active, constructive:

> In our cognitive as well as in our active life, we are creative. We add, both to the subject and to the predicate part of reality. The world stands really malleable, waiting to receive its final touches at our hand." ("Pragmatism and Humanism" 456)

As the motto for our introduction beautifully makes clear, James treasured openness, as this includes imagined alternatives; his openness in fact is an open-endedness. With this volume we want to enliven and enhance this open-ended dialogue, the search for pragmatism's fruits, engaging fresh perspectives. In the spirit of William James, we see the following articles as part of pragmatism's ceaseless experimentation. Since James's philosophy calls for an ongoing, never-ending series of descriptions and diagnoses, each from a particular vantage point, never fully grasping, yet approximating reality, we have collected intriguing articles coming from a variety of disciplines, all of them devoted to approximating or re-imagining James's pragmatism. Due to this, there is no single perspective, only a pragmatic verification of shared experiences, no unity, only continuity, no universe, only an unfinished multiverse, charged with novelty and possibility. Therefore, as James would have it, we believe both in the present and the future of pragmatism. And belief, as is well known, is another of James's key aspects. Characterized by trust, affection and hope, James's belief can be placed midway between an arrogant certitude and a pessimistic nihilism.

As James wrote in *The Will to Believe:* "We must go on experiencing and thinking over our experience, for only thus can our opinions grow more true" (14). Similarly, with the volume of various voices, we want to think over James's ideas and the consequences of his philosophy, thereby becoming true – yes, more true – to his pragmatism.

In our first section we turn to pragmatism's foundations. Joseph Margolis opens the discussion by bridging pragmatism's original achievement with what to him seems pragmatism's best promise. He argues that while Peirce's and Dewey's versions of pragmatism should be read in terms of their Hegelian bent, James favored a very different third route, in order to consolidate his idea of an introspective method that relied on, but at the same time exceeded, the limits of mere phenomenology. Margolis further argues that the unity of pragmatism in its classic period lies with its descent from the main force of Hegel's correction of Kant and its own promise in advancing a possible rapprochement among all the principal descendant developments from that same source. Accordingly, he claims pragmatism as the only continuously viable American contribution to the naturalizing of Idealist themes, to abandoning *apriorism* and cognitive privilege. Pragmatism, to Margolis, has entrenched the inclusive primacy of the practical within the flux of history, within conceptual amplitude that admits the continuities of the empirical and the transcendental, and the factual and the normative, within the terms of the continuity of the animal and the specifically human.

In the next article, Joan Richardson reminds us that William James's pragmatism speaks prominently about religion, in fact one of James's main concerns, and that these relations have been forgotten and consciously or unconsciously blurred over time. Following the method of imaginative or playful reading of James's texts, Richardson experiences pragmatism as a "self-reflexive activity of imagination in its essential aesthetic function." Focusing on this function, Richardson then brings the poet of pragmatism, Wallace Stevens, into the game and discusses the references to William James's philosophy in Stevens's poems. In her reading, Richardson establishes a conversation that the poet was continuing with the philosopher over the question of how to redefine and preserve religious experience without metaphysics. To Richardson, this dialogue was also about James's and Stevens's ideas about the patterns of the mind's activity.

The next chapter analyzes the function of images in William James's thinking, images being the outstandingly significant rhetorical mode and argumentative method employed throughout by James to reveal and to think Being. In order to do so, Herwig Friedl elaborates, James defines images as verbal indicators of pre-conceptual awareness, of a *sense* of the event of beings coming into experiential presence. As he shows, James's philosophy privileges the imaginative, the visionary, and – by extension – the visual in the widest sense; the percept and the image over the word, the concept, the text, the *logos*. As Friedl's reading reveals, James's ontology is not a series of insights, of teachings, or a system of metaphysical statements, but rather a sequence of motions on a way, a leading of our imaging and thinking towards conceptualization and back again into primary awareness. James's thinking Being thus is a being on the way, a departure, a coming-forth and a return in ceaseless circular reiteration or a forever innovative renewal.

Heinz Ickstadt complements this section with his responses entering into a lively dialogue with both Joan Richardson's and Herwig Friedl's essays.

The second part of this collection turns to major concepts in James's work. In his essay, Helmut Pape tackles one of the central ideas (if not *the* key concept) of pragmatism's theoretical layout: James's understanding of truth. Notoriously misinterpreted on the European philosophical scene, James's theory of truth was arguably the most important factor for pragmatism's hostile reception in European philosophy. It was accused of voluntarism, subjectivism, relativism, or the destruction of truth and rationality. Pape is not concerned with examining the traditional discussions of the eternal nature of Truth in Western philosophy in comparison with pragmatism's concerns. He rather proposes to follow James and ask how to "comprehend the role of small, situational truths and the meaning for our life of both the value of and the psychodynamical force of truth." In other words, Pape wants to interrogate how everyday truths affect our mental development and interaction with each other. He furthermore explains the conditions of the individual acquisition of truth according to James.

Kai-Michael Hingst turns to a different key concept, namely James's idea of man and its impact on his philosophy, distinguishing it from concepts of other thinkers in order to show that James reflects the *conditio humana* in a particularly realistic manner and, therefore, neither underestimates human beings nor expects too much from them. As Hingst contends, in terms of the construction of concepts in general, pragmatism holds that human beings orient themselves by concrete consequences for their future life rather than by abstract conceptual frameworks; in terms of morals pragmatism grants human beings the opportunity to make their life worth living through what James calls meliorism, thus avoiding ethical nihilism as well as moralistic dogmatism; in terms of religion, pragmatism views religious experience as conceivably real and affirms the possibility of transcendence instead of prohibiting religious beliefs.

Ulf Schulenberg seeks to answer the question why, after decades of an unfavorable and critical reception, pragmatism saw its revival in the so-called "pragmatist turn." Which elements of its theoretical layout render pragmatism attractive to theoretical thinking after post-modernism? By discussing conflicting positions such as the view that pragmatism's strength lies precisely in its not offering a clear method, in its theoretical vagueness, or the opposing perspective that pragmatism can act as an instrument of social reform, Schulenberg shows that pragmatism embraces various approaches. Pragmatism's axiomatic openness, he argues, corresponds to both James's role as public philosopher as well as his idea of the "worldliness" of pragmatism. According to the latter concept, understanding the world means to creatively interpret it and to engage in the world of practice. The essay closes with a discussion of the possibilities James saw for the "strong poet" and the power of individual initiative to change the world of practice.

The third part revisits and reimagines James in an arena of cultural politics. In her essay, Patricia Rae continues and expands her project of exploring the correspondences between James's concepts of truth and verification and the "tensional structure" of modernist poetry, most notably that written by Ezra Pound and Wallace Stevens. In both the processes of pragmatist truth-making and interacting with modernist poetry, Rae claims, certain patterns of provisional truths become discernible in the flux of experience. In her contribution to this collection, Rae now extends the scope of this project by considering modernist prose as well. In discussing George Orwell's and William James's reasoning about truth, Rae establishes Orwell as a "Jamesian modernist" and "public philosopher." Both Orwell and James, Rae writes, want to "unstiffen" categories in light of the evidence of experience.

Miriam Strube turns more explicitly to cultural politics. In her article, she explores pragmatism's potential to be useful for critical race theories. She shows how particular interpretations of pragmatism can help theorize race and ethnicity in sophisticated ways that surpass approaches that are either essentialist or color-blind. Strube argues that black thinkers in the pragmatist tradition such as Alain Locke, W.E.B. DuBois or Cornel West enrich classical pragmatism with an important dimension traditionally neglected by white pragmatists, namely the discourse on racial domination and empowerment. Finally, Strube shows how Paula Moya, while not an explicit or self-declared follower of pragmatism, can be placed in the same tradition of critical thinking with her concept of "doing difference differently" that brings the concepts of identity, knowledge, and race in a pragmatist interplay.

Georg Schiller also explores intersections between pragmatism and ethnicity, focusing on the connection between James's concept of radical empiricism and particular forms of lived experience such as indigenous knowledge. Native American thinking and American pragmatism share surprising correspondences, Schiller contends, such as the emphasis on cross-cultural learning or on feeling reality rather than understanding it in cognitive acts. He thus proposes to use James's deliberations on lived or pure experience as a bridge towards a better understanding of indigenous rituals and perspectives. James's concepts of the dissolution of the self and his portrayal of the mystical experience as an emotional insight are of particular interest in this regard.

The book's final section raises questions in current debates within politics, ethics and the sciences. Trygve Throntveit characterizes president Barack Obama as a pragmatist, albeit in practice as an imperfect one. According to James, however, there is no other kind, as the idea of imperfection is what defines pragmatist theory at its core, recognizing "both human idealism and human fallibility as preconditions of an eternally improvable world." Thus, if pragmatism means doing what works, Throntveit argues, and if it means making informed decisions and judging ideas and acts by consequences, not ideological origins, then Obama's politics can be called pragmatist. By way of a critical examination of Obama's 2006 book *The Audacity of Hope*, Throntveit unfolds what he sees as the pragmatist dimension of Obama's political philosophy and he asks why, if Obama's views echo important traditions from America's past, they come as a "revelation" or surprise to many Americans today.

Andrew Flescher's article tackles another of James's key concepts, that of overbelief. He sees hope as a functioning example of the Jamesian concept of overbelief, arguing that in believing one actually has the capacity to impact the "truth" of the believed thing in question. Approaching James from the perspective of medical humanities, Flescher unravels the effect of hope on the hoper's own recovery from illness and injury, thus extending James's notion from the *Will to Believe* that faith in a fact can help to create that fact. However, Flescher carefully points to the difference between overbelief and delusion or false hope, and furthermore to the fact that this difference manifests itself precisely in the pragmatic 'fruits' borne out of faith in a future, the actuality of which no one yet has the objective insight to dispute.

Robert Main also approaches James by looking at ethics, specifically environmental ethics and their connection to philosophical naturalism. He argues that the central questions of both environmental ethics and philosophical naturalism require abandoning the traditional disjunction between the 'natural' and the 'artificial' (along with corollary disjunctions such as 'nature' and 'culture,' *'physis'* and *'nomos,'* etc.) in favor of a model that views people, their culture, practices and productions as 'natural artifacts,' *continuous* with 'non-human' nature. As Main claims, pragmatic naturalism offers a promising way to escape the dichotomy between the natural and the artificial, in a manner that also enables a new approach to environmental problems. What this means for environmental ethics and policy is a pragmatist middle way between preservation and used-based valuations of the natural world.

Michael Anacker explores a current debate in the philosophy of science. In his article he shows that it is through the debate on scientific realism and instrumentalism that the underdetermination thesis has recently reappeared on the philosophical agenda. In the context of this debate Anacker presents a new argument, namely that both discussions, the old and the new one, miss an important point about underdetermination: In discussing the metaphysical implications of scientific theories and concepts, they fall short of explaining the role these very concepts play within the scientific progress. In turning to James, above all his *Principles of Psychology*, Anacker argues that underdetermination is not an effect of the symbolic nature of theories, but rather a central step within the scientific process, as it is the result of successful research. Consequently, the pragmatic change of perspective allows us to see science as the practice of research. It furthermore may also help us to understand the dynamics of theoretical changes within the scientific deep-structure as a part of a continuous process of empirical research of reality in order to serve our purposes, needs, and interests.

Works Cited

Croce, Paul. *Science and Religion in the Era of William James: Eclipse of Certainty, 1820-1880*. Chapel Hill: U of Carolina P, 1995.

James, William. "Pragmatism and Humanism." *The Writings of William James: A Comprehensive Edition.* Ed. John J. McDermott. New York: Random House, 1967. 449-461.

—. "What Pragmatism Means." *The Writings of William James: A Comprehensive Edition.* Ed. John J. McDermott. New York: Random House, 1967. 376-390.

Kloppenberg, James. *Reading Obama: Dreams, Hopes, and the American Political Tradition.* Princeton: Princeton UP, 2010.

Margolis, Joseph. *Pragmatism's Advantage: American and European Philosophy at the End of the Twentieth Century*. Stanford: Stanford UP, 2010.

McDermott, John. *The Culture of Experience: Philosophical Essays in the American Grain.* New York: New York UP, 1976.

WILLIAM JAMES: FOUNDATIONS

Reclaiming the Pragmatists: This Time, a Piece of William James

Joseph Margolis

I have a reflection for you regarding William James's *Principles of Psychology*. But may I postpone it for a bit to introduce myself with a small clutch of memories and a confession that may lend color to what I have to say. In fact, I can't quite separate the first from the second, which bears on my remarks.

I completed my doctorate at Columbia University, in 1953, when pragmatism was already pronounced moribund. I had attended John Dewey's final lecture, several years earlier, on the occasion of his 90th birthday. He was in excellent form, appealingly committed to a settled vision, steady and assured. But the movement he'd championed seemed to have vanished beneath his feet. The Columbia naturalists had become increasingly impatient anti-pragmatists, though the Department manfully contrived an air that exhaled nothing contrary to pragmatism's continuing primacy in a wayward land. When I left New York to start my own career, there was hardly a niche in academic America where pragmatism might claim an important stronghold. Charles Sanders Peirce remained little more than an honored name trotted out for some uncomprehending pieties; and James, who was credited with rescuing pragmatism from its first oblivion some twenty years after Peirce's pioneer papers first appeared in print, and who was himself immensely successful as a psychologist and pragmatist in his own right, came to be regarded, at least locally, as an unreliable, lightweight, second-tier companion to both Peirce and Dewey. (I'm speaking of appearances here.)

There was no definable common program to collect the classic figures, though it was never denied that the three of them belonged together as pragmatists. Each owed his reputation to undertakings the others never shared. Peirce remained essentially a mathematically-minded German Idealist mysteriously dropped into America. Dewey was a passionate liberal apart from his philosophical claims, a social critic and educational innovator whose systematic writings gradually afforded a passably pertinent but hopelessly dull defense of his many causes. James risked being used up by the unfinished, almost unmanageable invention of a terribly cluttered, possibly misconceived science of psychology that was poised to gain its promised unity by deliberately breaching the boundaries and sewing up the mismatched fringes of established disciplines expected to contribute to the executive vision of what James came to call "the self of selves" – somewhere between the uncertain questions of the American philosophical academy and the fractious loyalties of a would-be nascent psychology.

The science of James's *Principles* was never a system, and James never pretended that his philosophical forays could be counted on to yield a system to match even the scattered system of his psychology. Through it all, for about forty years until Dewey's death, the sum of these penny complaints against the novelty of his new science (which still seems worth recovering in, say, clinical and self-educative contexts) nagged also at pragmatism's *bona fides* and were never rightly stilled. In fact, psychology turned functional and then increasingly behaviorist (at Harvard) and began to lose the introspective focus James brought back to the United States from his studies with Wilhelm Wundt in Germany. An introspective strategy is indeed the nerve of James's *Principles* and very possibly the least understood feature of his original contributions: it's plainly missed, for instance, by Ludwig Wittgenstein, Edmund Husserl, and John Dewey.

The truth is, pragmatism's classic phase came to a close before it produced a perceptive picture of its own achievement – and a future that could be of interest to more than local partisans. It needed a second provocation to find its shared strength; and when that provocation appeared (in a distinctly minor dispute between Richard Rorty and Hilary Putnam), it inadvertently conveyed such a clear sense of a more general malaise in Eurocentric philosophy at large that it had no difficulty in finding its own advantage: that is, under one guise at least, the dawning significance of its having pragmatized Georg Wilhelm Friedrich Hegel's critique of Immanuel Kant and naturalized or Darwinized Idealism – all without quite grasping the inner congruity of the various parts of its collective undertaking under that description.

By the 1950s, American philosophy witnessed the incipience of a new version of an older analytic commitment ready to replace the failing fortunes of the unity of science program and the dimmed memories of logical positivism, which found its own new prospect in the eclipse of figures like Bertrand Russell, Rudolf Carnap, Hans Reichenbach, Carl Gustav Hempel, the Wittgenstein of the *Tractatus*. It came to rest of course in the canny economies packaged by W.V. Quine and Quine's associates. Quine displaced Carnap at a stroke with the publication of

"Two Dogmas" and, by 1960, assumed without significant resistance the effective leadership of Anglo-American analytic philosophy (at least as viewed from the American side).

Quine dismissed nearly all the most strenuous undertakings of the analytic movements of the 20s and 30s, required little in the way of loyalty beyond a soft adherence to a Fregean-like attitude toward the analysis of language (*sans* logicism), and therefore saw no purpose in resurrecting any of the familiar, thoroughly exhausted complaints against the supposed inadequacies of natural language. In 1968, Quine gave his John Dewey lectures at Columbia and acknowledged that he had, in 1931, during his own graduate student days, attended Dewey's William James lectures at Harvard. He added that he'd been directly influenced by Dewey's pragmatism – one supposes, favorably. It smoothed the acceptance of a rather neat joke: he co-opted Dewey as a more or less faithful behaviorist – a companion, say, to himself and B. F. Skinner! But the reductionists and scientistically-minded analysts of the second half of the last century were entirely content to work within the terms of the official stalemate Quine had clearly fashioned, even where they ventured beyond Quine's own uncertain vision.

Truth to tell, late pragmatism had failed for decades to bother to remain competitive with the best forces of the newer or established movements of the day, both in America and Europe. Although, in my own opinion, it was always pragmatism's subterranean attraction to the main lines of Hegel's critique of Kant, however muted, textually inexplicit, and difficult to decode it always was, that finally defined the secret strength (ignored or condemned by the new as well as the older analysts) and that confirmed its being at least as nimble and resourceful as any other of the going philosophical sects. So that when the minor skirmish between Rorty and Putnam surfaced during the last decades of the last century, pragmatism simply roared back into prominence with an unbelievable energy no one could have anticipated.

I think it's true that its new career has almost nothing to do with the chance spark struck by Rorty and Putnam's quarrel: it answers rather to the philosophical vacuum of the post-War years of Eurocentric philosophy, which, I would argue, were almost entirely inspired by the need to redefine the holism of post-Kantian and post-Hegelian thought. Quine's lax revival of an ideal language faltered visibly. Edmund Husserl and Martin Heidegger never achieved more than a token recognition in the United States before and shortly after World War II. What, however, proved surprising about pragmatism's revival was the sheer ardor with which it was welcomed and restored worldwide. As I read the event, pragmatism signifies an answer to diverse appraisals of Eurocentric stalemate: that is, the promise of a breakthrough. It can no longer be identified as a form of homage to a merely parochial American product and, therefore, it cannot be expected to adhere to any unique, agreed-upon direction.

Accordingly, I found myself obliged, in the 1950s, to abandon the pragmatist idiom in order to master the seeming precision of analytic practices; although quite apart from its scientistic tendencies, American analytic philosophy was always disconcertingly marked by an extreme indifference to the contextlessness and constancies of ideal languages. But, of course, that is precisely what pragmatism and the precursors of contemporary continental philosophy have always shunned: the loss of the primacy of practical and existential life, the sane institutions of a gifted human self under the condition of evolving experience and history. That's to say: the loss of the seminal orientation of the new beginnings of Eurocentric philosophy in the Idealist – preeminently, the Hegelian – reinterpretation of Kant's radical subject-centered world. (The pragmatists Darwinized that conception and the strongest continental movements tended to remain suspicious of naturalism itself.)

Seen in these terms, the entire purpose of James's *Principles of Psychology* and the hybrid birth of his new science at Harvard was already somewhat 'Hegelian' though hardly perceived to be – in a sense not altogether unlike the sense in which the Wittgenstein of the *Investigations* and the T.S. Kuhn of the *Structure of Scientific Revolutions* are also distantly 'Hegelian.' There's every reason to believe that neither Wittgenstein nor Kuhn was well-informed about Hegel's undertakings. But then, it may be not unfairly said that neither James nor Peirce had an adequate grasp of Hegel's purpose or running argument.

Consider the following excerpt from *Principles*:

> [T]he 'integration' of a thousand psychic units must be either just the units over again, simply rebaptized, or else something real, but then other than and additional to those units; that if a certain existing fact is that of a thousand feelings, it cannot at the same time be that of one feeling; for the essence of the feeling is to be felt, and as a psychic existent *feels*, so it must *be*. […] These assumptions are what the monists will seek to undermine. The Hegelizers amongst them will take high ground at once, and say that the glory and beauty of the psychic life is that […] it is just because the facts we are considering *are* facts of the self that they are both one and many at the same time. With this intellectual temper I confess that I cannot contend. […] So I leave this school to its devices. (165)

This is surely pure James, the James of the new psychology. But isn't it also, obviously, an empiricist rephrasing of selected elements of Hegel's *Phenomenology*, reflecting James's, but not Hegel's, preference for an earlier analytic phase of what James calls introspection: which grounds the work of the later synthetic phase of dialectical reason continually collecting ('sublating') what emerges from the other? (What James says here sounds better, directed against Josiah Royce than against Hegel.)

For his part, Peirce was able (quite remarkably) to anticipate by spare intuition – what he would later learn (under Royce's instruction) – had already been more floridly integrated by Hegel himself. In much the same sense, James was never entirely clear about the Hegelian aspects of the so-called 'scientific' and 'spiritualist' perspectives of figures like Herrmann von Helmholtz, Wundt, and Herrmann Lotze, whose views he cobbled in various ways, from time to time, for some advantage, in lobbying for Harvard's support of the new discipline (psychology) viewed as a benign conjunction of disparate parts. The concatenation proved to be an alternative to the Hegelian option, expressed in the broadly 'empiricist' idiom James favored, itself a variant of the larger idiom pragmatism applied in naturalizing Hegel's Idealism. What we now need is a clearer sense of what James meant by "introspection."

I have, it turns out, already sidled into the space of my intended reflection on James. I need a word more in general about bridging pragmatism's original achievement and what now seems its best promise, in order, precisely, to capture something of James's contribution. I'm drawn to the gathering verdict that, although Peirce's and Dewey's versions of pragmatism should be read in terms of their Hegelian bent (though they don't draw on Hegel in the same way and though they oppose Hegel for different reasons) – Peirce, in order to articulate what he means by Firstness, Secondness, and Thirdness within the bounds of his fallibilism and phenomenology; Dewey, in order to articulate his instrumentalist reading of Peirce's pragmatic maxim – James favored a very different third route, in order to consolidate his idea of an introspective method that relied on but exceeded the limits of mere phenomenology, bracketed as far as possible from philosophy, but not from naturalism.

The picture is not entirely accurate. First, because James subscribes to something like Peirce's pragmatic maxim, though it makes no appearance in *Principles*. Second, because Hegel was bent on co-opting the empiricists. Third, because (as we have just seen) James misreads the affinity between Hegel's phenomenology and his own treatment of mental events. Fourth, because he would certainly have benefited from a close reading of Hegel's treatment of thought with regard to the analysis of feeling and sensory perception. And, fifth, because, both in his primary undertaking as a psychologist and philosopher and in coming to terms with Hegel's more than passing relevance, James would have shared more explicitly a larger division of labor with Peirce and Dewey, which might then have yielded a more perspicuous reading of pragmatism as a commanding continuation of the original intuition that runs from Kant to Hegel. Pragmatism's best prospects, I believe, still run along these lines.

My thought is that the unity of pragmatism in its classic period lies with its descent from the main force of Hegel's correction of Kant and its own promise in advancing a possible rapprochement among all the principal descendant developments from that same source. Neither of these suggestions is quite standard. But pragmatism is the only continuously viable American contribution to the naturalizing of Idealist themes; to abandoning apriorism and cognitive privilege; entrenching the inclusive primacy of the practical within the flux of history, within a conceptual amplitude that admits the continuities of the empirical and the transcendental, and the factual and the normative, within the terms of the continuity of the animal and specifically human, and within the continuum of finite and infinite inquiry. American pragmatism is also committed to searching out the leanest legitimative grounds for science and morality that concedes at the start the indissoluble contribution of the subjective and objective sides of experience and the constructivist standing of every form of realism and objectivity. This is indeed the genealogical fuse of James's introspective psychology.

I hazard the thought that it's the promise of pragmatism's intuition (along the lines sketched) that explains its resurgence: the suddenness of all that, I suppose, is in some way due to an opportunistic use of the chance skirmish between Rorty and Putnam. But its new importance also spells the end of its parochial career. This is already clear in the recent reception of Peirce and Dewey. Peirce, of course, is closest to the post-Kantian Idealists. His conception of fallibilism and infinite inquiry is more than merely contrived: it's presciently convergent, for instance, with Ernst Cassirer's important analysis of the symbolic role of the notion of a "physical object" as "the idea of 'limit'" in the natural sciences. Both Peirce and Cassirer are Hegelianized Kantians here: but unlike Cassirer, Peirce is an unqualifiedly naturalized Idealist – I know of no one quite comparable. Peirce's example shows how pragmatism may be effectively pursued along more empiricist lines, without explicit

Hegelian concessions of any kind, by theorists as interesting as Ian Hacking, Nancy Cartwright, and Kuhn.

Dewey erases his original Idealist idiom and renders his fluxive themes in instrumentalist terms: their application to the sciences is no more than programmatic, often in fact terribly vague. Dewey's better skills lie, rather, with a pragmatist reading of the continuity of the factual and the normative (particularly, with the moral and valuational), which was never more than perfunctorily aired by Peirce – and resisted in James's account of his introspective discipline. One has only to compare Dewey with Jürgen Habermas: Habermas's difficulty in abandoning his Kantian universalism betrays his retrograde intent. But what is more intriguing for our present purpose is the sense in which James's sanguine attraction to the empiricists, expressed pragmatically, is certainly more congruent with the main thrust of Peirce's and Dewey's Hegelian tendencies than his own dismissal of Hegel suggests. I take that to begin to limn both the deep diversity of the original pragmatists and the deeper unity of their still-scattered program.

I'm persuaded that James was mistaken in his neglect of Hegel. If Hilary Putnam was justified (I think he was) in construing James's image of "the trail of the human serpent" as a neo-Kantian sign, then it's hardly farfetched to see James yielding in the direction of Hegelian themes, particularly those regarding the initial data of the *Phenomenology*. James always made his own way intuitively – not always perspicuously – in attempting to reconcile his sprawling thoughts about discrete feelings and perceptions, "the stream of thought," and the ubiquity of the self. The force of James's *Principles* lies, I think, with working out a schema for managing all these notions coherently.

Everyone says that James influenced both Wittgenstein and Husserl. It's true, of course, but both Wittgenstein and Husserl misjudged James's dawning comprehension of his own labor. He was not primarily interested in the "grammar" (or "philosophical grammar") of pains, emotions, feelings, sensations, perceptions, and transient thoughts: he seems genuinely naïve about all that.

Wittgenstein makes some stunning advances, of course, along these lines in his own extended reflections on psychology – largely at James's expense. But when James unequivocally affirms in the famous chapter on "the stream of thought":

> The only states of consciousness that we naturally deal with are found in personal consciousness, minds, selves, concrete particular I's and you's.
> Each of these minds keeps its own thoughts to itself [...]. Absolute insulation, irreducible pluralism, is the law. It seems as if the elementary psychic fact

> were not *thought* or *this thought* or *that thought*, but *my thought*, every thought, every thought being *owned.* (221)

James combines a 'grammatical' rule that anticipates Peter Strawson, goes against the extreme empiricists, *and* isolates the essential methodological constraint on the limits of rigor possible in his own introspective psychology. Wittgenstein, whom I greatly admire, simply misunderstood James's project here – and, of course, its viability. By the same token, James obviously favored 'the natural attitude' Husserl meant to supersede in his own supposed phenomenological recovery of what was alienated by the natural attitude itself. James couldn't have been a proto-phenomenologist of Husserl's sort, though he was a phenomenologist of a sort akin to that of Hegel's and Peirce's taste. He was his own man in this, however, since he favored the somewhat makeshift rigor of thought's hewing to a pragmatist account of the causal regularities of practical life that justify our tolerating the sheer transience of the stream of thought itself. Here, too, James asserts unqualifiedly: "No psychology can question the existence of personal selves" (221). It's still an open question how much rigor can be counted on within James's discipline. Certainly his insight regarding the emotions shows its best prospects: it hovers between an introspective psychology in search of causal recipes that may be intelligently applied along pragmatic lines and a phenomenology that must be grasped but need never be relied on as more than transient or provisional. Nevertheless, its larger contribution reminds us of the ineliminable importance of first-person reports of inner mental life. It shows the way to a full-service naturalism of the pragmatist stripe.

Works Cited

James, William. *The Principles of Psychology.* Boston: Harvard UP, 1983.

Pragmatism … *She Widens the Field of Search for God*

Joan Richardson

Near the close of "What Pragmatism Means," the second chapter of *Pragmatism*, William James describes as a heroine the method he unfolds in the pages comprising what is effectively a script for the performance of the eight lectures he will later collect as his 1907 volume. This personification is telling, pregnant with the meaning he is at pains to demonstrate. After noting that his Italian colleague, Giovanni Papini, had commented that pragmatism "'unstiffens' our theories," James continues:

> She has in fact no prejudices whatever, no obstructive dogmas, no rigid canons of what shall count as proof. She is completely genial. She will entertain any hypothesis, she will consider any evidence […].
>
> In short, she widens the field of search for God. Rationalism sticks to logic and the empyrean. Empiricism sticks to the external senses. Pragmatism is willing to take anything, to follow either logic or the senses and to count the humblest and most personal experiences. She will count mystical experiences if they have practical consequences. She will take a God who lives in the very dirt of private fact—if that should seem a likely place to find him.
>
> Her only test of probable truth is what works best in the way of leading us, what fits every part of life best and combines with the collectivity of experience's demands, nothing being omitted. If theological ideas should do this, if the notion of God, in particular, should prove to do it, how could pragmatism deny God's existence? She could see no meaning in treating as 'not true' a notion that was pragmatically so successful. What other kind of truth could there be for her, than all this agreement with concrete reality?
>
> In my last lecture, I shall return again to the relations of pragmatism with religion. But you see already how democratic she is. Her manners are as various and flexible, her resources as rich and endless, and her conclusions as friendly as those of mother nature. (James, *Pragmatism* 522)

I shall have occasion before closing to consider James's conclusions in that last lecture/chapter, but first it is important to remark starkly and simply that the centrality of religion to his notion of pragmatism, a connection that James here and elsewhere foregrounds, has been all but erased in discussions of pragmatism as they have come down to us. Or, should we say, better, that these relations to religion have been forgotten, repressed?[1] But to begin, before talking about pragmatism and the search for God, we need to take account of James's figure for his method as fecund and nurturing female, quite promiscuous in her habits of mind yet practically stringent in her judgments. Figures are used to create effects.

The Abracadabrant Power of Words

When, for example, Wallace Stevens titled the lecture/essay in which he suggests that poetry surpasses philosophy in showing us "how to live, what to do," "The *Figure* of the Youth as Virile Poet," he was deliberately "messing with our heads," so to speak, turning words to confuse our usual sorting categories: rather than "the figure of the *youth* as virile poet" (Stevens 666), we would have expected "the figure of the *poet* as virile youth." Stevens's little exercise in categorical dyslexia calls attention to the way figures work: they are designed to call and hold attention to themselves as embodying aspects of experience that cannot be described or articulated as effectively in any other way. (In this connection, it seems to me not accidental that the phrase "how to live, what to do," which Stevens used to title one of the poems of his early middle period – from *Ideas of Order* (1936) –, appears in William James's *The Varieties of Religious Experience*, the phrase emphasized in his text and indicating his own borrowing from Leo Tolstoy. There is, in other words, a conversation going on among these users of the phrase.) The use of a figure is a product of an aesthetic judgment, not a logical one. A figure causes a stir, creates a space of consideration and expectation, of possible action, sets the stage for an imagined drama. When, then, after announcing the title of his lecture, "The Figure of the Youth as Virile Poet," Stevens observed in opening the fifth section of his piece, "The centuries have a way of being male," his audience had already been primed, prompted, cued, to imagine myriad ways of "being male," and some listeners were no doubt entertaining what might have to *happen* to human nature and behavior to effect a sex change for future centuries: "Truth is what *happens* to an idea." By the time Stevens closed his talk describing how "the simple figure of the youth, in his character as poet, as virile poet," always voices the words "all of us have thought and which all of us have felt with such intensity," female and male alike, his audience had partici-

1 One of the few who has reminded us of the centrality of religion to William James's pragmatism is Linda Simon, most recently in "Active Tension" in *100 Years of Pragmatism: William James's Revolutionary Philosophy*. Ed. John J. Stuhr. Bloomington and Indianapolis: Indiana UP, 2010. 174-184.

pated in creating this new hermaphrodite being, adding their own facts of feeling to make the idea come alive (Stevens 685).

From the time of his own youth Wallace Stevens had attended carefully to William James, commenting in a late letter that for his generation the notion of James's "will to believe" had hung over everything. In this 1943 lecture, the poet invoked James repeatedly, acknowledging him as one of the "studious ghosts" with whom he continued to be in conversation (Stevens 11).

In considering James's personification of pragmatism, we must not forget his profound understanding of the nature and behavior of language and its effects on our perceptions and beliefs: "[...] what a great part in magic *words* have always played," James remarks in this lecture (the emphasis his) where he introduces pragmatism as his heroine, the lecture which opens famously, or infamously, with the example of a squirrel "going round" a tree, tracked by a man trying to get sight of the squirrel by moving as rapidly as he can around the tree, the lecture in which the idea of the "cash-value" of a word is introduced as well (James, *Pragmatism* 509). James's understanding of the figural and "abracadabrant" power of words began while he was still a child, a citizen of the James family," as his brother Henry described himself, both of them, together with their siblings, persistently reminded by their father always to frame their words precisely and to maximize aesthetic effect. William James never forgot his father's "constantly repeated" injunction to his children: "Convert, convert, convert [...] to convert and convert [...] everything that should happen to us, every contact, every impression, and every experience" (Henry James, *Autobiography* 123). They were instructed to "design" all manners of reporting their experience as "aesthetic reactions."[2] In particular, as Gerald Myers has astutely observed, "Religion [...] William's main concern all his life [...] was a further aspect of the aesthetic and impressionistic [...] [a] way of giving meaning to impressions recorded in letters, diaries, memories" (Myers, Introduction to *The Correspondence of William James*, vol. 3, xxxi). We should remember, too, that as a young man William had aspired to become a painter and had studied with William Morris Hunt; as a mature philosopher, James imported the pictorial into the way he used words. Lessons about shape, shading, balance, image, and scene were not lost. Indeed, it would not be

[2] For an extended discussion of the centrality of the aesthetic in shaping all aspects of James's thinking, see Joan Richardson, *A Natural History of Pragmatism: The Fact of Feeling from Jonathan Edwards to Gertrude Stein* (Cambridge: Cambridge UP, 2007), pp. 99-104 and to the additional sources pointed to therein.

an exaggeration to say that it is the attention James gave to the shape and sound of words, to their aesthetic effects as much as to their functions in the calculus of argument, that animated pragmatism and allowed it to continue engendering lively offspring. Had we been dependent primarily on C. S. Peirce's contribution – as central and major as it is – pragmatism would certainly not have come to be identified as America's defining philosophy. As Peirce was the first to acknowledge, he simply didn't have a way with words, in spite of spending his life elaborating "How to Make Our Ideas Clear." We could say that James was Melancthon to Peirce's Luther, not forgetting that James described the work of pragmatism as continuing that of the Protestant Reformation. In closing the third lecture/chapter of *Pragmatism*, "Some Metaphysical Problems," James observes:

> The really vital question for us all is, What is this world going to be? What is life eventually to make of itself? The centre of gravity of philosophy must therefore alter its place. The earth of things, long thrown into shadow by the glories of the upper ether, must resume its rights. To shift the emphasis in this way means that philosophic questions will fall to be treated by minds of a less abstractionist type than heretofore, minds more scientific and individualistic in their tone yet not irreligious either. It will be an alteration in the 'seat of authority' that reminds one almost of the protestant reformation. (James, *Pragmatism* 540)

While James would never fail to acknowledge Peirce's seminal role in drawing up pragmatism's master-plan, he himself recognized that Peirce's Luther did indeed need his Melancthon. As Paul Jerome Croce has observed, Peirce, "true to his unteacherly style," repeatedly realized "his limits as a popular communicator," commenting again in closing his published essays, that his "reasoning [was] somewhat severe and complicated." In order for the continuing Reformation project to succeed, in order for each individual to be prepared to experience what Ralph Waldo Emerson called "an original relation to the universe," to justify the ground for "personal religion," the points Peirce outlined would have to be "clarified […] with metaphor and vivid application" (Croce 222). William James, "that adorable genius," as Alfred North Whitehead characterized him in *Science and the Modern World* (1925), took on this charge, becoming in his time one of those the Puritan divines named "doers of the word," performing the task of "making the invisible visible."

Attention of the Mind in Thinking

In this context and turning our attention back to considering James's pragmatism as the figure of the woman as nubile philosopher, I shall recount my own scene of instruction as I reread the lecture where she is thus drawn, its closing lines those I have quoted here in opening. As I read, then, and remarked, too, on my earlier marginalia and the sentences, passages, words I had variously underlined in pencil and different colored inks over the many times through the years I had come back to this text, I was attentive simultaneously to memorial flickerings, glinting associations. I allowed myself to pause in reading to see if I could catch these wraiths, hear these whispers, hold them still long enough to listen, follow, the directions they offered. This practice, which Jonathan Edwards described as giving close "attention of the mind in thinking" (Edwards 384), is, I have come to recognize, key to pragmatism's method. It is a practice James himself had internalized from his own close reading of Edwards and of Emerson, both of whom had preceded him in beginning to translate the lessons of mysticism into the nascent discipline of psychology, which emerged as a distinct area of study only during the late nineteenth century, in America and in Germany (before then being regarded a branch of philosophy).

As I was reading, stopping periodically, "musing the obscure" in Stevens's words – so perfectly descriptive of this activity – it *happened* that after I had begun to reflect on James's having personified pragmatism as "she" who, in her "go-between" function, "marr[ying] old opinion to new fact" (James, *Pragmatism* 513), could be imagined as a kind of procuress, I found myself hearing repeatedly, silently echoing, the phrase, "the figure of the poet as virile youth." As repeatedly, I dismissed it. But the phrase persisted, with additional commentary offered in another register – a kind of different voice –, that there was something wrong, something off, something that didn't sound right. Yet when I imaginatively tried out the implicitly suggested, inverted form, "the figure of the youth as virile poet," I thought to myself that this phrasing could not be right. How/what would that figuration mean? The irritation caused by this flitting back and forth about a title I thought I knew by heart finally sent me to my bookshelf to pull down and open my Library of America edition of Stevens. There "The Figure of the Youth as Virile Poet" presented itself pristinely, without the underlinings and marginalia that, until the reading prompted by this occasion, remained confined to my original Vintage paperback copy, which I first read in 1970 and had reread several times over the years, though never – I realized at this moment – alongside close readings of William James. The juxtaposition brought astonishments, lessons from a scene of instruction evidencing how right it is to describe Stevens – as Richard Poirier was the first to do – as a poet of pragmatism, heir to James, but also illustrating pragmatism itself "as [...] a self-reflexive, recursive activity of imagination in its essential aesthetic function" (Richardson, *A Natural History* 135), or, in Stevens's more graceful phrase, as an "activity of the most august imagination," for him identical with what we mean by God. The function of this activity, the aesthetic, is "to restore temporary balance within a system, individually in mind, collectively in a society when the offered imaginative solution, whether in the form of a religious system, poetry, music, or a scientific hypothesis, *happens* to work in the larger order" (ibid. 135). Finding myself, "more truly and strange" indeed – to borrow from Stevens once more (Stevens 51) – then, back in his text, took my breath away as I found, seemingly by chance – *happen*stance – the words I needed to illustrate the story I am telling here.

While in my earlier readings of Stevens's essay I had, of course, registered the references to William James, I had not *experienced* this text as the script of an almost hidden dialogue that the poet – in his persona as "Professor Eucalyptus" ("eucalyptus" in its original Greek meaning "well-hidden") – was continuing with the philosopher of pragmatism. In short, I had not *heard*, not yet *sounded* it. We can begin overhearing Stevens's conversation with James from the outset when the poet takes for granted that "the nature of the truth changes" before he goes on to name William James and comment on the philosopher's finding "in Bergson a persistent euphony" (Stevens 667). The conversation's stream of thought then goes underground for a bit to re-emerge pages later in a way that made me realize that James had been accompanying Stevens all along, as Virgil Dante, calling attention to other voices adding their parts to this scriptural journey of descent and ascent. Bergson contributes, significantly, the sustaining bass, as it is the voice of his *Two Sources of Morality and Religion* that serves as the *noeud vital* for both James and Stevens, the concern of all three being how to redefine and preserve religious experience but without metaphysics – how, that is, to "widen the field of search for God." It is in the service of this redefinition that Stevens drew his figure of the youth as virile poet and James his of the woman as nubile philosopher.

Stevens quotes a passage from Bergson speaking of "the morality of aspiration" – in the translation the poet read, "The emotion [...] is the enthusiasm of a forward movement" (Stevens 673). Stevens goes on to say that "There is nothing rare about it [this feeling] although it may extend to degrees of rarity." He has just before quoting Bergson observed that "the way a poet feels [...] after he has written a poem that completely accomplishes his purpose [...] is shar[ing] the transformation, not to say apotheosis, accomplished by the poem" (ibid.). Then after noting that there is nothing rare about the enthusiasm of a forward movement, he introduces his figure, linking it centrally to Bergson's having offered that this feeling characterizes "the simpler representations [...] of the founders of religion, the mystics and the saints [...]. They begin by saying that what they experience is a feeling of liberation." Stevens continues,

> [...] so we may refer to the simpler representations of an aspiration (not the same, yet not wholly unlike) occurring in the lives of those who have just written their first essential poems. After all, the young man or young woman who has written a few poems and who wants to read them is merely the voluble convert or the person looking in the mirror who sees suddenly the traces of an unexpected genealogy. We are interested in this transformation [...]. (Stevens 673)

We should not forget at this juncture in connection with Stevens's evocations, within the repeated emphasis on "transformation," of *apotheosis* and *enthusiasm* – the words calling on the idea of God in their roots – a detail crucial to William James's conclusion to *The Varieties of Religious Experience*, which he offers in his "Postscript," where he also points ahead to "a later work" in which he hopes to "be enabled to state [his] position more amply and consequently more clearly;" this "later work" will be *Pragmatism.* After yet once more loosening the hold of metaphysics, James observes:

> [...] the practical needs and experiences of religion seem to me sufficiently met by the belief that beyond each man and in a fashion continuous with him there exists a larger power which is friendly to him and to his ideals. All that the facts require is that the power should be both other and larger than our conscious selves. Anything larger will do, if only it be large enough to trust for the next step. It need not be infinite. It need not be solitary. It might conceivably even be only a larger and more godlike self [...]. (James, *Varieties* 468)

We return now to Stevens's foregrounding the feeling of the morality of aspiration as "enthusiasm," "apotheosis," and his further particularization of his figure in the next section of his lecture, that which opens with "The centuries have a way of being male":

> [...] a younger figure is emerging, stepping forward in the company of a muse of its own, still half-beast and somehow more than human, a kind of sister of the Minotaur. This younger figure is the intelligence that endures. It is the imagination of the son still bearing the burden of the obscurities of the intelligence of the old. It is the spirit of its own self, not out of some surrounding myth, delineating with accurate speech the complications of which it is composed. (Stevens 675)

The muse of this "younger figure" is "still half-beast and somehow more than human, a kind of sister of the Minotaur," because she is post-Darwinian and though clearly not metaphysical, she provides access to the invisible: "Nothing that is not there and the nothing that is," the mysterious process by which we come to know, re-*cognize*, ourselves and the planet of which we are a part, "delineating with accurate speech the complications of which [a self] is composed." This "accurate speech" incorporates what Henry David Thoreau called the "mother tongue" acquired, beginning in infancy, as we now have learned from recent work in developmental linguistics, by prosodic imitation of sound streams, each individual being a kind of echo chamber resonating with the voices of its group.[3] This process links us to many other species and so to a "larger" – "beyond each man [...] there exists a larger power" –, "more than human" order: "the complications of which [a self] is composed" (Stevens 673). We can see in Stevens's turning back to recall William James, and through him Bergson, and Emerson, and Milton as well – recognizing in them his own best thoughts returned with a certain majesty – and equally in my recalling Stevens while reading James, the same process scaled up. In reflecting on this process, finally, "all mean egotism vanishes" as the individual comes to "see the traces of an unexpected genealogy," realize more and more its identity with "the larger power" Pragmatism is the method, belonging to "mother nature," that describes the activity of mind figured as "the clear intelligence of the young man still bearing the burden of the obscurities of the intelligence of the old" *transforming* this intelligence into a new truth, a new "agreement with reality": "old wine in new bottles," "a new name for some old ways of thinking," "an ancient aspect touching a new mind" (James, *Pragmatism* 572, 479; Stevens 676, 13).

The "story of the story" of figuration I am telling in these pages, in "slow motion" as it were, a rendering of my experience of giving

[3] See Steven Mithen, *The Singing Neanderthals: The Origins of Music, Language, Mind and Body* (Cambridge and London: Harvard UP, 2006) for a comprehensive treatment of recent research.

attention to my mind thinking as I was rereading James and hearing Stevens echoing, details the self-reflexive, recursive, recuperative activity that is the method of pragmatism and of nature: repetition and variation, imperfect replication. We know today, largely as a result of continuing research following observations and suggestions James offered in *The Principles of Psychology* (1890) – observations that could not have been tested during his lifetime – that the manner in which the mind works is dependent on electro-chemical signaling, the patterns of which in neuronal firing are products of wave functions having feedback and feedforward features moving literally at lightning speeds. More particularly, James realized within this activity how words work. He understood that our thoughts, before we voice them or set them down in words, do not come marching out in sequence, but rather fire simultaneously and radiantly, that words are, in fact – in the terminology of science not yet articulated in his time – *wave packets* in which thoughts as quanta hiss and spin, superpositioned, moving at or on different frequencies. James – following and extrapolating from the work of Hermann von Helmholtz in optics and acoustics – described how it is the sound of words that activates in the brain circuitry all the possible alternative "meanings"/*uses*, actual resonances, an individual has stored, as though in a charged battery. From this store, turning, tuning through various frequencies, a channel is selected, opened, through which the pulsing signals are sparked by a particular occasion or context – making what John Dewey would later generalize into his corrective description of the "reflex arc" as "circuit" (1896). Writing about pragmatism in letters to his brother Henry before and just after *Pragmatism* appeared as a volume, James notes that it "grew up from a more subtle and delicate theoretic analysis of the function of knowing," that it is "a way of thinking," that it is not anything new but that its message had to be *told*, *sounded* in a particular way to make it "representative" – to make it *work* within the "stream of thought," to make it *true to* and *in its time* – and that he has supreme confidence that if communicated in this way it will effect "something quite like the protestant reformation," as he also observes within the text of his volume, as indicated above (James, *Correspondence* 339).

The Way the Mind Works

My rereading "What Pragmatism Means," thinking about the *figure* James drew, *sparked*, brought to mind, Stevens's lecture/essay, whose title tantalized me with its Necker-cube effect. (It is worthwhile to mention that James described the activity of acutest consciousness as this kind of flickering uncertainty.) This unsettling beckoned for at least temporary rest. We recall another of James's brilliant figures, of consciousness as a bird's life –

> As we take […] a general view of the wonderful stream of our consciousness, what strikes us first is this different pace of its parts. Like a bird's life, it seems to be made up of an alternation of flights and perchings. The rhythm of language expresses this, where every thought is expressed in a sentence, and every sentence closed by a period. The resting-places are usually occupied by sensorial imaginings of some sort, whose particularity is that they can be held before the mind for an indefinite time, and contemplated without changing; the places of flight are filled with thoughts of relations, static or dynamic, that for the most part obtain between matters contemplated in the periods of comparative rest. (James, *Principles* 236)

The mind works to reestablish homeostasis by offering these temporary resting-places, "sensorial imaginings of some sort" drawn – as they can only be – from the store, the battery, of experience, where attention searches, looking for a fact, a figure, of feeling.

> Through this hovering of the attention […] the accumulation of associates becomes so great that the combined tensions of their neural processes break through […] and the nervous wave pours into the tract which has […] been awaiting its advent. And as the expectant, sub-conscious itching there, bursts into the fullness of vivid feeling, the mind finds an inexpressible relief. (James, *Principles* 113)

Even if we are not immediately aware of it, when we do reflect on the mind's process, give attention to the mind in thinking, we realize that this activity is recursive, recuperative, and that it, in fact, puts us *in touch with* aspects of ourselves, of our lived past, that were significant enough to have made a difference, to have *affect*ed us, to have registered what Jonathan Edwards called our "*consent* to being" – "consent," literally, a *feeling with* – drawing a line of relation between the individuals we happen to be and the environment in which we have found ourselves. This return to something learned, something that has not been forgotten, grounds us, the current opened by present circumstance temporarily closed by re*member*ing, re*mind*ing us that we are "part or particle" of larger, wider being, with "resources […] rich and endless." We remember that the meaning of the Greek word for "truth," *aletheia*, is "what is not forgotten." The feeling accompanying this return is that of coming back home, drawn by the voice of a "mother sleeplessly waiting," as Stevens phrases it: "pragmatism … she widens the field of search for God."

The pattern of the mind's activity as it continues its search for the particular meaning called for by a present occasion is musical, sounding a repetition of imperfect returns and variations until finding the closing resolution. This recursive, recuperative activity of the mind in thinking – holding the object of attention still enough to allow the various ideas associated with it to come into play with it – is a form of spiralling, a manner of progression identified, significantly, with the fugue in music, most notably in Bach's "Art of Fugue." This pattern is identified mathematically as the Fibonacci Series, the progress of which depends on the internalization of an earlier pattern projected onto what will come next, a pattern which also describes, in its spiralling, the activity we now know to be integral to the information exchange between the generative DNA and messenger-RNA molecules and which has been observed to be at work, as well, in phyllotaxis (maximizing the exposure of leaves to light), in the formation of galaxies, crystals, snowflakes, and other inorganic forms. Pragmatism figured as the activity of the most august imagination: "her conclusions are as friendly as those of mother nature."

The manner of this process as it happens in the brain exceeds rational description or, at least for our time, physical measurement. My mind reading James, finding itself recalling Stevens – "The meaning not the name I call," as John Milton announced in *Areopagitica* – obeyed an order larger than I could have intentionally set out: it turned itself, its own tropism searching for what it needed, for "what would suffice," in Stevens's phrasing. As he expressed in "The Noble Rider and the Sound of Words," another lecture deeply informed by James:

> The slightest sound matters. The most momentary rhythm matters. You can do as you please, yet everything matters. You are free, but your freedom must be consonant with the freedom of others. To insist for a moment on the point of sound […]. You have somehow to know the sound that is the exact sound; and you do in fact know; without knowing how. Your knowledge is irrational. In that sense life is mysterious; and if it is mysterious at all, I suppose that it is cosmically mysterious […].What is true of sounds is true of everything: the feeling for words, without regard to their sound, for example. There is, in short, an unwritten rhetoric that is always changing and to which the poet must always be turning. (Stevens 662)

James opened the famous "Stream of Thought" chapter of *The Principles of Psychology*, observing that it would be far more accurate to say of the way the mind works simply that "thought goes on," that *it thinks* rather than "he thinks" or "she thinks." The method of pragmatism was designed to attend to this major fact of the matter of being human, "part or particle of" the "cosmic weather" otherwise known as "God."

James's figure of the woman as nubile philosopher for the method of pragmatism foregrounds what Stevens describes above, what he elsewhere names "the irrational element" animating poetry. The nubile female, "as friendly as mother nature," in the state of nature, optimizes her chances for conceiving healthy offspring by entertaining as many various mates as present themselves, competing for attention and selection. The mind, as James realized, works somewhat in the same manner. Prompted by a present occasion, an end, an "object," attention hovers, hawk-like, over its field of search for what will satisfy its appetite, provide the best fit, answering the implicit question always posed by the mind. The subtitle of *Pragmatism, A New Name for Some Old Ways of Thinking*, is itself a gesture demonstrating the recuperative activity of thinking which points back to its generating feature, characterizing its continuity with all life forms, that it is a *quest*. This aspect is centrally presented in Plato's dialogue *Cratylus* where Socrates reminds his interlocutors of the common etymology of the words for quest, questing, adventure, eros and the erotic in the verb meaning "to question." The manner in which the mind finds what Emerson described in the signally important "Language" chapter of *Nature* (1836) as "a material image, more or less luminous" that answers to the idea, the question opened and suspended in the mind's "radiant and productive atmosphere" (which Stevens describes as the residence of the "youth as virile poet") is too quick for us to track in its cloud chamber: it thus has seemed and continues to seem "irrational," and in the culture of the West, at least until now, associated with "night, the female, obscure" – in Stevens's phrase (Emerson 23; Stevens 680). This aspect of human being, intrinsically "sensorial," has been sorely unacknowledged in the West – particularly in philosophy (with rare exceptions) and in science – left, as it were, unnamed, emerging only in poetry and in "mystical" varieties of religious experience. That in rereading James's *Pragmatism* I found myself recollected in the "sensorial imaginings" of Stevens demonstrates how this essential fact of feeling of the mind's life works, that "the activity of the most august imagination" is "beyond us, yet ourselves," endlessly moving (Stevens 471, 135).

In Between

The model of musical composition offered above as an analogue for the process I am delineating is particularly useful in providing accommodation to an evolutionary view of development, the major shift in negotiating the "cosmic weather" that prompted the quest that Peirce, James and the other members of what came to be known as The Metaphysical Club would pursue and that would issue in "pragmatism." A variation on a particular melodic line in music will lead to other possible variations from which yet others branch, all having an organic connection with the opening theme but with no one progression predetermined. Possibilities present themselves as the composition grows. The finished piece is one of many potential forms. It can be read backwards to demonstrate how the design developed from its opening, but its shape could have been another. Its rightness, the pleasure derived from hearing it, has to do with what we are capable of hearing, what we are prepared to hear, quite accidentally, from the relations in pitch and time that we have grown used to hearing. A new scale is a sounding of a new spatio-temporal relation, a finding of something *in between* relations that were in place but not heard before, a new adaptation, the issue of a marriage of sorts: "We have no questions to ask which are unanswerable," Emerson reminded us (7). As Plato exquisitely laid out in the *Cratylus* and as noted just above, the seed of the erotic is the question, the source without which the satisfaction of resolution would be impossible, the concealed spring of all imaginings, asking what is possible between this and that, moving into spaces opened, feeling at sea, responding with full attention and with the animal need to survive and come to rest for a while: pleasure, renewal. This activity is beyond us, yet ourselves in the most profound sense: "The crude aboriginal character of direct perception is inheritance," Whitehead observes. "What is inherited is feeling-tone," he notes, echoing James, "with evidence of its origin" (119).

A new aesthetic form, the use of a particular figure embodying the "unwritten rhetoric" towards which we are always turning, forces spaces of attention to open, breaches of reality. We do not first know what to make of what we hear or see. We are in new territory, questioning, alert, interested, literally *inter-esse*, between being one way and another. Coming to understand a new form requires time, *standing under* it, suffering its discipline, asking questions of it, engaging it again and again until we become fluent in its speech, dressed in a new habit of mind. We map the new space, repeat its contours, its relations. Our responsive accommodation to it shapes a template. We imitate the form while preserving the difference each of us is, theme and variation, DNA and messenger-RNA. This response expresses our translation of the past into the "feeling-tone" of our moment: *Pragmatism: A New Name for Some Old Ways of Thinking*, its method designed to make us attentive to the rhythmic continuity – what Peirce called "synechism" (from the Greek root, *syn-exw*, originally meaning *"to hold* or *keep together*" as "*to keep* the *rowers* together" [Liddel and Scott 676]) – between our thinking and the reservoir of the experience of life on the planet. As James describes in "The Consciousness of Self" chapter of *Principles*:

> Thought is a vehicle of choice as well as of cognition [...]. It appropriates *to* itself, it is the actual focus of the accretion, the hook from which the chain of past selves dangles, planted firmly in the Present, which alone passes for real, and thus keeping the chain from being a purely ideal thing. Anon the hook itself will drop into the past with all it carries, and then be treated as an object and be appropriated by a new Thought in the new present which will serve as a living hook in turn [...]. Its appropriations are [...] less to *itself* than to the most intimately felt *part of its present Object, the body, and the central adjustments*, which accompany the act of thinking [...] *These are the real nucleus of our present identity* [...] their actual existence, realized as solid, present fact [...] the "warm" parts of its present object [...] a firm basis on which the consciousness of personal identity would rest. (323; emphases in original)

In "The Figure of the Youth as Virile Poet" Stevens repeats an example offered by the French philosopher Henri Focillon in *The Life of Forms in Art* where he uses the example of Piranesi's etchings to illustrate the instinctive and mysterious process James describes above. Focillon observes that "a vocation recognizes its material by foresight, before experience," and Stevens continues:

> As an example of this, he refers to the first state of the *Prisons* of Piranesi as skeletal. But "twenty years later, Piranesi returned to these etchings, and on taking them up again, he poured into them shadow after shadow, until one might say that he excavated this astonishing darkness not from the brazen plates, but from the living rock of some subterranean world." (Stevens 672-73)

One could say that Piranesi returned to his early etchings as "a larger and more godlike self" having experienced in the twenty years before he came back to them increasing identification with the planet of which he was a part, feeling himself as having emerged, as all life, "from the living rock of some subterranean world."

In January 1907, months before *Pragmatism* was published, William James "gave the final lecture of his last course at Harvard […]. He closed with a careful consideration of the relation between mind and matter, arguing at last that they might be 'coextensive.' 'Matter might *everywhere* make mind conscious of what matter was doing, and mind might then everywhere either acquiesce in the performances, or encourage, hinder, or redirect them'" (Richardson, *William James* 491). It is not difficult to see in this formulation that "mind" = free will = chance. In the last lecture/chapter of *Pragmatism*, "Pragmatism and Religion," he asks his listeners/readers to consider their own individual "ideals," the goal any one of us "cherishes and is willing to live and work for," suggesting, as he extends the consideration, the continuity between us and "the world," between, that is, "mind" and "matter":

> Take, for example, any one of us in this room with the ideals which he cherishes and is willing to live and work for. Every such ideal realized will be one moment in the world's salvation. But these particular ideals are not bare abstract possibilities. They are grounded in *live* possibilities, for we are their live champions and pledges, and if the complementary conditions come and add themselves, our ideals will become actual things. What now are the complementary conditions? They are first such a mixture of things as will in the fulness of time give us a chance, a gap that we can spring into, and, finally, *our act.* [emphasis in original]
>
> […] Our acts, our turning-places, where we seem to make ourselves and grow [into, we could say "[…] a larger and more godlike self"], are the parts of the world to which we are closest, the parts of which our knowledge is the most intimate and complete. Why should we not take them at their face-value? Why may they not be the actual turning-places and growing-places which they seem to be, of the world – why not the workshop of being, where we catch fact in the making, so that nowhere may the world grow in any other kind of way than this? (612-13)

Works Cited

Croce, Paul Jerome. *Science and Religion in the Era of William James.* vol. 1: *Eclipse of Certainty, 1820-1880.* Chapel Hill: U of North Carolina P, 1995.

Edwards, Jonathan. "The Mind." in: *The Works of Jonathan Edwards.* vol. VI: *Scientific and Philosophical Writings.* Ed. Wallace E. Anderson. New Haven and London: Yale UP, 1980. 311-98.

Emerson, Ralph Waldo. *Essays and Lectures.* Ed. Joel Porte. New York: The Library of America, 1983.

James, Henry. *Autobiography.* Ed. Frederick W. Dupee. Princeton: Princeton UP, 1983.

James, William. *The Principles of Psychology.* rpt. Cambridge: Harvard UP, 1983 (1890).

—. *Writings 1902-1910.* Ed. Bruce Kuklick. New York: The Library of America, 1987.

Liddell and Scott's Greek-English Lexicon. Oxford: The Clarendon Press, 1979.

Mithen, Steven. *The Singing Neanderthals: The Origins of Music, Language, Mind and Body.* Cambridge and London: Harvard UP, 2006.

Richardson, Joan. *A Natural History of Pragmatism: The Fact of Feeling from Jonathan Edwards to Gertrude Stein.* Cambridge: Cambridge UP, 2007.

Richardson, Robert D. *William James: In the Maelstrom of American Modernism.* Boston and New York: Houghton Mifflin, 2006.

Stevens, Wallace. *The Collected Poetry and Prose*. Ed. Frank Kermode and Joan Richardson. New York: The Library of America, 1997.

The Correspondence of William James. vol. 3: *William and Henry 1897-1910*. Ed. Ignas K. Skrupskelis and Elizabeth M. Berkley. Charlottesville and London: UP of Virginia, 1994.

Whitehead, Alfred North. *Process and Reality: An Essay in Cosmology.* Corrected Edition. Ed. David Ray Griffin and Donald W. Sherburne. New York: The Free Press, 1985.

Response to Joan Richardson

Heinz Ickstadt

I am somewhat embarrassed that I feel in the same position I felt in responding to Herwig Friedl, namely that of an almost uncritical admirer. In the case of Joan Richardson, especially, I am predisposed to admiration since I once had the pleasure of participating in one of her graduate seminars on Henry James that also included a large dose of William. That experience, as much as reading her book on *The Natural History of Pragmatism*, has turned me into one of her many fans. It is easy and not embarrassing, after all, to admit this since her densely beautiful text, by exploring so eloquently and so persuasively the aesthetic dimension of William James's work, has confirmed this predisposition.

However, some of the counter-arguments I made on Herwig Friedl could also be made here: the absence of a cultural context and, possibly, of the cultural thrust of James's pragmatism. Here, Joan Richardson appears to follow the example of Richard Poirier who argued, first in *The Renewal of Literature* (1987) and, later, in *Poetry & Pragmatism* (1992), that with all the writers he calls "Emersonian pragmatists" (among whom William James figures prominently) the imagery of working and doing does not really lead into culture, even less so to society, but right back into the language they use. It should be perceived as referring to work done *in* and *through* language, specifically through what he calls strategies of troping. Poirier thus deals with James's pragmatist texts almost exclusively in aesthetic terms – they are, or rather: they "work" like poetry since they are products of a poetic imagination: "It needs to be kept in mind," he writes in *Poetry and Pragmatism*, "that the philosophers Emerson and James write less like philosophers or theorists than like their own poetic inheritors. They are like poets in their frequent resort to dizzying metaphors, in an allusiveness and elusiveness of phrasing that is to become a feature of the poetry of Frost, Eliot, and Stevens […]" (92); and again in a subsequent passage: "This imagination of work, power, and self is, insofar as I can describe it, indistinguishable from what is imagined by these same writers as the ideal operation of writing and reading, the operation by which a poem is created […]"

(ibid. 123). Accordingly, James's language "is subject to the same degree of metaphorical proliferation, slippage, and excess" (ibid. 131).

With this Joan Richardson would, I think, agree. She, too, discusses William James predominantly in aesthetic terms. Yet she also believes that the aesthetic cannot be separated from the religious and the scientific. If, on the basis of his strategy of troping, James can be placed among the poets, he may also, and for the same reason, be put into the company of mystics and modern scientists since, according to James, "the existence of mystical states absolutely overthrows the pretension of non-mystical states to be the sole and ultimate dictators of what we believe" (*Varieties of Religious Experience* 335). There is "the reality of the unseen" and it becomes evident in the powers which we possess. Accordingly, he embraces the "Darwinian facts" and intends, as Richardson writes in her chapter on William James in *The Natural History of Pragmatism*, to "unfold their implications in considering the evolution of the mind" (101). "His signal contribution," she continues, "was to articulate the identity of aesthetic with religious experience within the Darwinian framework" (ibid. 105). She defines her own interest as wanting to further elaborate "his identifying the scientific with religious and aesthetic experience specifically around what he realized as the actual power, energy, of language, in its performative function of translating imagination's products understood as expressions of the act of feeling" (ibid. 122).

The evanescent 'truth' James conveys through his fluid language of transition, a language placed on the borderline of consciousness ("like the thin line of flame advancing across the dry autumnal field," as James phrased it with great visual precision in "A World of Pure Experience," *Writings* 1181), is thus not only a poetic truth but, as an expression of effervescent as much as evanescent states of awe, ecstasy, or wonder (i.e. of religion not as doctrine but as a transitional, as a transmarginal state of consciousness), it is also congruent with, perhaps even verified by, the ongoing revelations of scientific inquiry. In fact, "imagination," Joan Richardson argues,

> is the organ through which chance operates on the human scale; its function, to effect variability. The uncertain space of imaginative projections, what James came to call, *the vague*, is [...] what today's physicists describe [...] as a wave packet, a probability amplitude composing a range, a scale of possibles, of action potentials.

"The important act which this 'field' formula commemorates," she quotes James, "is the indetermination of the margin [...]. It lies around us like a 'magnetic field,' inside of which our center of energy turns." (*NHP* 120f.) In other words, the aesthetic, the religious and the scientific are related as creative expressions of the human mind. In pragmatist thinking as embodied in 'verbal performance,' i.e. in a 'pragmatist method' of writing, the mind becomes aware of the rhythms of its own unfolding and, in doing so, recognizes itself in the structures, processes, and contingencies of 'mother nature.'

In her article, Richardson links those analogous yet different levels of discourse with great subtlety in the performative unfolding of her own argument: In reading James's text on "What Pragmatism Means," she creates her own text of pragmatist meaning by enacting a Jamesian method of associational drifting (3-19). In connecting two theoretical texts by James and Stevens through a halo of vague memories and "obscure relations, which," in the words of James, "like an horizon [...] spread about its meaning," she projects, through the weavings and meanderings of her personal consciousness, a text in which the aesthetic, the religious and the scientific interact and overlap; and in that process she gradually transforms the 'she' of James's personification of pragmatism into the 'she' of her own reflective agency.

It is, of course, no accident that this process of associational linkage would take her from James's reflections on Pragmatism to Stevens's essay "The Figure of the Youth as Virile Poet," his meditation on the relation of philosophy and poetry (cf. *Necessary Angel* 39-67). The latter he calls an "approach [...] to being by way of the imagination" (ibid. 41). At its beginning, Stevens quotes from a letter William James wrote to Bergson in which James links – in a manner quite similar to that of Joan Richardson – his reading of Bergson's *L'Evolution Créatrice* with his reading of Flaubert's *Madame Bovary*: "[I]n finishing it I found the same after-taste remaining [...] such a flavor of persistent *euphony*" (40; emphasis in original). For Stevens the fact of such "euphony" was evidence – as it most likely also was for James – that poetry's radiating power of suggestiveness (its power to express experience as felt and reflected) was superior to philosophy's "gaunt world of reason." The truth it produces and communicates *in* and *through* the words it uses is a rapturous confirmation of life, evidence of a godlike "incandescence of intelligence." In a passage that echoes Emerson as well as James Stevens writes:

> [...] and standing in the radiant and productive atmosphere, and examining first one detail of that world, one particular, and then another, as we find them by chance, and observing many things that seem to be poetry without any intervention on our part, as, for example, the blue sky, and noting, in any case,

> that the imagination never brings anything into the world but that, on the contrary, like the personality of the poet [...], it is no more than a process, and desiring with all the power of our desire not to write falsely, do we not begin to think of the possibility that poetry is only reality, after all, and that poetic truth is factual truth [...]? From that point of view, the truth that we experience when we are in agreement with reality is the truth of fact. (*Necessary Angel* 59)

A reality of fact, to be sure, transfigured by the light of the imagination; and perhaps also by the delight the mind takes in the awareness of its own working, for – as Stevens quotes the French poet and art historian Henri Focillon – "[t]he chief characteristic of the mind is to be constantly describing itself" (Stevens, *Necessary Angel* 46). Such delight in how the mind works and in the linguistic expression it gives to its working is of course part of the Emersonian tradition shared by James and Stevens – but also by Joan Richardson whose argument cannot be separated from the method of her presentation of it: In its own proliferating network of intertextual references and associations her text, "she," indeed widens "the field of search for god" – or for a new consciousness of the godlike or divine.

In a posthumously published essay, Stevens had written that "in an age of disbelief, when the gods have come to an end, when we think of them as the aesthetic projections of a time that has passed, men turn to a fundamental glory of their own and from that create a style of bearing themselves in reality. They create a new style of a new bearing in a new reality" ("Two or Three Ideas" 209). I am pretty sure that Richard Poirier (and Joan Richardson as well) would identify that new style – that "new name for some old ways of thinking," as James called it – with the pragmatist method of expressing the mind's self-reflective explorations on the borderline of concept and percept, of the potency and evanescence of the word. The territory of consciousness and language is thus extended to, or even beyond, its margins, not with any certainty of name and knowledge but always with an assumption of 'as if.'[1]

In James and Stevens as well as in Joan Richardson there is an evolutionary dimension to these processes of thinking and their linguistic expression. But I am not sure whether that evolutionary movement just

[1] In reflecting a passage from Emerson's "Self-Reliance," Poirier writes: "That is, the soul appears or occurs only as something we feel compelled to live into or to move toward as if it were there; it is like James's will to believe, it hints at Stevens's supreme fiction [...]" (*Poetry & Pragmatism* 24). "William James's feeling of if" is the title of Richardson's chapter on William James (*The Natural History* 98–136). See also *The Varieties of Religious Experience* 60.

denotes continuous change or a progressive unfolding of a cosmic consciousness: of the mind increasingly discovering itself as part and parcel of the universe, an Emersonian vision of unity slowly coming to fulfillment through "the activity of the most august imagination" (as Stevens says) – the working presence of God in mind and nature. This struck me especially when Richardson writes about the "mind's activity of thinking" and links it to the spiraling structures in music and mathematics, to Bach's "Art of the Fugue," the structures of DNA and "messenger-RNA molecules" as well as relating it to "the formation of galaxies, crystals, snowflakes and other inorganic forms."

My second question concerns Poirier's (and Richardson's) easy subsuming of James among the poets and their practice. No doubt, his use of imagery is at times stunning and statements like the following seem to anticipate Gertrude Stein's linguistic practice:

> There is not a conjunction or a preposition, and hardly an adverbial phrase, syntactic form, or inflection of voice, in human speech, that does not express some shading or other relation which we at some moment actually feel to exist between the larger objects of our thought [...] the relations are numberless, and no existing language is capable of doing justice to all their shades [...]. (James, "Stream of Thought" 189)

But his effort to escape conceptual speech still operates within a frame of philosophical discourse, of logical argument. In my reply to Herwig Friedl, I refer to James's language as an "embodiment" of his thinking. Friedl, even he, later raised objections by stating that James did not use language as an embodiment but as a mediation of thought – even though there are passages of amazing metaphoric power in his essays, and his desire of extending language to the borderlines of consciousness certainly resembles the project of many works of modernist poetry.

At the beginning of her text Richardson argues that in "considering James's personification of pragmatism, we must not forget his profound understanding of the nature and behavior of language and its effects on our perceptions and beliefs: '[...] what a great part in magic *words* have always played.'" But the passage is more ambivalent than she admits: "Metaphysics has usually followed a very primitive kind of quest," James writes:

> You know how men have always hankered after unlawful magic, and you know what a great part, in magic, *words* have always played. [...] So the universe has always appeared to the natural mind as a kind of enigma, of which the key must be sought in the shape of some illuminating or power-bringing word or name. (*Writings* 509)

The words he connects with "magic" are those of a very primitive kind of "quest," the quest of the "natural mind" for metaphysical certainty, attempting, in fact, to end all metaphysical quest. It would seem, then, that he uses words *against* magic – the magic of 'holy' names as well as of "stiff" metaphysical concepts. Opening up conceptual speech by what he calls "following the pragmatic method" is to "bring out of each word its practical cash-value, set it at work in the stream of your experience. It appears less as a solution, then, than as a program for more work, and more particularly as an indication of the ways in which existing realities may be *changed*" (James, "What Pragmatism Means" 7).

What this entails is not entirely clear to me. Evidently it does not mean trying to grasp a reality independent of human thinking for that would be attempting, as he writes in "Pragmatism and Humanism," to catch something that

> is just entering into experience, and yet to be named, or else to some imagined aboriginal presence in experience, before any belief about the presence had arisen, before any human conception had been applied. It is what is absolutely dumb and evanescent, the merely ideal limit of our minds. We may glimpse it, but we never grasp it; what we grasp is always some substitute for it which previous human thinking has peptonized and cooked for our consumption. If so vulgar an expression were allowed us, we might say that wherever we find it, it has been already *faked*. (Poirier, *Poetry and Pragmatism* 48)

Creating awareness of how far the field of consciousness and language in fact extends toward the "limit of our minds" is therefore only one part of his enterprise;[2] the other is finding form and concept, yet avoiding closure and an end to the quest. He aims at extending the center toward its margins, not to replace it by the marginal. Talking about mystical experience in *Varieties of Religious Experience*, James writes:

> In mystical literature such self-contradictory phrases as "dazzled obscurity," "whispering silence," "teeming desert," are continually met with. They prove that not conceptual speech, but music rather, is the element through which we are best spoken to by mystical truth. Many mystical scriptures are indeed little more than musical compositions. (330)

[2] Although, admittedly, he conceives the self-creating individual as anchored in this dark area of primary feelings where world is at once apprehended and made: "Individuality is founded in feeling; and the recesses of feeling, the darker, blinder strata of character, are the only places in the world in which we catch real fact in the making, and directly perceive how events happen, and how work is actually done" (*Varieties* 389).

But he is neither a mystic nor does he want to turn his texts into a form of musical composition (i.e. the music of poetry). He places himself on borderlines, Janus-faced, between poetry and philosophy, between his fascination with the irrational and his need to put it under the control of reason and of habit: He always looks into both directions: toward the margins *and* the center, intending to bring out form and yet conceiving of form as something temporary, 'worked' out of fluid experience.

Joan Richardson might answer perhaps somewhat impatiently: "But that is precisely what Stevens had in mind and not much different from what I tried to make you understand!" To which I would reply in the enigmatic manner of William's brother Henry: "Then there we are."

Works Cited

James, William. "The Stream of Thought." Selected Writings. Ed. G. H. Bird. London: Orion, 1995. 170-204.

—. *Varieties of Religious Experience.* London: Macmillan, 1961.

—. "What Pragmatism Means." Selected Writings. Ed. G. H. Bird. London: Orion, 1995. 3-19.

—. *Writings 1902-1910.* Ed. Bruce Kuklick. New York: The Library of America, 1987.

Poirier, Richard. *Poetry & Pragmatism.* Cambridge: Harvard UP, 1992.

—. *The Renewal of Literature.* New York: Random House, 1987.

Richardson, Joan. *A Natural History of Pragmatism: The Fact of Feeling from Jonathan Edwards to Gertrude Stein.* Cambridge: Cambridge UP, 2007.

Stevens, Wallace. *The Necessary Angel: Essays on Reality and the Imagination.* New York: Alfred Knopf, 1951.

—. "Two or Three Ideas." *Opus Posthumous.* New York: Alfred Knopf, 1957. 202-216.

The Ontology of William James: Thinking in Images and Images of Thinking

Herwig Friedl

In my attempt to characterize the function of images in William James's thinking, ontology should not be understood as a subdivision or version of metaphysics. The term ontology should rather indicate a thinking of and about Being in the post-metaphysical sense implied by Martin Heidegger's *Seinsfrage*, the question of Being. At the same time I do not propose to deal with images as the subject matter of *Bildwissenschaft* which arose with and after the so-called pictorial or iconic turn announced by W.T.J. Mitchell in 1992 (Mitchell 89-94). Images are here understood neither as exclusively mental and visual representations nor as pictures, a distinction which is basic for the relevant research advanced by, for example, Horst Bredekamp (15-26).

In a preliminary way, I would like to define images for my purpose as verbal indicators of pre-conceptual (not necessarily and not exclusively visual) awareness, of a *sense* of the event of beings coming into experiential presence. I would like to approach the problem at hand in four steps: part I '*About* Ontology' will deal with the limited range of explicit, almost exclusively conceptual, approaches to the question of Being in William James; part II 'Images and Philosophy' is designed to present heuristic tools which may be useful in dealing with images as modes of experiencing and means of thinking based on observations and suggestions from Aristotle to Hans Blumenberg; William James's specific and original use of images in dealing with the question of Being is discussed in part III 'Images and Ontology in William James,' and part IV 'A Philosophy, an Ontology of the Future' tries to do justice to the momentous break in the history of thought which manifests itself in James's intuition of Being. It is this break which Alfred North Whitehead had already analyzed and appreciated in 1925 as the true beginning of philosophical modernism in his interpretation of James, which focused not so much on Being as on James's innovative, revolutionary re-interpretation of the idea of consciousness (Whitehead 143-144).

About Ontology

For William James, the existential and the intellectual, i.e. philosophical worth and dignity of a human being and his thinking manifest themselves primarily in his vision: "a man's vision is the great fact about him," he claims with aphoristic emphasis in *A Pluralistic Universe* and later in the same book he elaborates and urges the reader of philosophy:

> Place yourself [...] at the centre of a man's philosophical vision and you understand at once all the different things it makes him write or say. But keep outside, use your post-mortem method, try to build the philosophy up out of the single phrases, taking first one and then another and seeking to make them fit "logically," and of course you fail. (14, 117)

The reader of philosophy needs "living sympathy," James says in *A Pluralistic Universe* (117) and in a letter to a doctoral student he insists that in reading philosophy you should first grasp the "centre of vision, by an act of imagination" (*Letters* II 355). Doing and reading philosophy, then, are primarily acts of existential engagement and significance, they privilege the imaginative, the visionary, and – by extension and amplification – the visual in the widest sense, the percept and the image, over the word, the concept, the text, the *logos*. Writing and speaking, terminologies and logical sequence as well as consistency merely follow, they depend on the *a priori* of the intuited, on that which reveals itself without mediation in the intensity of significant experiential awareness. The center of vision in James's philosophy, his primary and foundational intuition, is, I argue simply here, his radically innovative, his modernist, ontological insight. If one considers the way in which the *Seinsfrage*, the question of Being, obsessively informs and, in endless permutations, pervades the projected 95 volumes of Heidegger's collected works, it seems both daring and naïve to insinuate that William James may have anticipated and possibly even rivaled Heidegger's grandiose project in depth and dimension. It is true, the *term*, the *concept* of Being, is marginal in James. The *Sache des Denkens*, Being as the very matter of thought, however, may be shown as foundational, of primary and ultimate importance. This importance is manifest, it shows, I maintain, above all *in* and *as* the *function* of images – images which are the outstandingly significant rhetorical mode and argumentative method employed throughout by James to reveal and to think Being.

By comparison, important abstractly conceptual discussions of Being in James may be found in hardly more than two relatively inconspicuous places. The, at first sight, disappointingly brief third chapter on "The Problem of Being" in James's last, unfinished book, *Some Problems of Philosophy* is announced in these not exactly encouraging terms: "I will start with the worst problem possible, the so-called 'ontological problem' or question of how there comes to be anything at all" (25). The conclusion of James's meditations is seemingly as disappointing:

> So the question recurs: How do our finite experiences come into being from moment to moment? [...] Who can tell off-hand? The question of being is the darkest in all philosophy. All of us are beggars here [...] For all of us alike, Fact forms a datum, a gift, or *vorgefundenes*, which we cannot burrow under, explain or get behind. It makes itself somehow, and our business is far more with its *what* than with its *whence* or *why*. (29-30)

The implications of these few meager statements are, however, significantly more than a mere shrugging of shoulders or the expression of a wondering awe at the enigma. Firstly, Being is seen as event, "as coming to be." Being is inescapably temporal, it emerges from "moment to moment." Secondly, our thinking finds itself always already indebted to Being as to a *Vorgefundenes* in a way which makes it impossible to ground, find or identify it objectively and thus metaphysically as a *substantia* which is thought to be independent of its being experienced. James's characteristically modest statements imply these intuitions: a proper response to the question of Being would have to be anti-foundationalist and acknowledge Being as temporal event or as ceaseless ungrounded transition into and out of itself. James says: "There are novelties; there are losses. The world seems [...] really to grow" (ibid. 29). Making sure that we have not missed these understated points, James adds a footnote: "[...] one may say that fact or 'being' is 'contingent,' or matter of 'chance' so far as our intellect is concerned. The conditions of its appearance are uncertain, unforeseeable when future, and when past, elusive" (ibid. 29). One should emphasize that from the point of view of conceptual reasoning (i.e. intellect or *logos*) Being is contingent, ungrounded, and radically temporal. In a later chapter of *Some Problems of Philosophy*, James briefly returns to the question of Being and states that "being gives *it*[!]self to us abruptly [...]" (84; my emphasis, HF). Being then, may be understood as a given or rather as a gift – humans are existentially and intellectually at its mercy, "all of us are beggars here," James had said; if Being thus shows itself, as I have here suggested, as an ungrounded, contingent, always temporal self-presentation – you may, if you wish, read this as a premonition of Heidegger's "*Es* gibt Sein und *es* gibt Zeit" in the late essay "Zeit und Sein" (9, my emphasis, HF) with its meditation on the event- or *Ereignis*-character of Being as radically temporal emergence that *knows* no agent, only agency. James justifies the scarcity of his conceptual elucidations concerning the question of the coming to be of Being and beings by pointing to the wonder, the puzzlement, the *thaumazein* occasioned by the problem: "Philosophy stares, but brings no reasoned solution, for from nothing to being there is no logical bridge" (James, *Some Problems* 27). This does not mean, as is often assumed, that the question, the problem is abandoned or that we deal with a kind of 'negative philosophy' which knows its theme only by a series of negations: James merely argues that Being as the event, the *Ereignis* of "coming to be" is not a matter of reasoning, of a logical bridge. If *ratio* and *logos* do not provide answers, maybe the mandatory, the ideal imaginative reader of James's central vision should look for different modes of approaching the problem, for different bridges to think the emergence of Being out of nothing.

Before I consider these alternative approaches and test other than logical bridges let me remind you of the second of the two major conceptualist attempts to articulate Being in James. Probably James's most concise and most profound definition or, more appropriately, conceptual interpretation of Being occurs in the entry "Experience" for J.M. Baldwin's *Dictionary of Philosophy and Psychology* of 1902: Experience signifies, James begins his definition, and it signifies

> the entire process of phenomena, of present data considered in their raw immediacy, before reflective thought has analysed them into subjective or objective aspects or ingredients. It is the summum genus of which everything must have been a part before we can speak of it at all. [...] If philosophy insists on keeping this term indeterminate, she can refer to her subject-matter without committing herself as to certain questions in dispute. But if experience be used with either an objective or a subjective shade of meaning, then question-begging occurs, and discussion grows impossible. (95)

Experience designates, to repeat James, "the summum genus of which everything must have been a part before we can speak of it at all." This means that, for James, experience, or better, as he was to discuss it a few years later, pure experience, is a name for Being in general. As such it necessarily precedes all verbal articulation – like Charles Sanders Peirce's Firstness it does not fall under the jurisdiction of the *logos*. Peirce's version of the experience of Being as Firstness both clarifies and deepens our understanding of James's intuition of Being as pure experience:

> The idea of the absolutely First must be entirely separated from all *conception* of or reference to anything else. The First must therefore be present and immediate […]. It must be fresh and new, for if old it is second to its former state. It must be initiative, original, spontaneous and free; otherwise it is a Second to a determining cause. It is also something vivid and conscious. […] It cannot be *articulately thought*; assert it and it has already lost its characteristic innocence. […] Stop to *think* of it, and it has already flown. (Peirce 1.357; my emphases, HF).

For both James and Peirce, Being as pure experience or Firstness is an event, an emergence, it occurs before the subject-object split so dear to traditional metaphysical and epistemological modes of thinking and their conceptual apparatus. James's radically modern ontological thinking therefore demands – in a wonderful pun – that the *term* experience and thus the word for Being be kept inde-*term*-inate, i.e. that it be both spoken and unspoken, asserted and denied, maintained and abandoned. Experience as Being is the togetherness of an awareness and its "contents," contents or objects which only emerge as such once "reflective thought," as he states in the dictionary entry on "Experience," approaches the simple *this* and *there*, the *thatness* of the really real, namely Being as the experiential event. Strictly speaking, experience or Being as such in their immediacy cannot be talked about; they may issue in nameable aspects and elements only when they have been retrospectively focused in the context of a new event of experience called reflection. Experience as Being is or shows as, what James often called, "knowledge by direct acquaintance" as distinguished from retrospective, reflexive knowledge or "knowledge *about*." James's conceptualist approach to Being, his presentation of knowledge *about* it, then, offers these severely limited results: Being as contingent and temporal emergence entails a monistic understanding of a pre-linguistic entity or prelinguistic entities, called experience or, rather, experiencing, that cannot be spoken, i.e. conceptually articulated. Critics of James legitimately call this either a neutral monism or, as both Ruth Anna Putnam (5) and Felicitas Krämer (167) would prefer, a neutral pluralism which implies Being or Experience as signifying a multiplicity of experiential events, within each of which an intimately unified, *lebensweltliche* totality of – in traditional metaphysical dualist parlance – mind and matter emerges. Despite their terminological precision and academic dignity, or maybe because of that, terms like "neutral monism or pluralism" strike the imaginative reader of James as the dry husks of a vital ontological vision, as the ossified, static placeholders of that intuitional awareness in James which sets out to allow Being to manifest, to reveal itself primarily in a dynamic philosophical discourse replete with ever newly productive images. Ultimately, this implies not merely a radically novel, a truly modernist departure in ontology, it also prepares the way for a fundamental revaluation of what it means to do philosophy.

Images and Philosophy

By way of preparing my interpretation of the ontological function of imagery in James's thinking, I would like to present a sketch of some representative philosophical positions concerning the functions of imagery in philosophy.[1] This may help one see how James's imagistic practice draws upon, utilizes, and transforms established classical and also contemporary, i.e. late nineteenth-century interpretations of philosophical imagery and, at the same time, foreshadows major twentieth-century work in this field. My highly selective readings of Aristotle, Rudolf Eucken, and Hans Blumenberg cannot pretend to do justice to the respective inner consistency of each of these three philosophical analyses and interpretations of what images may do in and for thinking. The three thinkers will provide me with a series of heuristic devices which, hopefully and pragmatically, will prove their hermeneutic value in reading James's use of images for and in ontology.

Aristotle's *Peri Psyches* (or *De Anima*) discusses the soul as the vital principle, as "that whereby we live and perceive and think in the primary sense" (II 2, 414a13-15; 79)[2] – the soul in Aristotle is an equivalent of the existentially self-aware dynamic which James in *The Principles of Psychology* described as the "*first fact for us, then* [...] *that thinking of*

1 Three relatively recent German publications are devoted to interpretations of the theories and the functions of philosophical imagery in predominantly European philosophers: Bernhard H. F. Taureck. *Metaphern und Gleichnisse in der Philosophie. Versuch einer kritischen Ikonologie der Philosophie*. Frankfurt am Main: Suhrkamp, 2004, Ralf Konersmann, ed. *Wörterbuch der philosophischen Metaphern*. Darmstadt: Wissenschaftliche Buchgesellschaft, 2007, and Simone Neuber and Roman Veressow, eds. *Das Bild als Denkfigur. Funktionen des Bildbegriffs in der Geschichte der Philosophie*. München: Wilhelm Fink, 2010. It is only in Taureck that we find a few remarks on imagery in James (and Peirce). Taureck limits his observations to the Jamesian pragmatist conception of truth and – predictably in a somewhat prejudiced European critical stance – the monetary imagery whose antecedents in Franklin (and Plato and Cusanus) are dwelt upon; the more significant indebtedness of James to the philosophy of Leibniz and his use of monetary imagery is not discussed (Taureck, 360-361).

2 References to Aristotle will identify the Greek text in the traditional manner and this is followed by the page number for the English text in the Loeb Classical Library edition after the colon.

some sort goes on" (I, 219). The intimate connection between existence, in the *primary* sense and as *first* fact, and perception and conception – between Being and perceiving and thinking – in Aristotle's view is the theme that appears most intriguing for my present concern. For Aristotle the object *of* or *within* the mere percept is in Blumenberg's later terminology "das Unbegriffliche" – the a- or non-conceptual: "The object of sight […] has in fact no name" (Aristotle, *Peri Psyches* II 7, 418a26-28; 103). It is, in James's terminology, a mere *that* (James, "The Thing and Its Relations" 46). As such, however, Aristotle concludes: "the perception of proper objects is true […]" (III 3, 428b19-20; 163). It is only when language begins to articulate attributes that error may arise, or in James's view: "language works against our *perception* of the truth […]" (James, *Principles* I, 234, my emphasis, HF). Mind itself, the conceptualizing faculty, is interestingly not seen as an entity by Aristotle, but rather as a function (as in James's essay "Does Consciousness Exist?"). Aristotle says: "That part of the soul, then, which we call mind […] has no actual existence until it thinks" (Aristotle, *Peri Psyches* III 4, 429a22-24; 165). Thinking as a function, however, is intimately tied to and conditioned by both percepts and images in this way: "Now for the thinking soul images take the place of direct perceptions […]. Hence the soul never thinks without a mental image" (Aristotle, *Peri Psyches* III 7, 431a15-17; 177) and Aristotle adds in the summary of the book: "[…] no one could ever learn or understand anything without the exercise of perception, so even when we think speculatively, we must have some mental picture of which to think; for mental images are similar to objects perceived […]" (III 8, 432a6-11; 181). The image then is the vital and indispensable *bridge* between the silent, the speechless, and thus selfevidently true presence (Being) of the object *of* and *in* perception and the conceptual articulation in the speculative play of truth and error. The image is primarily a *function* within thinking as it goes on from awareness through imagination to conceptualization. One might say that it is an event rather than a mental fact. The modernist ontological implications of the Aristotelian interpretation of thinking the presence of beings through the function of *images* (in the wide sense of the term, which I prefer) can be briefly sketched with the help of two subtle readings of Aristotle's ontological profundity of vision by Heidegger and Agamben, respectively. Heidegger discusses Aristotle's mode of thinking the essence of beings (German: *Wesen*) and concludes:

> Was dies ist, jenes Beständige, wird gleichwohl im vorhinein und zwar notwendig gesichtet. Sehen heisst griechisch *idein*; das Gesichtete in seiner Gesichtetheit heisst *idea*. Gesichtet ist das, als was sich das Seiende im vorhinein und ständig gibt. Das *Was es ist*, das Wassein, ist die *idea*; und umgekehrt die 'Idee' ist das Wassein und das Wesen. *idea* ist genauer und griechisch gedacht: der *Anblick*, den etwas bietet, das Aussehen, das es hat und gleichzeitig vor sich her zur Schau trägt, *eidos*. (Heidegger, *Grundfragen* 62)[3]

The awareness of what and how something, a being, shows itself, its phenomenal aspect (*Anblick*), has the unwavering (*ständig*) quality of an image in the wider sense. The image is given, is presented by the being in question (*zur Schau trägt*), it is the individual being itself which manifests, i.e. shows or makes visible (*Aussehen*) the ontological dimension of essence. In his *Metaphysics* Aristotle had strongly emphasized the unquestionable quality of that which presents itself thus for human awareness, of essence or *quidditas*, before it is thought about and then, *a posteriori*, becomes open to questions, to decisions about right and wrong: "With respect then, to all things which are essences and actual, there is no question of being mistaken, but only of thinking or not thinking them" (IX 10, 1051b, 40-32; 473).[4] It is this strong interpretation of the ontological dimension of the function of imagistic awareness and self-presentation of beings in Aristotle which is remarkably seconded and amplified in a very short essay by Giorgio Agamben. In *L'amico* Agamben reads a passage from Aristotle's *Nicomachean Ethics*. The passage, he argues, amounts to a statement of a *prima philosophia* and that is to say that it deals not only with beings and their essence but with the question of Being itself, with *existentia* in the aboriginal and in the recovered modern sense which may, after all, apply to James. "Es gibt" Agamben says, "eine Wahrnehmung des reinen Seins, eine *aisthesis* der Existenz" (5) because Aristotle speaks of the *perception* that we are: "*aisthesis oti estin* […]" (5). The phrase "perceptual awareness of pure Being, an *aisthesis* of existence" bears an

[3] I refrain from attempting to translate Heidegger into English here and will paraphrase the quotation to the best of my ability in the subsequent paragraph. The same will apply to the short passage from Agamben below.

[4] My reading as supported by Heidegger presents a strong contrast to and contradicts the analysis by Stephan Herzberg who reduces images (Gr. *phantasmata*) in Aristotle to examples, to instantiations or exemplifications, of the generalizing mind; this, it appears to me, is a way of imposing traditional metaphysical patterns unquestioned on Aristotle's vision; such patterns tend to obscure the very ontological complications that are discussed here (Herzberg 63-65).

uncanny similarity to Emerson's evocation in "Self-Reliance" of "the *sense of being*, which in calm hours rises, we know not how, in the soul, [and which] is not diverse from things [...] and proceeds from the same source whence their life and *being* also proceed" (64; my emphases, HF).

The Aristotelian interpretation suggests the function of images as indicators of Being itself and of the *whatness* or essence of beings. Images work as *bridges* which mediate the silent self-presence of what shows as experience *and* our later conceptualizations of this primary undivided awareness or *sense of being*. This interpretation, Aristotle's primary ontology, has the potential of being recovered in a modern re-enactment: the Aristotelian echo in Emerson's just quoted proto-pragmatist intuition points the *way*. It prepares the *method* which will come to full fruition in James's use of functional imagery in reading Being. Images, the linguistic place-holders of the *sense of being*, do not re-represent, they do work as events, as indispensable occurrences in the ceaseless and continuous temporal and experiential self-manifestation of beings in their Being on the way towards potential conceptual renderings.

James's contemporary Rudolf Eucken (1846-1926), the 1908 Nobel Prize Laureate for Literature, whom James sporadically quoted with mild approval of his activist idealism (e.g. James, *Pragmatism* 123), published a concise treatise *Bilder und Gleichnisse in der Philosophie* (*Images and Comparisons in Philosophy*) in 1880. Eucken is acutely aware of a shift in philosophical rhetoric and terminology as the indication of an imminent fundamental historical re-orientation of thinking, i.e. of the emergence of modernism. On the one hand Eucken still believes in the primacy of the concept, in Descartes' maxim (inherited from Cicero, Augustine, and Thomas Aquinas) that the foremost duty of thinking consists in *abducere mentem a sensibus*, that is, to move towards ever clearer and more distinct concepts and thus away from the senses and from percepts and images. Eucken's great good sense of historical change, however, forces him, even if ever so uneasily and reluctantly, to acknowledge a constitutive role of imagery for philosophy. Images, Eucken the historian of philosophy argues, proliferate especially in times of paradigm changes in thinking as, for example, in the late Middle Ages and the Early Renaissance, between, say, Cusanus and Francis Bacon, or, for that matter, in Eucken's present, i.e. the late nineteenth century (Eucken 8). Images, Eucken insists, are trailblazers ("Pfadfinder und Bahnbrecher" 9) for future innovative conceptualizations on the one hand and, more importantly for my purpose, necessary correctives of the analytic production of discrete ontologies or of a scientific world of factual, empirical singularities on the other hand. This is because images alone are apt and necessary to lead thinking and intuition back to visionary synthesis, to the non-mediated experiential awareness of a coherent and continuous totality. In other words, images have the power to re-direct conceptual differentiation towards the intuition of synthesis ("Einheit einer Anschauung" 27) and towards the actual experience of the world realized in terms (i.e. images) of an indiscrete ontology.[5] This imagistic practice, Eucken reasons, shows itself in particular in the leading and creative, that is historically innovative, thinkers (7). The philosophically significant image is both inexhaustible for subsequent conceptualizations and, at the same time, it functions as a means of literally liquifying thoughts and concepts: "die Gedanken in lebendigen Fluss zu bringen" ['to immerse thoughts in a living stream' tr. HF] (29). The image may serve in leading the rigid and static discreteness of a world analyzed conceptually back into the dynamic and vital continuities and the flow of active perceptual and experiential engagement.

Arguments like these, from which, as I stated, Eucken again and again shies back in order to almost ritualistically invoke the ultimate superiority of a Cartesian language of pure ideas, do indeed read like some of the antiintellectualist passages in James's *A Pluralistic Universe* or like parts of the chapters on percepts and concepts in *Some Problems of Philosophy*. In this way, Eucken's vision of the philosophical image as, firstly, trailblazer of a new epoch in thinking and, secondly, as the guarantor of the intuitive vision of a world synthesized by way of a dynamic and indiscrete ontology, and his understanding of the image, thirdly, as a resource which guides active thought without ever being exhausted by its conceptualizations, these three aspects may help to properly read the possible function of Jamesian imagery in an innovative, a modern ontological context. Images can then be understood as a means of correcting the deficiencies of predominantly rationalistic and conceptual ways of thinking, but also as alternatives to traditionally atomistic and empiricist philosophical stances. Summarily stated, images tend to erode the dogmatic validity of all discrete ontologies.

Despite the more detailed and concrete recent analyses of philosophical imagery by Bernhard Taureck (2004), by Ralf Konersmann (2009), and in the essay collection by Simone Neuber and Roman Veressow (2010), Hans Blumenberg's work on images, metaphors, and the significance of the nonconceptual ("das Unbegriffliche") in philosophy stands unrivalled in depth and sophistication. The central insight of Blumenberg's work concerns the

[5] I use the term "indiscrete ontology" as defined in Hogrebe, 122-123.

ultimate and necessary failure of the Cartesian project of a fully conceptual language of clear and distinct ideas, a project which, once realized, would have entailed the end of the history of philosophy, a problem already discerned by Leibniz and, of course, re-interpreted by Peirce (Blumenberg, *Unbegrifflichkeit* 10-12, 105-106). Niggardly reason, Blumenberg says pointedly, is always negatively contrasted with the lavish profusion of creation,[6] i.e. of Being in its fullness (20). One is reminded here of James's opposition between the thin reductionism of conceptual, rationalist thinking and the thick plenitude of perceptual awareness (James, *Pluralistic Universe* 64-68). While the concept will never be able to fulfill all of the demands of reason according to Blumenberg (11),[7] its successes often consist in the inversion of its function: it may help to lead thinking back to a freely chosen encounter with the riches of the un-mediated self-presentation of empirical, perceptual reality in the widest sense (27); in a similar fashion James had argued that all (conceptual) talk ultimately may and should serve as a means towards an enriched "return to life," a re-immersion into the plenitude of ongoing reality most intimately realized in direct perceptual awareness and active (inner) participation (James, *Pluralistic Universe* 131). Blumenberg's thinking contrasts this subordinate, menial role of the concept with the powerfully irreducible function of some images in the conduct of thinking. He calls these images or metaphors "absolute metaphors." Absolute metaphors arise out of the profusion of images provided by our *lebensweltliche* background, a profusion richer and more comprehensive and inescapable than that of verbal language (Blumenberg, "Paradigmen" 288). Sentences beginning with, for example, the noun-phrase "Das Sein", i.e. Being, sentences and arguments dealing with the totalities of either the cosmos or the *Lebenswelt*, the life-world, a preconceptual realm in which the thinking subject always already finds herself (Blumenberg, *Lebenswelt* 14-15 and *passim*), such statements will necessarily have to issue in metaphors or images that resist a fully satisfactory translation into a conceptual argumentative context (Blumenberg, *Unbegrifflichkeit* 65); rather, thinking of and about and within total horizons will persistently find itself indebted to such absolute metaphors or even worlds of metaphors. Absolute images, world-metaphors, reveal a pre-philosophical a-conceptual ("unbegriffliche") space of thinking awareness, the given and inescapable sub-structure of later conceptualizations, a catalytic sphere,

[6] "Die sparsame Vernunft steht gegen die verschwenderische Großzügigkeit der Schöpfung."

[7] "Der Begriff vermag nicht alles, was die Vernunft verlangt."

Blumenberg says, where concepts are ceaselessly being gene-rated without ever fully consuming and annihilating the foundational reservoir of perceptually generated imagery ("Paradigmen" 288). Here we find the nutrient solution out of which the crystallizations of a rational discourse emerge and which is unable to totally consume and transform the background to which it owes itself. Blumenberg's own images are intended, or have this function, to testify to the validity of an insight into experiential totalities and processes which refuse to find rationalistic closure. His images gesture towards the foundational and irreducible "Unbegriffliche" which both necessitates and forever frustrates all conceptual transformations (Blumenberg, *Unbegrifflichkeit* 107).

In turning to William James's use of images for and in thinking Being, I would like to employ *these* insights from Aristotle, Eucken, and Blumenberg as heuristic guidelines: namely, images may function as indispensable bridges between the mute and true ("unbegriffliche") presence of reality in or as perceptual awareness on the one hand and later conceptual articulation on the other; images herald open vistas of un-precedented, i.e. modern thinking, they have the potential to act as trailblazers of the new, the essentially novel, and they may guarantee the intuition of indiscrete ontological continuities easily sacrificed by conceptualist analytical discernment; lastly and perhaps most importantly, images as absolute metaphors are the indispensable instruments that help convey the meaning of total contexts to which any philosophical questioning always already finds itself indebted, be they called *Lebenswelt*, cosmos, or Being.

Image and Ontology in William James

Undoubtedly, a considerable number of images employed by James are primarily and merely rhetorical: they serve as illustrations, as elegant seductions of the reader or listener into following and assenting to abstract propositions and challenging insights: in chapter IX of *The Principles of Psychology*, the comparison of the rhythms of the stream of consciousness as it unfolds with the "alternation of flights and perchings" of a bird's life (*Principles* I, 236) may serve as a representative example. However, absolute metaphors and images, with which I am concerned, images which do ontological work, may come in two major ways which definitely go beyond rhetorical persuasion and embellishment: 1. absolute ontological images in James may occur as an open-ended series of at first sight incompatible alternatives or 2. as a unified world of internally related, proliferating metaphorical images, in Blumenberg's sense, i.e. as a *leitmotif* with possibly endless variations.

James's *Essays in Radical Empiricism* provide impressive examples for the first variant of allowing images to function in ontological thinking: here a series of alternative images is employed to convey the meaning of Being as pure experience which is not to be exhausted by one single perspective or experientially grounded visualization emerging from immediate awareness. In "Does Consciousness Exist?" James argues: "My thesis is that if we start with the supposition that there is only one stuff or material in the world, a stuff of which everything is composed, and if we call that stuff 'pure experience,' then knowing can easily be explained as a particular relation into which portions of pure experience may enter" (4). I do not want to enter in detail into the central *epistemological* concern of the essay, the question of the existence of an independent faculty called consciousness. The *ontological* implications of the text, however, become apparent once you focus on the controlling image in the text just quoted. The image of the stuff, the material, gr. *hyle*, arises out of the awareness of an a-conceptual *that*, which precedes all relations of cognition; as such pure experience is "perceived" in the Jamesian sense which goes far beyond mere perception in the exclusively sensualist meaning of the word. As in Aristotle, the nameless given calls for, it elicits or helps provide, a quasi-visual dimension within the perceptual awareness. The shapeless *that* acquires a certain specificity in generating, in allowing, in insinuating the image of the stuff which now and in turn guides or leads towards possible conceptual differentiations. Again, as in Aristotle's *Peri Psyches*, the image serves as the hinge or bridge which mediates the wordless presencing of undifferentiated Being and possible arguments about it.

Somewhat later in "Does Consciousness Exist?" James offers this alternative image: "The instant field of the present is at all times what I call the 'pure' experience. It is only virtually or potentially either object or subject as yet. For the time being, it is plain, unqualified actuality or existence, a simple *that*. In this *naif* immediacy it is of course *valid;* […]" (13). Pure experience, Being, is now a temporal spread: this imagistic vision of the ever-present field of nowness allows or facilitates thinking, even conceptualizing, Being as spatialized time. At the same time, the image supports Aristotle's point about the unquestionable truth of anything that is purely given in direct awareness: the naive immediacy is valid, James says, and precedes as well as supports both image and concept. In "The Thing and Its Relations" James begins his argument in this way:

> 'Pure experience' is the name which I gave to the immediate flux of life which furnishes the material to our later reflection with its conceptual categories [...]. Its purity is only a relative term, meaning the proportional amount of unverbalized sensation which it still embodies. (46)

The stuff, the instant field of the present, pure experience, Being, now shows as the ever-productive source of its own later verbalization: Being presents itself as the image of a ceaseless continuity, a flux, which allows for and always encompasses an internal structuring which we call language, conceptualization, knowledge, *logos*. As such the flux is immediate, a temporal phenomenal self-presence without static substantial grounding. The three images, and one might add the odd vision of the mosaic organically growing by its edges in the essay "A World of Pure Experience" (42), the three or four images show that the encounter with the mere *there* or *that* of Being, an encounter which James would have qualified as perceptual, as irreducible awareness, activates the thinking imagination and helps produce an open-ended series of images. What Blumenberg would call a world of metaphors, provides for a potentially endless series of conceptualizations without, Blumenberg argues, exhausting or replacing, consuming or eliminating the validity of the images which guide, as in Aristotle, the mind in its speculative ontological endeavor. These images, as Eucken had it, are trailblazers of all *a posteriori* intellectualist, rationalist, analytic differentiations, which always follow in James's essays on the imagistic passages quoted, while still retaining the vision of an indiscretely cohesive and unremittingly challenging pre-verbal totality.

The second mode in which images help to think Being in James, the unified world of internally related visualizations, is not at all surprisingly represented by the vision of water, of flow, of streams, of liquefaction. The majority of a plethora of variations on this imagistic theme, however, are verbs. As Joan Richardson has pointedly observed, James's "shifting attention away from a substantive-based language" toward a "language animated by the predominance of transitives" (19) may have been actually more successfully implemented by Henry James, but the transitives representing and enacting and pointing towards flow and its cognates in William James nevertheless, I believe, deserve more attention. The chapter on "The Stream of Thought" and its central imagery is so well-known that I think I may forego illustrations here. A far from exhaustive, a frankly unsystematic selection of quotations from other writings, may serve as the basis for the decisive point, the contribution of the world of water-imagery towards an, again, indiscrete modernist ontology. In *The Varieties of Religious Experience* we read:

"Philosophy lives in words, but truth and fact *well up* into our lives in ways that exceed verbal formulation" (360, my emphasis, HF). The agency of truth and fact, "experience," i.e. Being as event, which, as James says in *Principles*, remoulds us incessantly (228), this agency shows itself as an irrepressible spring or fountain. In *A Pluralistic Universe* James argues: "Reality, life, experience, concreteness, immediacy, use what word you will, exceeds our logic, *overflows* and surrounds it" (96, my emphasis, HF). The *logos* appears inundated and ultimately submerged by the abundance of the ceaseless self-presencing of Being. In another chapter of the same book, James argues that you "can no more *dip up* the substance of reality" with concepts "than you can *dip up water with a net*" (113, my emphasis, HF). This, in turn, may remind readers of the wonderful image in *Principles of Psychology* where James intuits conceptual entities as pots and barrels surrounded by *the swirling waters* of the really real, the ongoing flow of ontic continuity as experience (246). If we understand Being as experience, this statement from *A Pluralistic Universe* will further manifest the irrepressible power of the images of flow to convey ontological truth: "Every smallest state of consciousness, concretely taken, *overflows* its own definition" (129, my emphasis, HF). Images of *confluence* with "higher consciousnesses" (131) widen the horizon of ontological intuition towards the realm of religious modes of experience or Being.

The foundational quality of the vision of insuperable flow becomes manifest most succinctly, however, in the opening statements of chapter IV in *Some Problems of Philosophy* concerning percept and concept: "[…] concepts *flow out of* percepts and *into them* again, they are so interlaced […] that it is difficult to impart a clear notion of the difference meant" (31, my emphasis, HF). The difficulty of presenting a clear notion, a concise and distinct Cartesian idea of a difference between percept and concept, argues for a vision of flowing continuity that submerges the very tools of a discrete ontology in the irrepressible dynamic of Being as relentless inundation that admits of no final or static conceptual articulation. The percept, once again not to be limited to mere visual appropriation of experience, as experiential awareness, as individual enactment of Being as ongoing event or *Ereignis*, can be had only as the mute presence, the wordless *this* or *there* of which Aristotle spoke. Or it can be seen as the image which provides – functioning like a bridge – the basis for, again in Aristotle's view, speculative thinking, for the arsenal of rationalizations according to Blumenberg, an arsenal which can never be replaced by any single concept or system of concepts emerging from it.

The profusion of ontological images in James evokes a total vision which may be qualified as initiating a major change in ontology, a paradigm change in thinking, of which, as Eucken surmised in general terms, the very prominence of images in James's text is a significant testimony. The water images reveal an irrepressible tendency in Being which we may qualify, using a Heideggerian term, as *Abbau* (destruction). Being as self-generating emergence and flux consistently and relentlessly erases, destroys, removes, and submerges the very demarcation lines, the very boundaries or definitions which make (through which we make) things into things and concepts into concepts and that allow us to conceive identifiable single entities. Every single moment of experience, of Being as experiential moment of consciousness, James had argued in *A Pluralistic Universe,* "overflows its own definition" or as Bruce Wilshire has it, creatively expanding the reach of James's imagery of liquefaction, "[e]ssential to the supremacy of the *that*, the world, things finally overflow our pigeonholes and categories, and 'bleed' through their boundaries into the evolving surround" (118). This radical temporality of Being thus does away with the law of (definable) identity, with the law of the excluded middle, among other mainstays of traditional metaphysics. In a world of flowing transitionality self-identical entities and their conceptual definitions are necessarily and constantly eroded. The emergence of images out of the un-differentiated, 'begriffslose' *that* (according to Aristotle or Blumenberg) of pure experience may lead towards varieties of conceptualization, which, in turn, however, lead us back into the indiscrete fullness of Being as irrepressible temporal presencing and ultimate validity.

A Philosophy, an Ontology of the Future

My readings of William James's ontology have so far characterized it not so much as a series of insights, of teachings, let alone as a system of metaphysical statements but rather as a sequence of motions on a way, as a *methodos*, a leading of our imaging and thinking towards conceptualization and back again into primary awareness, towards that silent *thaumazein* which, according to Aristotle, sets all true thinking into motion, that staring of philosophy at the question of Being of which James spoke in *Some Problems of Philosophy*. James had insisted in *A Pluralistic Universe* that, ultimately, the thinker should "deafen" his readers or listeners to talk, and "make them return to life" (131) – into the immediacy of perceptive awareness and in *Pragmatism* he reminded one of the function of all knowing as a "leading" "into the particulars of experience" (98-99), that is, a move back into the fullness of Being as experiential event. In *Some Problems of Philosophy* James completed this image of thinking and knowing as a "leading" by reminding us that all our conceptualized worlds from the everyday to the mathematical have "flowered out" of the immediacy of awareness only to ultimately "return and *merge* themselves again in the particulars of our present and future perception" (34, my emphasis, HF). Thinking Being thus becomes, as I have said, a being on the way, a *methodos*, which, like the *structure* of emanations in Neo-Platonism, embraces a *proodos* and an *anodos* (or: *epistrophe*; Dodds, 62-64), a departure, a coming-forth and a return in ceaseless circular reiteration or a forever innovative renewal. In this (literal) *way of thinking Being* images are the bridges, or in Emerson's words, the conveyances ("The Poet" 37), which lead thought from amazed awareness through the momentary stasis of useful conceptualizations back again into the existentially practical engagement of the unmediated *thatness* or the once again silent wonder at the sheer fact of Being as it issues forth in and as pure experiences. James's ontology is a philosophy of the future not so much because, like Nietzsche's idea of it, it simply heralds a new era of thinking, but rather, because in its ceaseless issuing forth from the ever renewed and novel encounter with the mere *that* of emergent Being, it keeps the future open as the necessary condition of the possibility of its very existence as a thinking on the way.

Works Cited

Agamben, Giorgio. *L'amico. Der Freund.* Trans. Sabine Schulz. Berlin: Diaphanes, 2009.

Aristotle. *Metaphysics.* Vol. I: Books I-IX. Ed. and trans. Hugh Tredennick. Cambridge: Harvard UP, 1996.

—. *On the Soul. Parva Naturalia. On Breath.* Trans. W.S. Hett. Ed. Jeffrey Henderson. Cambridge: Harvard UP, 1957.

Blumenberg, Hans. "Paradigmen zu einer Metaphorologie." *Theorie der Metapher.* Ed. Anselm Haverkamp. Darmstadt: Wissenschaftliche Buchgesellschaft, 1983. 285-315.

—. *Theorie der Unbegrifflichkeit.* Frankfurt am Main: Suhrkamp, 2007.

—. *Theorie der Lebenswelt.* Frankfurt am Main: Suhrkamp, 2010.

Bredekamp, Horst. "Drehmomente, Merkmale und Ansprüche des Iconic Turn." *Iconic Turn. Die neue Macht der Bilder.* Ed. Hubert Burda and Christa Maar. Köln: Du Mont, 2004. 15-26.

Dodds, Eric Robert. "Tradition und persönliche Leistung in der Philosophie Plotins." *Die Philosophie des Neuplatonismus*. Ed. Clemens Zintzen. Darmstadt: Wissenschaftliche Buchgesellschaft, 1977. 58-74.

Emerson, Ralph Waldo. "Self-Reliance." *Essays. First Series*. The Works of Ralph Waldo Emerson. Vol. II. Boston: Houghton and Mifflin, 1883. 45-87.

—. "The Poet." *Essays. Second Series*. The Works of Ralph Waldo Emerson. Vol. III. Boston: Houghton and Mifflin, 1883. 7-45.

Eucken, Rudolf. *Bilder und Gleichnisse in der Philosophie*. Leipzig: Veit, 1880.

Heidegger, Martin. *Grundfragen der Philosophie. Ausgewählte 'Probleme' der 'Logik.'* Gesamtausgabe vol. 45. Frankfurt am Main: Vittorio Klostermann, 1984.

—. "Zeit und Sein." *Zur Sache des Denkens*. Frankfurt am Main: Vittorio Klostermann, 2007. 3-30.

Herzberg, Stephan. "Aristoteles und der Begriff des Bildes." *Das Bild als Denkfigur. Funktionen des Bildbegriffs in der Geschichte der Philosophie*. Eds. Simone Neuber and Roman Veressow. München: Fink, 2010. 51-65.

Hogrebe, Wolfram. *Metaphysik und Mantik. Die Deutungsnatur des Menschen*. Frankfurt am Main: Suhrkamp, 1992.

James, William. *A Pluralistic Universe*. Cambridge: Harvard UP, 1977.

—. "A World of Pure Experience." *Essays in Radical Empiricism*. Cambridge: Harvard UP, 1976. 21-44.

—. "Does Consciousness Exist?" *Essays in Radical Empiricism*. Cambridge: Harvard UP, 1976. 3-19.

—. "Experience." *Essays in Philosophy*. Cambridge: Harvard UP, 1978. 95.

—. *Pragmatism*. Cambridge: Harvard UP, 1975.

—. *Some Problems of Philosophy*. Cambridge: Harvard UP, 1979.

—. *The Letters of William James*. Vol. II. Ed. Henry James. Boston: The Atlantic Monthly P, 1920.

—. *The Principles of Psychology*. Vol. I. Cambridge: Harvard UP, 1981.

—. "The Thing and Its Relations." *Essays in Radical Empiricism*. Cambridge: Harvard UP, 1976. 45-59.

—. *The Varieties of Religious Experience*. Cambridge: Harvard UP, 1985.

Konersmann, Ralf. Ed. *Wörterbuch der philosophischen Metaphern*. Darmstadt: Wissenschaftliche Buchgesellschaft, 2007.

Krämer, Felicitas. *Erfahrungsvielfalt und Wirklichkeit. Zu William James' Realitätsverständnis*. Göttingen: Vandenhoeck & Ruprecht, 2006.

Neuber, Simone and Roman Veressow. Eds. *Das Bild als Denkfigur. Funktionen des Bildbegriffs in der Geschichte der Philosophie*. München: Fink, 2010.

W. J. T. Mitchell, "The Pictorial Turn." *Artforum* 30.7 (March 1992): 89-94.

Peirce, Charles Sanders. *Collected Papers of Charles Sanders Peirce*. Ed. Charles Hartshorne and Paul Weiss. Cambridge: Harvard UP, 1931-1935. Vol. I.

Putnam, Ruth Anna. "Introduction." *The Cambridge Companion to William James*. Ed. Ruth Anna Putnam. Cambridge: Cambridge UP, 1997. 1-10.

Richardson. Joan. *A Natural History of Pragmatism*. Cambridge: Cambridge UP, 2007.

Taureck, Bernhard H. F. *Metaphern und Gleichnisse in der Philosophie*. Frankfurt am Main: Suhrkamp, 2004.

Whitehead, Alfred North. *Science and the Modern World*. New York: Free P, 1967.

Wilshire, Bruce. "The Breathtaking Intimacy of the Material Word: William James's Last Thoughts." *The Cambridge Companion to William James.* Ed. Ruth Anna Putnam. Cambridge: Cambridge UP, 1996. 103-124.

Response to Herwig Friedl

Heinz Ickstadt

I admit that reading Professor Friedl's article for the first time left me awed and speechless. Here is a man, I thought somewhat nervously, a dear friend and inspiring co-worker in the field, who, for decades, has been living in the minds of Emerson and William James, has immersed himself in their texts; has, time and again, reflected their thought *in* and *against* a German tradition of ontological reflection (Nietzsche's as well as Heidegger's). He is largely responsible not only for the lively presence of American pragmatism in contemporary German American Studies but also for giving philosophy a distinguished place in it. After he has written so authoritatively, what is there left for me to say?

I am aware, however, that the function of a respondent *cannot* consist of simply saying "wow" – yet I *do* say it and want you to remember that I said it. In his effort to prepare a discussion, the respondent is also obliged to take issue, attempt to punch a hole or two into the armor of the speaker's intellectual and rhetorical persuasiveness. (As much as that is possible for someone like me who has dealt with William James's thought frequently, but for the most part instrumentally: i.e. who has used it as a kind of philosophical spectacles that would allow for a clearer reading of the late novels of William's younger brother.)

Right at the beginning you quote William James's advice: "Place yourself at the center of a man's philosophical vision and you understand at once all the different things it makes him write or say." You subsequently identify that center of vision as "his radically innovative, his modernist ontological insight," his deep fascination with the "question of Being." But you concede immediately that an "abstractly conceptual discussion of Being" can be found only in "relatively inconspicuous places," – implying that William (not unlike his brother Henry) dealt with the question of Being not via abstract speculation but through sensuous metaphor, the linguistic embodiment of his thinking. And yet, going through William James's texts once again, I did not find a single passage that could quite compare with Henry James's reflection on death and immortality. In his 1910 essay "Is There a Life after Death," Henry had written:

> I won't say that the world [...] grows more attaching, but will say that the universe increasingly does, and that this makes us present at the enormous multiplication of our possible relations with it; relations still vague [...], yet filling us [...] with the unlimited vision of being.[...]
>
> [I]n proportion as we [...] enjoy the greater number of our most characteristic inward reactions, in proportion as we do curiously and lovingly, yearningly and irrepressibly, interrogate and liberate, try and test and explore, our general productive and [...] creative awareness of things, in that proportion does our function strike us as establishing sublime relations. It is this effect of working it that is exquisite [...]; it is in a word the artistic consciousness and privilege in itself that thus shines as from an immersion in the fountain of being. Into that fountain, to depths immeasurable, our spirits dip – to the effect of feeling itself, qua imagination and aspiration, all scented with universal sources. (quoted in Matthiessen 602-614)

Does William deliver himself as unrestrictedly to these "depths immeasurable?" Is the center of his vision really that stream of "pure experience" out of which thought (or rather: thinking) is formed and linguistically made present as a process of continuous transition? A process that constantly and inevitably destabilizes its own stabilizations into form and meaning since, as you put it so eloquently, the "abundance of the ceaseless self-presencing of Being" inundates the *logos*? Toward the end of the famous "Stream of Thought"-chapter in his *Psychology* James writes from a radically pluralist perspective, but not in the rhetoric of "pure experience:"

> The mind [...] works on his block of stone. In a sense the statue stood there from eternity. But there were a thousand different ones beside it, and the sculptor alone is to thank for having extracted this one from the rest. Just so the world of each of us, howsoever different our several views of it may be, all lay embedded in the primordial chaos of sensations, which gave the mere matter to the thought of all of us indifferently. We may [...] by our reasonings unwind things back to that black and jointless continuity of space and moving clouds of swarming atoms which science calls the only real world. But all the while the world we feel and live in will be that which our ancestors and we, by slowly cumulative strokes of choice, have extricated out of this, like sculptors, by simply rejecting certain portions of the given stuff. Other sculptors, other statues from the same stone! Other minds, other worlds from the same monotonous and inexpressive chaos! My world is but one in a million alike embedded, alike real to those who may abstract them. (203f.)

My question would be, then, whether there is really only *one* center in William James's philosophical vision. Whether there isn't at least a counterpoint, or a counter-weight, to what he called his "flux philosophy;" or whether that center may not be conceived of as Janus-faced, as a tension between a pull towards immersion into Henry's "fountain of being" and a need to resist that pull – a resistance expressing itself in an abundant imagery of building and shaping. There is surely his appreciation of a Whitmanian "feeling of the sufficiency of the present moment [...] this absence of all need to explain it, account for it, or justify it" (James, "The Sentiment of Rationality" 21); but there is also a self-disciplinarian appeal for action, this urge to acknowledge that, as he wrote in *The Will to Believe*, "conduct, not sensibility is the ultimate fact" (quoted in Posnock 30).[1] Ross Posnock considers this to be a "rigorous commitment to self-creation" (29). I am thinking, too, of that frequently recurring image of a block of stone or marble whose form is yet to be brought out. "We receive in short the block of marble, but we carve the statue ourselves," as he writes in another chapter of *Pragmatism*; and, as a variation of the same idea: "Truth is *made*, just as health, wealth and strength are made, in the course of experience." As Posnock argues in *The Trial of Curiosity* – and it should be obvious that, by and large, I follow his argument in my response to Herwig Friedl: "Pragmatism's investment in control is easy to lose sight of amid James's extravagant rhetoric of endless process, vulnerability, risk and change. But without this investment pragmatism would cease to be the way to philosophize without lapsing back into wonder-sickness" (40f.).

I hope I do not veer too far from Friedl's focus on Jamesian ontology by harping once again on the complex relationship between the two brothers. I will give it a twist by bringing in a third figure, William Dean Howells. William James, as we so well know, disliked the opaqueness of his brother's late style and told him so – impatiently and condescendingly. But he gave lavish praise to the novels Howells wrote during the same period. He personally let Howells know how much he appreciated *The Kentons* (1902), which was poorly received by critics and the general public. On *Letters Home* (1903) he wrote with even greater enthusiasm:

> I've just read *Letters Home*, which raised me from the dead almost, and which is the most absolutely faultless piece of richness as well as veracity that ever flowed out of human pen. I bar no one and no language. It is nature itself, and the wit of it, and the humor of it, and the goodness of it! You may go – that will remain. (quoted in Brooks 195f.; fn 8)

[1] Posnock states the tension in James's thinking very acutely: "James's life and work are a monument to the self as a perpetual work of labor, a structure of repression. But this is not to deny that the repression is dialectical, issuing in a philosophy of pragmatism that celebrates repression's opposite: the fact of vulnerability in a world of contingency, uncertainty, risk, change [...]" (30).

Although, after having read *Pragmatism*, Henry wrote famously to his brother: "I simply sank down, under it. [...] I was lost in the wonder of the extent to which all my life I have [...] unconsciously pragmatised," he never commented on his brother's *Principles of Psychology* – yet it is hard to imagine that he did not know it or at least knew parts of it. *The Ambassadors* and *The Golden Bowl*, especially, show an equal fascination with the "stream of thought," with its rings and halos of suggestiveness, the elusive radiance of its vagueness. In contrast, Howells never called himself a pragmatist but he reviewed *Principles of Psychology* in his *Editor's Study* of July 1891. Ignoring almost completely what William James had written about the instability of self and the streaming of consciousness, he concentrates on the chapters on "Habit" and on "Will" from which he extracts as a lesson to be learned that "we are creatures of our own making." Against the ever-changing fluidity of our thoughts and "the dark underlying premises of the luminous consciousness that delights him," Howells quotes William James as sternly demanding that "[i]nstead of all this, more zestful than ever is the work, the work; and fuller the import of common duties and of common goods" (quoted in Simpson 323f.).

In these mutual interpretations, obviously, each reads the other according to his own different needs and purposes. But it should also be clear that all three are involved in a civilizing project which one may call, with William James, an "unstiffening" of (pre)given ideas, or of existing forms (be they cognitive, linguistic or narrative, ethical or social), and ultimately, of concepts of cultural order. In this project, which opens the notion of the "civilized" (without ever abandoning it) downward or outward towards "the dark underlying premises of consciousness," and where form – as William James believed – is to be worked out of the fluid stuff of experience, Henry James and William Dean Howells occupy opposite yet related positions. They are related in attempting to save a notion of order that is based on "reason," imagination, and/or "manners" by making it more fluid and flexible. Yet they are separated by the different degree of flexibility they each allow. While Howells confined himself to the ethical premises of his vision, he was yet determined to explore, within the limits he imposed on it, a world of social experience. It was a world grounded in an *ethics* of behavior; whereas Henry James emphasized, in his late novels, an *aesthetics* of behaviour that filtered (and thus refined) its ethical implications through the careful contemplation of social signs, through self-abandoning and world-transforming introspection.

William James stands curiously in-between: He is torn between a fluid, self-dissolving vision of the marginal, of the pre-conscious and pre-linguistic realms of the irrational which powerfully attracted (yet also repelled) him, and a felt need to control, through the reign of habit, this newly discovered contingent and chaotic territory of knowledge. It is precisely this double movement: the opening of "dumb and evanescent," yet creative areas of consciousness, on the one hand, and the channeling of their unpredictable energies in the service of the growth of mind and character, on the other hand, that makes James see pragmatism, with all its "unstiffening" and destabilizing tendencies, as a stabilizing and meliorizing cultural factor. "Willing to take anything," pragmatism functions like a very large net of thought in action (or: of thought into action) – a net that can, if flung out wide enough, profitably catch and bring into the realm of the culturally useful so many new, if sometimes strange, kinds of "fish" from the margins of consciousness as well as of society ("outcasts and eccentrics: mystics, mind-readers, mental patients, "primitives" of all provenance).

I imagine hearing you inwardly sigh now with some exasperation: "Good God, here I wanted to bring out the truly innovative elements in James's thought: to what extent writing and thinking coincide in the rich dynamics of his imagery; to what extent he, whom so many contemporary philosophers despised, anticipates modern philosophy's existential push toward the mind's reflection of Being (including its own). Yet my respondent wants to put him back into a narrow historical frame: William James as cultural hero, as a representative figure of American Progressive Culture – exactly the frame that, for a long time, has been a blindfold preventing us from seeing the innovative potential, the modernity of James's thought. I take that frame for granted (I still assume Herwig Friedl as thinking), and move from there into a more promising, a more interesting direction."

To which I would answer: fair enough. Conceiving the "question of Being" as *the* center of James's philosophical vision is your own, self-empowering act of imagination which surely gives James relevance beyond a specific historical context. And yet, I would argue, without that context, without that counterweight in James's thought, without this second engine of his thinking, the image you project – exciting as it is – is incomplete and slightly distorting. The center you discover in James is clearly the center of your own philosophical interest and vision.

To which you might then reply: Isn't that, precisely, what James's concept of a pluralistic universe is all about? "Other sculptors, other statues from the same stone" ("The Stream of Thought" 204).

Works Cited

Brooks, Van Wyck. *Howells: His Life and World.* New York: Dutton, 1959.

James, William. "Pragmatism and Humanism." Ed. Bruce Kuklick. *William James: Writings 1901-1910.* New York: The Library of America, 1987. 591-604.

—. *The Correspondence of William James.* Vol. 3. Eds. Skrupskelis, I.K. and E.M. Berkeley. Charlottesville: The U of Virginia P, 1994.

—."The Sentiment of Rationality," *Selected Writings.* Ed. G.H. Bird. London: Orion, 1995. 20-53.

—."The Stream of Thought." *Selected Writings.* Ed. G.H. Bird. London: Orion, 1995. 170-204.

Matthiessen, Francis Otto. *The James Family.* New York: Alfred Knopf, 1948.

Menand, Louis. "Pragmatism's Conception of Truth". *Pragmatism. A Reader.* New York: Vintage Books, 1997. 112-131.

Posnock, Ross. *The Trial of Curiosity: Henry James, William James, and the Challenge of Modernity.* New York: Oxford UP, 1991.

Simpson, James W. *Editor's Study by William Dean Howells.* Troy: Whitston Publishing Company, 1983.

The Truth and Nature of/in Pragmatism

William James on the Psychodynamical Force of Truth

Helmut Pape

What is truth? Is there a single, eternal truth? In everyday life, we do not pose these questions. "That is true" usually only serves to confirm small, situational truths such as "It's already raining," "My car is over there," or "It is dark now." For some philosophers, Hegel, for example, in the *Phenomenology of Mind*, these small truths do not count: They are worthless because they are ephermeral and transitory. "The Truth," spelled with a capital "t," that interests many philosophers is timeless, unchanging and perfect. Does William James give us a new, pragmatic theory of or argument against "The Truth?"

I do not think that in his 1907 lectures *Pragmatism: A New Name for Some Old Ways of Thinking*,[1] William James was interested in the question whether there is an eternal nature of truth, although this is insinuated by some of his critics as well as by his followers. He had various other things in mind, and he wanted his readers to focus on issues that have to do with the way we grasp, evaluate and use truth. I argue that one of his main concerns was to comprehend the role of small, situational truths and the meaning for our life of both the value of, and the psychodynamical force of, truth. By this force all sorts of truths – even the big ones are effectively embodied in one's own individual experience. Accordingly, in his book on pragmatism James states:

[1] The *Pragmatism*-Lectures, by far James's most famous and influential book, were originally published by Harvard UP, but are available today in a number of fairly good editions, including the one on www.Gutenberg.org. Of course the *Pragmatism* lectures published as Vol. 1 of the critical edition in *The Works of William James*, ed. by Frederick H. Burkhardt, Fredson Bowers and Ignas. K. Skrupsekelis, Harvard UP, Cambridge, Mass. 1975 - 1978, 17 volumes in 19 parts, will give you the definitive critical version of the text. In Germany the translation of "Pragmatism" in 1908 by Wilhelm Jerusalem, a friend of William's, is still available from Meiner Verlag, Hamburg, in its 2nd edition printed in 1994 with a new introduction and edited by Klaus Oehler. I will be quoting from an edition that combines *Pragmatism* with a volume of essays titled *The Meaning of Truth,* first published in 1909: *Pragmatism and The Meaning of Truth*, introduction by A. J. Ayer, Harvard UP, Cambridge, Mass. 1978. I will refer to this edition using the siglum "*P*".

> "The true," to put it very briefly, is only the expedient in the way of our thinking, just as "the right" is only the expedient in the way of our behaving. Expedient in almost any fashion; and expedient in the long run and on the whole of course; for what meets expediently all the experience in sight won't necessarily meet all farther experiences equally satisfactorily. (P^2 106)

What kind of process and what kind of value does James have in mind when he talks about truth being "expedient" for our way of behavior?

The Question of Truth: James on the Power of Truth

The Jamesian claim that truths are important is built on the idea that they advance us in our thinking and are "rewarding," "useful" and "satisfactory" in the long run of our course of experience. It has, therefore, not only provoked criticism and strong hostile reactions in philosophy but downright condemnation. All of this is still present today in the depths of the German understanding of pragmatism owing to the reception of James's thesis. Thus, the German philosopher Guthberlet wrote in 1908: "A new fashionable philosophy comes to us, this time from across the ocean from the land of the dollar that has to be regarded as the ideal of this philosophy. The very same degrades truth to utility [...]" (quoted in Joas 119). Bertrand Russell, Max Scheler, Heinrich Rickert, G.E. Moore, Josiah Royce – to mention only a few well-known philosophers – have accused the Jamesian theory of truth, of voluntarism, subjectivism, relativism, or the destruction of truth and rationality. The British philosopher and Nobel Prize laureate, Bertrand Russell, even claimed that James reduced truth to individual satisfaction: Pragmatism as a form of cognitive self-gratification?[3]

But how are the effect and the force of small, everyday, and situational truths to be understood? Surely, the individual's satisfaction and pleasure do not provide a reliable condition, but are instead influenced or depend upon the truth we find or accept. In preparing ourselves for a philosophical discussion of everyday truths using the Jamesian theory of truth, we should look at the characteristics of our own, contemporary problems in our everyday negotiations of truth.[4]

[2] Cf. footnote 1: "*P*" refers to *Pragmatism: A New Name for Some Old Ways of Thinking*, in the 1978 Harvard edition.

[3] In discussion with me Marxists have, time and again, attacked this notion of truth and pragmatism being an expression of "brutal American-style capitalism" or an expression of "the mentality of the slaughterhouses and gangsters in Chicago."

[4] In analytic philosophy, truth is understood as a logical property of assertions. The

Surely, today, there are not too few but too many truths: In some scholarly disciplines, the empirical knowledge available doubles every five to ten years. Moreover, the access to and the usage of knowledge has broadened in several new ways as, in the age of internet and e-mail, many people are overwhelmed by the ever-increasing flood of new, globally accessible scholarly and cultural knowledge. They know that they should always try to take more truths into account than they actually do. However, this is an impossible task, even when working selectively. The choice and the responsibility for the selectively used interests are then to be justified and decided on by each of us individually. That may be the reason why some of us reject the supply from the global network of knowledge as irrelevant and rather unimportant, and even refuse to deal with new ways of accessing knowledge. The question "How can truth help in developing the new knowledge being shared with other people?" is not being asked. Can such a way of dealing with possible truth be morally and epistemologically justified? How much value do truths have for us anyway?

What James does is to tell us how the value of truth and their effects on ourselves is effecting the structure of our experiential processes and how we approach truths in the course and development of biographically lived, strictly finite and contingent individual experiences. If I am right, the Jamesian theory of truth is concerned with the human, personal ways of how we acquire, trace out, deal with, and employ truths. That is, how they affect our mental development and interaction with each other. In contrast to some present-day neuroscientists, James balances psychological, neurophysiological, and practical aspects of the mental processes that lead to our understanding of new and old truths. In doing so, his argument combines the practical acquisition of truth through actions with exchanges of a successfully lived and shared life.

Consequently, this is one claim defended in this paper: James's concept of truth addresses and explicates the successful practice of truth and the situatedness of all truth in everyday life. The philosopher Rainer Marten has described a philosophical account of everyday production of and interaction with truth as follows:

> There is truth. As long and as far as people live and act, the results are necessarily fulfilled conditions of truth. In the everyday interaction of humans with each other, and the individual with him or herself, actually to master the

Tarski-Davidsonian semantic account of truth tells you that the property of truth of the assertion "grass is green" can be sufficiently captured by the equivalence "grass is green" if and only if 'grass is green'. But this neither tells us what truth means to us, nor what it means to realize truth in our individual experience.

> challenges of life in every assessment of one's own ability, practices of recognition and truth are being experienced in sometimes very short intervals. (Marten 18; my translation)

In everyday life, people are, above all, consciously concerned with the failure of actions and their understanding among each other. Therefore, they easily overlook that in the overwhelming majority of cases they succeed and their actions and habits are "true to the facts" when interacting with each other and their environment. They ignore that there is always a sound base for true understanding and successful action. This much truth is even contained in every failure and is successfully realized – even when failure, error or disaster occurs. What, then, is the basis for this successful realization of the everyday acquisition of world and truth?

In this paper, I can only sketch the ways in which James generalized his seminal research in psychology to philosophical insights into the conditions permeating mental processes in order to master and create truth for us, human beings living for a limited time. So my main and core thesis in this paper is as follows: When James speaks of "utility," "leading" and "advancing" in the pragmatic theory of truth, he is concerned with the cognitive conditions of the goal directed execution of human experience that embody truth or tend to bring about truth. This thesis holds only for those cognitive processes which connect together thinking and perceiving, feeling and sensing in the exchange with other people and the environment.[5]

James is concerned with the small, changeable, and context-dependent truths. Precisely because of this, however, they are able to become useful in a specific context of human activity and exchange, which is why their "benefit" and their "effectiveness" are much greater than those of eternal truths, since these would first have to be transformed in the contexts of their application. James's human conception of truth is a pragmatist one, for dealing with and experiencing truth can be connected. Already the experience of comprehending truth is an action in itself. Its result can only prove itself

[5] This also includes the neurophysiological and experiential structural characteristic of grasping the truth. James stresses that experience has a teleological structure which supports the activity of discovering truth. This is a success condition of cognition build into it. For humans to know truth is "essentially bound up with the way in which one moment in our experience may lead us towards other moments which it will be worth while to have been led to. [...] Our experience meanwhile is all shot through with regularities. One bit of it can warn us to get ready for another bit, can intend or be significant of that remoter object." (*P* 98f.)

gradually valid and applicable to situations other than those of the initial comprehension, if it can be confirmed. Confirming or acquiring the truth of a belief thus has a value in itself, namely the "workability." James, therefore, says about the pragmatist: "Truth, for him, becomes a class-name for all sorts of definite working-values in experience" (*P* 38).

"Being expedient," "utility," and "workability" are pragmatic characteristics of the psychodynamical force of truths which are employed in the acquisition, corroboration, and application of small truths in occasional experiences. The pragmatic theory of truth, however, thus claims to make truth comprehensible in the human sense of an open, constantly changing practice of truth. James, therefore, understands human truths also as an open process of sharing a world with one another, which he positions against the notion of unchanging Truth:

> The trail of the human serpent is thus over everything. Truth independent; truth that we *find* merely; truth no longer malleable to human need; truth incorrigible, in a word; such truth exists indeed superabundantly […] but then it means only the dead heart of the living tree, and its being there means only that truth also has […] petrified in men's regard by sheer antiquity. (*P* 37; emphases in original)

Pragmatism is also concerned with the small, transitory truths that are still alive and that become new truths when acquired so that truth takes control of the human being. These small, everyday truths highlighted by pragmatism are thus crucial because their dynamic role in opening up new experiences is indicative of their value:

> From this simple cue pragmatism gets her general notion of truth as something essentially bound up with the way in which one moment in our experience may lead us toward other moments which it will be worth while to have been led to. Primarily, and on the common-sense level, the truth of a state of mind means this function of *a leading that is worth while.* (*P* 98; emphases in original)

The small, contextual and specific truths that I have acquired by chance open up, nevertheless, a viable path of thinking and experience for me to lead my life in the here and now of my individual existence. Moreover, it is a path which orientates my future experience and which experience has to follow so that we can attain that which is worthwhile. This describes the small truths consisting of the experience of "workability" in daily life. If their function is to be understood, then what happens and what is supposed to happen in experiences and the thinking of human beings when they understand something successfully, experience it consciously or intuitively, and turn it into practical action, needs to be explained. To deal with the embodiment of truths in daily life theoretically, is far from easy because we have to consider contingent aspects of life, rather than psychological and physiological theories about them. In everyday life, facts and details, as well as the way we grasp them are decisive: We are engaged in a practical process, that is purposive, that successfully connects thinking, experience, and action in individual situations.

The Process of Truth: Conditions of the Individual Acquisition of Truth

How does James manage to explain the process whereby an individual acquires, embodies and constructively interprets small truths?

Being worthwhile

Let us start with arguably the most striking moment in the Jamesian characterization of truth. This aspect is the idea of "being worthwhile" which is made possible by the comprehension of truth. Behind this inconspicuous, everyday expression of "being worthwhile," which appeared twice in the quote above (cf. *P* 98), lies the concept of the transformation of an objective or principle in a preconscious or conscious mental process that guides a choice which traces out those arbitrary, contingent truths concerning the individual in some situation or other. Objectives, values and principles that are completely accepted by us allow us to choose or select preconsciously. This is a characteristic of human beings: The principles and objectives that they seriously pursue permeate all levels of their cognitive activity, as both conscious thinking and involuntary perceiving and feeling. That means that even when we are unaware of it, they control the perceptions, feelings, and sensations of the person believing in a principle and seriously pursuing an objective. From the beginning, the human mind and human sensibility are processes of choice and differentiation. If we describe something as true in daily life, this also means that what is described as true is valuable or at least important or interesting for us.

As we are permeated by certain objectives, values and principles, it is worthwhile for us to engage more deeply in certain features (and not in others) of people and objects. The reason for this is the significant fact of anthropology and life that connects "being worthwhile" with the understanding of truth. This fact is the finite and transient nature of each individual human life, for it is finiteness and life's transience determine which principles and objectives are meaningful for humans in the first place. I can only hint at that connection here.[6] Finite nature and transience have an important consequence for the indispensability of objectives and principles in the construction of the small truths of our experience: Because human experiences and thoughts are temporally and energetically limited by a lifespan, only those principles and objectives are in life useful that – during our lifetime's finite experience – select something effectively.[7] In any case, the meaning and success of our life is dependent on an accurate selection of what we spend the time and energy of our life on.

This leads us to human reason and the meaning of economy, a meaning that is easily overlooked, as it is easily confused with the abstract economic orientation of all areas of life prevalent today, which only recognizes the principle of profit maximization, possibly even in the form of "share-holder value." The human economy of life is based on the finite nature of the time and energy of our lives, a feature that we collectively share with each other. Only in the finite time of our lives can we effectively develop and share the principles, objectives, and goals of our lives with each other. They guide the meaningful selection of truths in our experience and our actions precisely only because we are finite and mortal. In short, whether we want to or not, we cannot help but engage in an interest and value-guided selection of truths, also limited by objectives and purposes.

Willpower and choice: The active, personal contribution to truth

Let us turn to another one of James's characterizations of the process of acquiring truth: The active contribution of the individuals themselves. This much is obvious so far: "Advancing," "leading to," and

[6] In his book *Lebenskunst*, Rainer Marten treats the relation between life's finiteness and the meaning of life-shaping objectives and encounters between human beings as the basis for the meaning of life as a truly human one. In his approach, being aware of one another by looking into the eyes of another human being creates human time and space. Seeing one another and needing another person then become essential ingredients of a meaningful human life.

[7] Speculative philosophy and mystic esotericism tend to ignore that it is obvious that even the infinite and eternal can only be acquired and constructed in the form of finite experiences. One or the other of us may possess more or less energy. But that does not change the fact of a necessarily strictly finite limitation of lifetime and life-energy. The capacity for abstraction and for poetical romantization in their own thinking and in their living with each other allows people to construe their selves in such a way that they largely devote their life only to the presumably infinite and eternal.

"orientating" can only be accomplished by individual thinking, enabling the experience of small, contextual truths that allow the comprehension of truth in the process of experience.

There are, however, some more constructive and actively action-oriented determinants of the process of truth than the ones already mentioned. These refer to the "making," "corroboration," and "creation" of truth. Both types of determinants describe the complex dependence of constructions of truths on people as well as the corroboration of principles and objectives for orienting the process of truth toward a goal. Yet, they place a very different emphasis on the contribution provided by a person's mental processes. While the first three determinants ("advancing," "leading to," "orientating") also describe the orientation of the experiential process on a truth that exists independently of the subject, the determinants of "assimilating," "corroborating," and "creating" add a constructive and selective perspective, as well as the idea of the self-controlled and self-reliant creation of truth.

These activist processual characteristics find their expression in the Jamesian term "verification." Only through verification is a concept or an opinion "made true." This concept means that truth is changeable and that, in a certain sense and up to a certain point, individuals are able to selectively "make" truths. "Verification" thus means the "making true" of the comprehension of truth that is controlled by the subject. This element is the core of the pragmatic characterization of truth. James states:

> *True ideas are those that we can assimilate, validate, corroborate and verify. False ideas are those that we cannot.* That is the practical difference it makes to us to have true ideas; that, therefore, is the meaning of truth, for it is all that truth is known-as. (*P* 97; emphases in original)

Such verification would be a complete and successful "leading" of the concept, for example, of the experience of a given topic through a "verification-process" (*P* 98).

Did James really want to claim that "verification" in an active, practical sense may create and produce truths by willpower only? In this case – and this has been criticized by Josiah Royce – the fact that a statement is true would only be dependent on whether I want it to be true or not and act accordingly. Josiah Royce, like James a professor of philosophy at Harvard, assumes that James actually wanted to argue this. Royce thus imputes the Jamesian theory of truth to voluntarism, which he defined as follows: "[…] the solving word of the theory of truth is Voluntarism. Truth is won by willing, by creative activities. The doer, or perhaps the deed, not only finds, but *is,* the truth. Truth is not to be copied, but to be created. It is living truth. And life is action" (Royce 67). Let us ignore the cases where we talk about our own future actions: For if I say "I will jump," it is only my jumping that will "create" the truth that my assertion predicts.

If James argued for a voluntaristic theory of truth, he would have had to claim that the truth of a statement is only or primarily contingent on the conscious will of a single, verifying person. Only then would it be correct to say that the use of the individual will is able to produce truth. However, we have already seen that James speaks about conditions that are preconscious and independent of will, and that are effective in our experiential processes. Moreover, James claims that when we experience truths, selective influences (for example, through focus of attention) emanate from the verifying person that determines which kind of truth we turn to. This selective influence is due to the stream of consciousness, experiences, perceptions, and feelings which are actively oriented toward the facts, relations, and things at hand. Yet, on the basic level of the stream structure of mental processes, conscious will is necessarily irrelevant: We perceive and feel these things involuntarily and sometimes even against our own will. Furthermore, it does not make sense to talk about "selecting" or "attending to" some situational truth (and not to some other), if truth is created through selection or attention.

But why did Royce accuse James of voluntarism? The root of this misunderstanding is James's attempt to do justice to both the human individual as well as the neurophysiological aspects of understanding the connections between the mental processes that a person has to go through to comprehend a truth. All truths have to be comprehensible for us in their particularities and in their temporal subdivisions. After all, James attempts to answer the question "What does it mean for the individual to comprehend truth with their very individual experiences and feelings?" His critics, however, usually presume that he answers the question of "What is a general definition of truth like that applies to all kinds of truth?" Every single person asking whether a belief is true or not, needs time, energy, and opportunities for life experiences in order to be able to confirm anything. James, therefore, emphasizes the inescapable human temporality of acquiring truth which is necessary for a contextual, situational truth.

However, it must be admitted that James's point would have been much stronger had he discussed how by expressing the same idea or assertion and thereby using it, it turns out to be true in some situation. But he prefers to state his view in terms of ideas or assertions changing their truth-value: "Truth *happens* to an idea. It *becomes* true, is *made* true by events. Its verity *is* in fact an event, a process: the process namely of its verifying itself, its veri-*fication*. Its validity is the process of its valid-*ation*" (*P* 97, emphases in original).

We have seen that James acknowledges the existence of absolute and unchanging truths but that he did not want to say anything about the nature of absolute truth. Instead, he is concerned with the process through which even absolute truths are translated into our experience and are thus comprehended in one form or another. For every person, this comprehension of truth is something that happens or occurs at a specific point in time and that requires specific individual experiential and representational processes. That means that truth is attained at a certain point in time and through certain individual experiences and reflections which have to be executed and experienced. If this is the case, then a concept has been "valid-ated" for a person.

Conclusion: The Practice of Truth and True Human Culture

In conclusion, I would like to turn to the psychological model that is generalized and pragmatically interpreted by James's theory of truth. What turns a truth into a human and individually comprehensible truth is a process of experience, reflection, and confirmation. We are thus concerned with the connection between our thinking and our actions and the lives that you, and I, would like to live amonga community of people in a way that is valuable to us. The meaning of eternal, enduring, or even only scientifically true laws and facts has to be translated into people's value structures and experiential biographies. Absolutely true facts and laws by themselves, even if they exist and we recognize them, are inconsequential to the value and meaning of human life if no such translation exists.

James's notion of the meaning of truth accounts for the unavoidable practical and experiential effects, arguing that all truths have to be cashed out in terms of the currency of small truths we are able to experience. However, this view also ensures that the meaning of human existence and life cannot be dismissed from a point of view of some eternal truth about the universe.

This is the argument James made in a letter to Henry Adams on June 17, 1910, shortly before his death. Henry Adams argued for a deterministic and pessimistic concept of history which he wanted to support by his interpretation of the Second Law of Thermodynamics.

The Second Law states that in a closed system the distribution of energy can only increase. According to Adams this implies that the universe is irreversibly headed toward heat death. Therefore, even now human life on earth has no meaning. James's reply to Adams relies on the inherent meaning of small truths:

> Certain arrangements of matter *on the same energy-level* are, from the point of view of man's appreciation, superior, while others are inferior. Physically a dinosaur's brain may show as much intensity of energy-exchange as a man's, but it can do infinitely fewer things, because as a force of detent it can only unlock the dinosaur's muscles, while the man's brain, by unlocking far feebler muscles, indirectly can by their means issue proclamations, write books, describe Chartres Cathedral, etc., and guide the energies of the shrinking sun into channels which never would have been entered otherwise – in short, *make* history. [...] The "second law" is wholly irrelevant to "history" – save that it sets a terminus – for history is the course of things before that terminus, and all that the second law says is that, whatever the history, it must invest itself between that initial maximum and that terminal minimum of difference in energy-level. (James, *Letter* 345; emphases in original)

This reply shows that James's understanding of the psychodynamical force of truth in our life can neither be refuted by some truth coming from physical cosmology, nor by other eternal truths. Transcending physicality, more comprehensive connections of everyday and cultural practices constitute the specific meaning of human life. These practical relations are as omnipresent as physical fact and logical truths. They are the trail of the human serpent which integrates and they cover everything, as long as they can be included in the communal practice of life which constitutes a meaningful human culture.

Works Cited

James, William. *Pragmatism and The Meaning of Truth.* Cambridge: Harvard UP, 1975.

—. *The Letters of William James.* ed. by H. James, Boston: The Atlantic Monthly P, 1920.

Joas, Hans. *Pragmatismus und Gesellschaftstheorie.* Frankfurt am Main: Suhrkamp, 1992.

Marten, Rainer. *Lebenskunst.* München: Fink, 1993.

—. *Menschliche Wahrheit.* München: Fink, 2000.

Royce, Josiah. "The Problem of Truth in the Light of Recent Discussion." *Bericht über den III. Internationalen Kongress für Philosophie zu Heidelberg, 1.-5. 9 1908.* Ed. Th. Eisenhans. Heidelberg: Winter, 1909. 62-90.

William James's Idea of Man: The *Conditio Humana* and the Philosophy of Pragmatism

Kai-Michael Hingst

Introduction

Why should philosophy deal with concepts of man? Should this not instead be a topic for descriptive psychology or anthropology? By no means is this the case. Each philosophy implicitly presupposes a certain concept of what man is. This concept or idea of man also essentially influences the subjects that a philosopher chooses to address.

However, this interrelation is hardly discussed by most philosophers; it is rare that an idea of man is formulated in advance, in most cases it remains unexpressed and is, in the best case, retroactively unfolded in a confirmatory and cursory manner.

Yet a particular idea of man, and one which seems to go without saying, forms the basis of philosophical thought, as some examples show. For instance, Plato (427–347) would not have written two dozen dialogues, if he had not been convinced that man is discursive, i.e., is willing and able to communicate with his peers in a conversation. Descartes (1596–1650) in his *Meditationes de prima philosophia* (1641) would not have looked for the archimedic point of knowledge in the shape of "*cogito ergo sum*," if he had not acted on the assumption that man generally strives for secure knowledge. Kant (1724–1804) in his *Grundlegung zur Metaphysik der Sitten* (1785) would not have searched for the basic principle of moral action, if he had not considered man as free, but as determined, not as possessing good will, but as intrinsically amoral or immoral. Whether or not these ideas of man – or rather strains of such an idea – rendered by Plato, Descartes and Kant are right or wrong is not the point here, but rather that a philosopher will hardly be able to philosophize at all without, consciously or unconsciously, having any such idea.

In this paper, I will first outline William James's idea of man. Secondly, on the basis of some fundamental themes of James's philosophy I will inquire, whether and how this idea of man is reflected in his philosophy. Thirdly, I will ask the question of whether, from James's perspective, there is a cogent relationship between his idea of man and philosophy. Finally, I will present my conclusion.

James's Idea of Man

What, then, is James's philosophical idea of man? Before we pursue this question, it has to be remembered that James studied medicine in order to become a doctor although he never practiced, and that for a long time he was a professor of psychology. He established the first psychological laboratory in America at Harvard University and became one of the leading psychologists of his time. His psychological *opus magnum* of nearly 1300 pages, *The Principles of Psychology* (1890), was a product of twelve years of work and became the leading book on psychology as a natural science rather than, as is the trend today, on general psychology. However, it makes sense to take account of James's psychological writings when looking for his idea of man.

To this end, an inventory of James's idea of man should emphasize six characteristics:

1. The teleological orientation of mind. James considers human thought as strictly teleological. He repeatedly states that "mental life is primarily teleological" (*PBC*[1] 11), that the "organism of thought [...] is teleological through and through" (*EP* 18), that "classification and conception are purely teleological weapons of the mind" (*PP* 961 = *PBC* 310) and that conceptions are "teleological instruments" (*WB* 62). Furthermore, he views "the mind as an essentially teleological mechanism" (*WB* 94). As his repeated emphasis indicates, the aspect of human behavior and experience driven by individual purpose and interests is the dominant reference point in James's pragmatism (cf. Oehler XXII*).

2. Practical bearing of human thought. If human thought is teleological, the question arises as to what the τέλος, or purpose, of this thought is. To James, the response is clear: the purpose which thought aligns oneself with is a successful practice (of life), since "man is primarily a practical being, whose mind is given him to aid in adapting him to this world's life" (*TT* 24). This practical orientation of man is underlined by James in his psychological writings when he states that "[w]e cannot escape our destiny, which is practical" (*TT* 26) and "[m]y thinking is first and last and always for the sake of my doing" (*PP* 960 =

[1] The abbreviations used for James's works refer to the bibliography at the end of this paper.

PBC 309). In general he also emphasizes "man's practical nature" (*WB* 106), while, corresponding to this practical conception of man, the formation of habits to which he dedicates a separate chapter in both *The Principles of Psychology* (1890) (*PP* 109–131) and *Psychology: Briefer Course* (1892) (*PBC* 125–138) plays a crucial role in his psychology[2]. One example will here suffice, when he states that "[a]ll our life [...] is but a mass of habits" (*TT* 47).

3. Sense of futurity. Another important aspect of James's idea of man is his contention that man is turned towards the future. James captures this reference to the future, ignored by most writers, with the apt phrase "sense of futurity," by which he means that a state of expectancy is a part of our consciousness at any given time (*WB* 67, cf. 68, 70; cf. Hingst, *Perspektivismus* 191f.). Reflecting this idea, he approvingly quotes the Danish philosopher Søren Kierkegaard (1813–1855): "We live forward, we understand backward" (*PU* 109).

The three characteristics of James's idea of man mentioned so far have been summarized by Suckiel as follows: "Aims, ideals, ends, the fulfillment of goals: the conative, striving human being is the hub from which James's world-view emanates and develops" (7f.). Additional moments accrue.

4. Religious need of man. Part of the *conditio humana* in general is that man wants to have his needs satisfied. Among these, James takes into consideration the need for transcendence, i.e. that need which his contemporary Friedrich Nietzsche (1844–1900) (critically) called man's "metaphysical need" ("[d]as metaphysische Bedürfniss") (III 494, cf. II 61). James sees the most essential manifestation of this in the need for religion (cf. Hingst, *Perspektivismus* 370f.), attesting that man has a "religious demand" (*WB* 40) or "religious cravings" (*WB* 41). In his view, the reason for this is a feeling of insecurity: "Our interest in religious metaphysics arises in the fact that our empirical future feels to us unsafe, and needs some higher guarantee" (*Pr* 61). James considered in detail how to deal with this religious need in his writings on the philosophy of religion *The Will to Believe* (1897) and *The Varieties of Religious Experience* (1902). It is certain for him that religion has "a vital function" (*ML* 375).

[2] This also applies to James's considerations of educational psychology in *Talks to Teachers on Psychology and to Students on Some of Life's Ideals* (1899), which contains a chapter on "The Laws of Habits." James states that "[t]he aim of education is to make useful habits automatic" (*TT* 7) and explains, "that the teacher's prime concern should be to ingrain into the pupil that assortment of habits that shall be most useful to him throughout life" (*TT* 48).

5. Moral openness of man. In regards to morals, James considers man as not determined. He considers man neither as thoroughly good nor as radically evil, but sees his moral nature as open. Admittedly, James deems the idea that mankind is capable of moral progress as illusionary: "There is a deep truth in what the school of Schopenhauer insists on – the illusoriness of the notion of moral progress" (*WB* 131).

6. Lack of a universal perspective (cf. Hingst, *Perspektivismus* 352–359). Eventually, not only the abilities which man possesses, but also those which he lacks, are important in an inquiry about man. An essential strain of James's idea of man can be described *ex negativo* as follows: "There is no point of view absolutely public and universal" (*TT* 4), "neither the whole of truth, nor the whole of good, is revealed to any single observer" (*TT* 149 [S II]). No point of view includes everything (*WB* 6), a "total perspective" does not exist (*WB* 201). "There is no possible superhuman view" (*ECR* 552). This human deficit, if you like, will prove important for James's philosophy.

7. Result. Essential strains of James's concept of man can be summarized as follows: Man is purpose and practice driven, turned towards the future, incapable of a universal perspective, inclined and in need to believe as well as morally open. I want to point out that each of these characteristics can be severely disputed. For the time being, I will consider them as I discuss them in the context of James's writings.

James's Philosophy

Turning to the question of whether and how James's idea of man has been reflected in his philosophy, one has to ask whether there is an *interrelation* between his idea of man and his philosophy. As a philosopher, James consistently advocates an inclusion of human actualities, a fact that is apparent if one singles out some major topics of his philosophy.

1. Thought and life as venture. First of all, James faces up to the fact that due to the lack of a universal perspective we can neither achieve unquestionable knowledge nor absolute certainty. Instead of despairing of this, he effectively makes a philosophical virtue out of this psychological necessity and argues in general for taking on ventures and living with personal risk: "a genuine pragmatist […] is willing to live on a scheme of uncertified possibilities which he trusts" (*Pr* 142f.). He supports the idea that "we [are] willing to go in for life upon a trust or assumption" (*WB* 19), emphasizes that "we are free to trust at our own risks anything that is not impossible" (*WB* 52), and stresses that "a man believes at his risk" (*Pr* 71). James praises "the pragmatic openness of mind" (*Pr* 3) and "the power to trust" (*WB* 76), and thus he advocates "faith-ventures" and demands that you "make your own ventures" (*Pr* 144). Summarizing these sentiments in sentence, he states: "The element of venture is a part of human life" (*ML* 414). Later on I will return to the so-called "faith-ventures" as a specific kind of venture.

It has to be emphasized that, for James, venture and risk, respectively, have a positive connotation and should not solicit any contrition. We do not know what the future, to which we orientate ourselves, will bring to us. In James's view, however, this should not prevent us from engaging with this future, but rather make us do so with enthusiasm.

It should be mentioned that this unsecured starting point only allows James to make, both for philosophy in general and his philosophy in particular, a reduced claim for validity. Philosophy can only form a hypothesis: "all philosophies are hypotheses" (*ERE* 143), "no philosophy can be more than a hypothesis" (*EP* 93).[3] By the way, a (moral) consequence of the lack of a universal perspective is tolerance, namely "tolerance of whatever is not itself intolerant" (*TT* 4; cf. 149).

2. *Value of thought for life.* How can we measure whether the ventures in which we involve ourselves via thinking and acting succeed? For James, of course, the answer is clear: We measure the value of thought by living life. James is much more interested in this than in the functionality of thought and logic, for it is thought that serves life and not the other way round. A typical statement of James in this regard reads: "On pragmatic principles we cannot reject any hypothesis if consequences useful to life flow from it" (*Pr* 131).

Whether this will be the case is not settled once and for all, but – bearing in mind the futurity of man – needs to prove its worth again and again. The value for life, to be sure, is not proven from a bureaucratic ivory tower, but is, in view of the practical bearing of thought, necessarily assessed in practical actions. It is practice where the struggle for correct hypotheses takes place, and the idea that practice is the standard of theory, and that thought proves its worth in action, runs like a thread through James's work from his first reviews in the 1860s to his posthumously published papers. It is virtually the *ceterum censeo* of pragmatism. This orientation by the value for life has three consequences, which will be outlined next.

3. *Conceptions as instruments.* True to the teleological conception of mind, James's understanding of concepts is firmly functional and related

[3] Cf. *PU* 39, 148 in relation to the "pluralism" advocated by James.

to actions. To him, concepts have a solely instrumental character: "*Theories* [...] *become instruments*" (*Pr* 32; emphasis in original). "All our conceptions are what the Germans call *denkmittel*" (*Pr* 84, German in the original; cf. 88). We have "to think of concepts as the merely practical thing" (*PU* 121). And we have "to interpret each notion by tracing its respective practical consequences" (*Pr* 28).

By the way, this orientation towards consequences corresponds to the pragmatic maxim, which is central to the entire philosophy of pragmatism, and to the watchword of pragmatism: "By their fruits you shall know them" (*MT* 7, 16) (cf. *VRE* 25). James has adopted both the pragmatic maxim and the slogan from his friend Charles S. Peirce (1839–1914).[4] James's basic conviction is that any thinking and belief separated from action cannot be explained and described; the meaning of each single thought can be tracked to a particular, concrete consequence in our future practical experience, provided that the respective thought has any meaning at all (Oehler XX*).

4. Use of truth for life. In particular, the theory of truth (cf. Hingst, *Perspektivismus* 139–186) shows how James's idea of man, being related to practice and life, is reflected in his philosophy. James writes: "[A]n idea is 'true' so long as to believe it is profitable to our lives" (*Pr* 42). For James, our ideas are in the service of life and survival: "Their truth helps our survival" (*MEN* 234).

Throughout, James's definitions of the true and of truth revolve around consequences which lie naturally in the future and around action: "The ultimate test for us of what a truth means is [...] the conduct it dictates or inspires" (*Pr* 259), as he says in the forerunner to *Pragmatism*, the essay "Philosophical Conceptions and Practical Results" (1898). For James "the name of it (scil. truth) is the *inbegriff* of almost everything that is valuable in our lives" (*MT* 48, German in the original). "'*The true,' to put it very briefly, is only the expedient in the way of our thinking*" (*Pr* 106; emphasis in original). A true idea leads us successfully, a false idea leads us astray. In the long run, man cannot afford to consider something false as true – not for the sake of "the truth" (or an idealized truth itself) or because of a moral imperative, but as reality threatens human beings to do so in spite of their wishes (Oehler XVI*).

5. Right to believe (cf. Hingst, *Perspektivismus* 249–266). James takes the religious need of man into account by granting man a license to believe. In other words, he defends the right of man to believe and holds that "we have the right to believe at our own risk" (*WB* 32). James

[4] Cf. Hingst, "James' Transformation" on these connections.

undertakes "a defense of our right to adopt a believing attitude in religious matters" (*WB* I) and emphasizes that faith "remains as one of the inalienable birthrights of our mind" (*ML* 415). James even goes so far as to consider religious thoughts as being really true if measured by the standard valid for all thoughts, i.e. the standard of a lived life. "If theological ideas prove to have a value for concrete life, they will be true" (*Pr* 40).

With this the way is free to volunteer for a very special quest, the so-called faith-venture (*Pr* 144). Using the graphic metaphor of the faith-ladder, James shows most clearly how we climb up to religious faith step by step (cf. Hingst, *Perspektivismus* 170–172). Accordingly, James supports a broad notion of reality[5], which includes religious facts. He grants man the opportunity of authentic religious experience, delineated in detail in his principal work on the philosophy of religion as well as the psychology of religion, *The Varieties of Religious Experience* (1902), which bears the notable subtitle *A Study in Human Nature*. All in all, James's religious philosophy keeps the gate to belief open (cf. Hingst, *Perspektivismus* 404).

6. Moral meliorism. James reacts to man's indifferent state of origin in the world with a doctrine positioned between optimism and pessimism, which he calls meliorism. By that he understands that man can and should try to improve his situation in the future by one's own moral efforts with a notion of a conceived good (Hingst, *Perspektivismus* 221). "Meliorism treats salvation as neither inevitable nor impossible. It treats it as a possibility" (*Pr* 137; cf. 60f.). "Pluralism is neither optimistic nor pessimistic, but *melioristic* rather. The world, it thinks, may be saved, on condition that its parts shall do their best. But shipwreck in detail, or even on the whole, is among the open possibilities" (*ML* 412). Although he is himself rather skeptical with regards to morals, James does not sink into pessimism as he believes that man has his moral fate in his own hands.

James draws the conclusion that we must act (*WB* 131–135, 134). In his article "The Moral Philosopher and the Moral Life" (1891) (*WB* 141–162) he claims: "Moral scepticism can no more be refuted or proved by logic than intellectual scepticism can" (*WB* 28). Accordingly, James promulgates "the active will" (*TT* 164) on the basis of which life becomes worth living, as he sets out in his article "Is Life Worth Living?" (1895) (*WB* 34–56): "This life *is* worth living […], *since it is what we make it, from the moral point of view*" (*WB* 55; emphasis in

[5] Cf., fundamentally, Krämer.

original). Exactly what someone does, everyone has to decide for himself.

Overall, pragmatism grants human beings the opportunity to make their life worth living through meliorism, thus avoiding ethical nihilism as well as moralistic dogmatism.

7. Result. James does not just come to terms with the *conditio humana*, but he approves of it and he does so, now and then, even euphorically. The gesture of wanting to change man, to make him a "new man," to overcome him and turn him into a "superman" (as Nietzsche had in mind) or – alternatively – to incessantly hold man's finiteness against him and, therefore, to have a low opinion of him – is a gesture totally alien to James.

The Relationship between the Idea of Man and Philosophy

For sure, pragmatism is a philosophy which suits James's idea of man *very well*. But is it also the philosophy which suits this idea of man *best*? In other words, is James's philosophy – in relation to this idea of man – "without alternative?"

"What sort of philosophy one chooses depends on what sort of man one is." This statement by Johann Gottlieb Fichte[6] (1762–1814), to which James would surely have agreed without reservation, suggests that there is not generally *one* philosophy which suits *all* men. However, can it be argued that, in relation to one *specific* idea of man, there is just one right or most suitable philosophy? James would probably answer this in the negative, because he considered – beyond the idea of man as an idea of man in general – two *subjective factors* of a person as relevant in the choice of a philosophy: the individual intellectual temperament and the individual preferences. In addition, the question of gaps in James's idea of man can be posed.

1. Impact of intellectual temperament. What, first of all, is the difference between temperament and *conditio humana*? *Conditio humana* describes the human nature common as to all human beings. Accordingly, there is just one (single) *conditio humana*. Temperament, in contrast, is different from man to man. Certainly human beings can in this regard be united in groups, a fact reflected, for instance, by the ancient doctrine of the four humors, which distinguishes between a sanguine, a choleric, a melancholic and a phlegmatic temperament. The

[6] My translation from the German original: "Was für eine Philosophie man wähle, hängt [...] davon ab, was man für ein Mensch ist" (Fichte 434).

same applies to the character of human beings which seems to be even more complex than their temperaments. In any case, James's thoughts on intellectual temperament can be seen to be in this tradition.

As is known, James believes that temperament impacts decisively on somebody's philosophy: "The history of philosophy is to a great extent that of a certain clash of human temperaments" (*Pr* 11). This creates a problem for a professional philosopher who will be tempted to conceal this fact, but James insists: "Yet his temperament [...] gives him a stronger bias than any of his more strictly objective premises" (*Pr* 11). However, "in the forum he can make no claim, on the bare ground of his temperament [...]: the potentest of all our premises is never mentioned" (*Pr* 11). Nevertheless, "[t]emperaments with their cravings and refusals do determine men in their philosophies, and always will" (*Pr* 24).

In *Pragmatism* (1907), James detects a "particular difference of temperament" (*Pr* 12) in human beings: He distinguishes "tender-minded" and "tough-minded" persons,[7] characterizing the former, among other things, as rationalistic, idealistic, religious and dogmatic and the latter, among other things, as empiricist, materialistic, irreligious and skeptical (*Pr* 13). Against this background, James recommends his pragmatism as a "mediating way" (*Pr* 26), as "a philosophy that can satisfy both kinds of demand" (*Pr* 23), the religious demand as well as the empiricist demand of man. Pragmatism "can remain religious like the rationalisms, but at the same time, like the empiricisms, it can preserve the richest intimacy with facts" (*Pr* 23). The temper which James attributes to *himself* is "the pragmatic temper" (*Pr* 133), which he recommends thoroughly but does not prescribe at all.

2. *Impact of sentiment.* Next to temperament, simple preferences and the passions of a human being guide his philosophy: "likes and dislikes *must* be among the ultimate factors of [...] philosophy" (*ERE* 141; emphasis in original). This influence has to be acknowledged. "A philosophy is the expression of a man's intimate character" (*PU* 14), "philosophy is more a matter of passionate vision than of logic" (*PU* 81). James does not hesitate to approve this impact: "Our passional nature not only lawfully may, but must, decide" (*WB* 20, cf. 24), given that "the whole man within us is at work when we form our philosophical opinions. Intellect, will, taste, and passion co-operate" (*WB* 77), as he frankly accepts in his most remarkable article "The Sentiment of Ratio-

[7] Wilhelm Jerusalem (1854–1923), the first German translator of James's *Pragmatism*, expressed this pair of opposites aptly in his translation of "tender-minded" as "*zartfühlend*" and of "tough-minded" as "*grobkörnig*" (cf. James, *Der Pragmatismus* 7f.).

nality" (1897) (*WB* 57–89). For James, it is consequently erroneous to "pretend that any philosophy can be [...] constructed without the help of personal preference" (*WB* 77). Furthermore, "what makes us monists or pluralists, determinists or indeterminists, is at bottom always some sentiment" (*WB* 119).

It is also important to note that different intellectual standards among human beings play a role in this. What is insufficient for "superior minds" may perfectly satisfy "the mind with the shortest views" or "the mind of the more shallow man" (*Pr* 56). The latter, "a mind content with little," is characterized by "a certain native poverty of mental demand" (*PU* 81). One may well suppose that James would see a superior mind as more suited to pragmatism than a shallow mind. However, the preferences of human beings are individual and cannot be generalized, so that James's idea of man enables a lot of different philosophical attitudes, none of which appear necessary to him, not even his own. This philosophical abstinence of James can surely be called into question. In spite of this, the human factor is in general always effective, as James expresses using a fine metaphor: "The trail of the human serpent is thus over everything" (*Pr* 37). In his view "it is impossible to strip the human element out from even our most abstract theorizing" (*ECR* 552).

3. Gaps in James's concept of man. The emphasis of these two decisive subjective factors, the second of which (sentiment) is possibly a variant of the first (temperament), makes it plausible that the claim for validity in James's philosophy is comparably – as well as realistically – small. In another regard, it can be asked whether essential parts of an idea of man have been "forgotten" or undervalued by James, and actually it appears that this is the case. There are thematic "gaps" in his philosophy, since he has occupied himself with certain philosophical disciplines less intensively than with others. Although James himself was a talented amateur painter, he has only marginally dealt with the *aesthetic sense* of man[8] and has thus developed no theory of aesthetic experience as, later on, John Dewey (1859–1952) succeeded to with his *Art and Experience* (1934). Besides, James lacked a sense for – and an interest in – *logic* as such, so that he gave little attention to this discipline[9] – acting as much under the deterrent as well as the authoritative example of his friend Peirce.

[8] Cf. the hints in the sub-chapter "Aesthetic and moral principles" in *The Principles of Psychology* (*PP* 1264–1268).

[9] Cf., however, the following remarkable note in his manuscripts: "It is obvious that aesthetic connexion might cover logical connexion as a special case" (*MEN* 44).

Conclusion

William James's philosophy of pragmatism is in most parts an adequate philosophical expression of human nature and essential human needs. In terms of the construction of concepts in general, pragmatism holds that human beings orientate themselves by considering concrete consequences for their future rather than abstract conceptual frameworks. In relation to religion, pragmatism views religious experience as conceivably real and affirms the possibility of transcendence instead of prohibiting religious beliefs. In terms of morals, pragmatism grants human beings the opportunity to make their life worth living through what James calls meliorism, thus avoiding ethical nihilism as well as moralistic dogmatism. Given the world as it is, James realizes that life is a venture, which, if embarked upon, is also rewarding.

In doing so, James reflects the *conditio humana* in a particularly realistic manner and, therefore, neither underestimates human beings nor expects too much from them.

Works Cited

Fichte, Johann Gottlieb. *Werke*. Vol. I. Ed. Immanuel Hermann Fichte. Berlin: Walter de Gruyter, 1971.

Hingst, Kai-Michael. "James' Transformation der Pragmatischen Maxime von Peirce." *William James: Pragmatismus*. Ed. Klaus Oehler. Berlin: Akademie Verlag, 2000. 33–67.

—. *Perspektivismus und Pragmatismus: Ein Vergleich auf der Grundlage der Wahrheitsbegriffe und der Religionsphilosophien von Nietzsche und James*. Würzburg: Königshausen & Neumann, 1998.

James, William. *A Pluralistic Universe* (*PU*). Eds. Frederick Burckhardt, Fredson Bowers and Ignas K. Skrupskelis. Cambridge and London: Harvard UP, 1977.

—. *Der Pragmatismus: Ein neuer Name für alte Denkmethoden*. 2nd ed. Trans. Wilhelm Jerusalem. Ed. Klaus Oehler. Hamburg: Meiner, 1994.

—. *Essays, Comments, and Reviews* (*ECR*). Eds. Frederick Burckhardt, Fredson Bowers and Ignas K. Skrupskelis. Cambridge and London: Harvard UP, 1987.

—. *Essays in Philosophy* (*EP*). Eds. Frederick Burckhardt, Fredson Bowers and Ignas K. Skrupskelis. Cambridge and London: Harvard UP, 1978.

—. *Essays in Radical Empiricism* (*ERE*). Eds. Frederick Burckhardt, Fredson Bowers and Ignas K. Skrupskelis. 3 vols. Cambridge and London: Harvard UP, 1976.

—. *Manuscript Essays and Notes* (*MEN*). Eds. Frederick Burckhardt, Fredson Bowers and Ignas K. Skrupskelis. Cambridge and London: Harvard UP, 1988.

—. *Manuscript Lectures* (*ML*). Eds. Frederick Burckhardt, Fredson Bowers and Ignas K. Skrupskelis. Cambridge and London: Harvard UP, 1988.

—. *Pragmatism* (*Pr*). Eds. Frederick Burckhardt, Fredson Bowers and Ignas K. Skrupskelis. Cambridge and London: Harvard UP, 1975.

—. *Psychology: Briefer Course* (*PBC*). Eds. Frederick Burckhardt, Fredson Bowers and Ignas K. Skrupskelis. Cambridge and London: Harvard UP, 1984.

—. *Talks to Teachers on Psychology and to Students on Some of Life's Ideals* (*TT*). Eds. Frederick Burckhardt, Fredson Bowers and Ignas K. Skrupskelis. Cambridge and London: Harvard UP, 1983.

—. *The Meaning of Truth* (*MT*). Eds. Frederick Burckhardt, Fredson Bowers and Ignas K. Skrupskelis. Cambridge and London: Harvard UP, 1975.

—. *The Principles of Psychology* (*PP*). Eds. Frederick Burckhardt, Fredson Bowers and Ignas K. Skrupskelis. Cambridge and London: Harvard UP, 1981.

—. *The Varieties of Religious Experience* (*VRE*). Eds. Frederick Burckhardt, Fredson Bowers and Ignas K. Skrupskelis. Cambridge and London: Harvard UP, 1985.

—. *The Will to Believe* (*WB*). Eds. Frederick Burckhardt, Fredson Bowers and Ignas K. Skrupskelis. Cambridge and London: Harvard UP, 1979.

Krämer, Felicitas. *Erfahrungsvielfalt und Wirklichkeit: Zu William James' Realitätsverständnis*. Göttingen: Vandenhoeck & Ruprecht, 2006.

Nietzsche, Friedrich. *Sämtliche Werke: Kritische Studienausgabe*. Eds. Giorgio Colli and Mazzino Montinari. München, Berlin and New York: Deutscher Taschenbuch Verlag and Walter de Gruyter, 1980.

Oehler, Klaus. "Einleitung." *William James, Der Pragmatismus: Ein neuer Name für alte Denkmethoden*. Trans. Wilhelm Jerusalem. Ed. Klaus Oehler. 2nd ed. Hamburg: Meiner, 1994. XI*–XXXIV*.

Suckiel, Ellen Kappy. *The Pragmatic Philosophy of William James*. Notre Dame and London: U of Notre Dame P, 1982.

Poets, Partial Stories, and the Earth of Things: William James and the Worldliness of Pragmatism

Ulf Schulenberg

As a method, conceptual instrument, or form of redescription, pragmatism has been severely criticized since its inception in the late-nineteenth century, having been attacked for supporting American imperialism (James), for being anemic and ineffectual (Dewey), or for being frivolous, decadent, and cynical (Rorty). Nowadays, however, it seems that pragmatism's fate has changed as demonstrated by the much-debated revival or renaissance of pragmatism, for which Rorty, despite his reservations, prepared the ground in the late 1970s and early 1980s. The revival has demonstrated the multilayered complexity of this way of thinking and of grasping the relation between theory and practice, but in view of pragmatism's undeniable success in various fields, from literary studies to law, the question inevitably arises: Why pragmatism? To put this somewhat differently, one wonders what exactly pragmatism has to offer. What is pragmatism good for? One answer is certainly that this way of thinking offers the possibility of bringing everything together, as it were: antifoundationalism, antiessentialism, nominalism, historicism, fallibilism *and* antiskepticism, meliorism, and an antitheoretical stance which at the same time ought to be seen as a resistance to the general resistance to theory. Whereas a materialist theoretician such as Fredric Jameson, for instance, has always emphasized the utmost importance of the conceptual instrument of mediation, pragmatism, in its anti-systematicity and governed by an anti-Hegelian gesture, seeks to make clear that one does not need any of these old-fashioned instruments in order to recognize the intimate interwovenness of pragmatic (anti-) theory and liberal pluralism.

However, it is not only Hegelian Marxism and Marxist literary and aesthetic theory which are defunct, if one follows most neopragmatists, but also poststructuralist and deconstructive approaches. Concerning the relationship between pragmatism, Marxism, and poststructuralism, Morris Dickstein underlines how "pragmatism has come to be seen as an American alternative, an escape from the abstraction of theory [Marxism] and the abyss of nihilism [poststructuralism]" (16). Giles

Gunn contends that "over the next decade or two pragmatism may well prove to be the most intellectually resilient American response to the quicksands and carapaces of cultural postmodernism" (7).

Dickstein and Gunn suggest that pragmatism as a theoretical practice strengthens our position in confronting other theoretical approaches. Not only is pragmatism a philosophy which critiques abstractions and absolutes and which is clearly oriented toward practice and action, but it also helps and guides us in our own search for method. Following Dickstein, pragmatism in its contemporary version "is less an attack on the foundations of knowledge, as it was portrayed by its early critics, than a search for method when the foundations have already crumbled" (16). It is crucial to note that Stanley Fish would object to this that it comes close to another version of what in *Doing What Comes Naturally* he calls antifoundationalist theory hope. What we finally have to understand, in other words, is that pragmatism does not offer anything to us, not even a method. Concerning Fish's interpretation of pragmatism, his essay "Truth and Toilets" is surely the most valuable text and was originally the afterword to the volume edited by Dickstein. In it Fish makes clear that "pragmatism should itself know enough not to promise anything, or even to recommend anything. If pragmatism is true, it has nothing to say to us; no politics follows from it or is blocked by it; no morality attaches to it or is enjoined by it" (295).

According to Fish, pragmatism has no firm outline, and this vagueness or amorphousness has two advantages. First, it offers a way of thinking that is so protean as to be a difficult target for its enemies because they do not know what to hit and where to attack it. Second, because of its vagueness, pragmatism is incapable of serving as a successor theory, a new foundation, to replace the foundationalist theories whose shortcomings and inadequacies it has illuminated. One of the most interesting aspects of this text is that one could almost speak of a disappearance of pragmatism with regard to Fish's depiction of it: "Pragmatism may be the one theory – if it is a theory – that clears the field not only of its rivals but of itself, at least as a positive alternative" (299). Discussing essays by Richard J. Bernstein, Richard Poirier, and James T. Kloppenberg, Fish stresses that "nothing follows from pragmatism, not democracy, not a love of poetry, not a mode of doing history" (304). In view of the fact that pragmatism provides no method, the question as to what it can be good for returns with a vengeance.

The answer to this question, if one follows Fish, consists of two parts. First, pragmatism teaches us that all we need can be found in the world of practices (and it thus shows us that we already have everything we need due to our embeddedness in locally specific situations). Second, pragmatism teaches us that we live in a rhetorical world. As regards the first point, Fish's stripped-down version of pragmatism emphasizes the sufficiency of human practices, as well as the idea that this way of thinking, despite the fact that it delivers no method, assures us "that in ordinary circumstances there will usually be something to be done" (307). Pragmatism as an (anti-)philosophy of little steps, of small patchwork solutions, temporary stopgaps, and creative and experimental tinkering, inevitably leads us back to the solidity and plasticity of the world which is shaped and constantly reshaped (or redescribed) by human beings. The way we are in this world of practice is utterly independent of the theoretical account we sometimes, in certain situations, give of those practices. Our theoretical narratives or vocabularies will never have the desired consequences in the world of practice. In the confrontation with the solidity of this world of practice (and solidity here paradoxically means contingency, transience, and history), theory can only be considered a blurry fantasy.

Whereas Fish would answer the aforementioned question "Why pragmatism?" by calling attention to pragmatism's disappearance as a positive alternative or method, Mark Bauerlein, in *The Pragmatic Mind*, argues that (Rortyan) pragmatism should be regarded as "a justification for making criticism into an instrument for social reform" (xi). Bauerlein speaks of an "appealing political impulse of the new pragmatism," and he avers that while Nietzschean, Foucauldian, and de Manian forms of antifoundationalism, antirealism, and antirepresentationalism inevitably lead to "a nihilistic assertion of the loss of transcendence," neopragmatism "interprets antirepresentationalism as the happy foreground of a reconstruction of culture and criticism" (xv). Although Bauerlein ignores the political side of deconstruction, which has become increasingly obvious in the last two decades (think of the questions of deconstruction and ethics, deconstruction and law, and deconstruction and Marxism), his emphasis on the political impulses of neopragmatism is particularly valuable. All of this of course concerns the question of pragmatism's worldliness. Is it possible, and legitimate, to advance the argument that one ought to see pragmatism as a worldly and oppositional criticism (somewhat in the Saidian sense)? William James's understanding of the worldliness of pragmatism is of utmost importance in this context. In this article, I will discuss James's brand of pragmatism by focusing on its worldly aspects in two steps. First, I will analyze the worldliness of James's version of radical empiricism and his function as a public philosopher. Second, I will complicate my results by underscoring that one may see James, together with Emerson and Whitman, as a strong poet who prepared the establishment of a postmetaphysical literary or poeticized culture in the Rortyan sense. In other words, there are two intertwined narratives here. On the one hand, one possibility of framing the history of American pragmatism would be to argue that there is a connection between the Jamesian understanding of worldliness and Cornel West's leftist version of neopragmatism as he developed it in *The American Evasion of Philosophy* and other texts. On the other hand, one might feel inclined to see a similarity between James and Rorty's liberal brand of pragmatism insofar as both stress the importance of creative and innovative redescriptions offered by a strong individual or poet. It is the fruitful tension between these two narratives which is my primary concern in this article.

James's Worldly Pragmatism

William James's version of pragmatism, or what he also termed radical empiricism and what might be called scientific romanticism, is still fascinating for many reasons. His idea that all theory is practice, that all distinctions of thought can in the end be reduced to differences in practice and that what really deserves our attention are the consequences of our beliefs; his strong emphasis on pluralism, particularity, contingency, open-endedness, and vagueness; his insistence on the importance of meliorism, (Peircian) fallibilism, change, and pragmatism's future-orientation; his (implicit) suggestion that only pragmatism is capable of fruitfully combining fallibilism and antiskepticism; his notion of truth; his relentless attempt to underline the human mind's creativity and inventiveness; and his writing style that reflects his understanding of democracy – these are all elements that characterize James's thinking. A main reason for the fact that James's version of pragmatism still fascinates us is that pragmatism strives to have an effect on the world we live in. It desires to change our world, to make it a better place.[1] Pragmatism, as James seems to hold, is about the attempt to change the actual world by interpreting it. His radical empiricism, what he calls "a mosaic philosophy, a philosophy of plural facts" (315) in "A World of Pure Experience," constantly calls attention to its worldliness. At the beginning of *Pragmatism*, for instance, he speaks of

[1] In this context, see Richard J. Bernstein. "The Ethical Consequences of William James's Pragmatic Pluralism." in *The Pragmatic Turn*. Malden: Polity, 2010, 53-69.

the necessity of looking abroad on "this colossal universe of concrete facts, on their awful bewilderments, their surprises and cruelties, on the wildness which they show" (15). Furthermore, in the context of a discussion of rationalism's abstractness he warns against the danger of substituting "a pallid outline for the real world's richness" (ibid. 36). One must not neglect "this real world of sweat and dirt" (ibid.). Further below in his text James avers that "[t]he earth of things, long thrown into shadow by the glories of the upper ether, must rescue its rights" (ibid. 57).

In an almost Whitmanian way, James seems fascinated by the confrontation with "the mere spectacle of the world's presence" ("On a Certain Blindness" 280). Neither Whitman nor James are radically antimetaphysical authors, of course. Yet both illustrate that one ought to refrain from reaching a position which would attempt to unify the world, a position which offered the possibility of permanently or only temporarily leaving the world of practice, the world of biased beliefs and daily desires, behind. The worldliness of the Jamesian brand of radical empiricism is explained as follows in the preface to *The Will to Believe*:

> Real possibilities, real indeterminations, real beginnings, real ends, real evil, real crises, catastrophes, and escapes, a real God, and a real moral life, just as common sense conceives these things, may remain in empiricism as conceptions which that philosophy gives up the attempt either to "overcome" or to reinterpret in monistic form. (194)

It is crucial to understand that pragmatism's worldliness not only means that one ought to pay attention to the aforementioned richness of the real world and its concrete facts, but it also signifies that this real world is incomplete, malleable, and thus waiting or asking for interpretation. In other words, the question of pragmatism's worldliness inevitably concerns our activity as interpreters of the world's stories. Following James, this task is a seemingly difficult one since "[t]he world is full of partial stories that run parallel to one another, beginning and ending at odd times. They mutually interlace and interfere at points, but we can not unify them completely in our minds" (*Pragmatism* 65; see also *Some Problems of Philosophy* 1048). In contrast to rationalists or idealists as monists, radical empiricists contend that the world is not eternally complete but incomplete and therefore subject to further change, addition, or modification. We cannot unify the world's partial stories, but we can try to creatively interpret them and thereby to achieve consequences in the world of practice. It is our activity and creativity as interpreters, as people who realize the complexity and opacity of their material but who still desire for consequences of their (interpretive) actions, that are of utmost concern for James. In *Pragmatism* he formulates as follows:

> In our cognitive as well as in our active life we are creative. We *add*, both to the subject and to the predicate part of reality. The world stands really malleable, waiting to receive its final touches at our hands. Like the kingdom of heaven, it suffers human violence willingly. Man *engenders* truths upon it. (112; emphases in original)

It is important to recognize that our worldly interpretations must not center on concepts such as correspondence, imitation, mimesis, or copying, but that they ought to lead to "the enrichment of the previous world" (ibid. 158). In James's opinion, "thought's mission [is] to increase and elevate, rather than simply to imitate and reduplicate, existence" (ibid.). This idea seems more pertinent than James's later suggestion, in *Some Problems of Philosophy*, that philosophers, after many aberrations, eventually "may get into as close contact as realistic novelists with the facts of life" (996).

Concerning the question of worldliness, it should also be mentioned that it seems legitimate to advance the argument that James functioned as a public philosopher in his time. Like, for instance, Cornel West and Edward Said after him, James accepted responsibility for addressing public problems, i.e. he grappled with cultural, social, and political forces in the public sphere (think of his vehement anti-imperialist stance).[2] He was not content with presenting himself exclusively as a professional philosopher solving abstract problems, but he always put a premium on the importance of a fruitful tension between technical work and public issues, the professional and the popular. As so very often, James saw his primary role as *mediator*, as someone who tried to creatively blur the traditional lines between professional and public philosophy. He did not declare the demand for philosophical depth as obsolete, but sought to balance it with the needs of a public presence, an oppositional voice in the public sphere. Applying insights from his complex technical work to public issues and problems, James's texts show that these popular concerns and public issues in turn also had a strong impact on his professional philosophy. In particular, this

[2] In this context, see Robert B. Westbrook, Democratic Hope: *Pragmatism and the Politics of Truth.* Ithaca: Cornell UP, 2005. 52-73. In addition, see James T. Kloppenberg, "James's Pragmatism and American Culture, 1907-2007." in *100 Years of Pragmatism: William James's Revolutionary Philosophy.* Ed. John J. Stuhr. Bloomington and Indianapolis: Indiana UP, 2010. 7-40.

reciprocity can be detected in his work during his most successful period as professional and public philosopher from 1890 to 1910. Of primary concern here is his constant attempt to call attention to the interplay of theory and practice or the fruitful and productive tension between professional and partly abstract philosophy, on the one hand, and public philosophy as political practice, on the other.

George Cotkin, in *William James, Public Philosopher*, convincingly argues that James actually reached his audience and successfully fulfilled his role as public philosopher. According to Cotkin, James's case demonstrated that "public philosophy furnished the philosopher with an audience and a cause; it permitted him to manufacture a world view that combined personal experiences and philosophical expressions with an eye toward the era's social and cultural issues" (14). Moreover, the public philosopher, as Cotkin maintains with reference to Rorty, "engaged philosophy as an act of edification and education rather than one of systematization and abstraction" (ibid.). James as public and edifying philosopher

> wanted philosophy to be a conversation, a playful yet serious and enlightening confrontation with philosophical and cultural issues. Truth with a capital *T* was not the concern of the edifying philosopher; self-knowledge, playful probing, and fuller intercourse with the world were his imperatives. In setting up familiar divisions between the tough- and tender-minded, or the one and the many, James sought, in the style of philosophy as edification, to mediate and question. His resolutions to philosophical and cultural problems were at times more passionate than precise, more methodological than systematic. To a degree, philosophy as edification was also philosophy as therapy and jeremiad. For James, the philosophical statement, even when presented in its most technical form, responded both to perennial philosophical conundrums and to deeply held private tensions and public concerns. (ibid. 14f.)

Since James sought to present his thinking in an accessible fashion in his numerous lectures, for traditional, rationalist and abstract philosophers he had to pay much too high a price. Yet to James, the lack of systematization, technical exactitude, and logical rigor did not appear as a disadvantage or problem. As a public philosopher attempting to confront worldly problems in their historical and cultural specificity, he was highly critical of the pretensions of professional philosophy and its desperate search for what is more than another human invention.

James's public philosophy and his thinking in general were of great importance to many turn-of-the-century political theorists and reformers. His radical theory of knowledge, meaning, and truth, i.e. his anti-foundationalist critique of traditional epistemology, proved useful and suggestive to those who fought for progressive change in America around 1900. His meliorism, voluntarism, future-orientation and his emphasis on concerted action apparently corresponded with the reform agenda of American progressives and social democrats that steadily gained power in the first decade of the twentieth century. Contributing to the willingness to reform and to the acceptance of change in the social and political realm, James helped to create a new political sensibility which would eventually reach fruition in Dewey's writings and those of other reformers and radicals. One only has to think in this context of James's influence on W.E.B. Du Bois and Alain Locke, two of his students at Harvard.[3] While James's worldly pragmatism has proven to be very influential, and a seemingly direct line runs from the Jamesian version of pragmatism with its emphasis on practical activism and moral strenuousness to West's leftist neopragmatism who nonetheless criticizes his predecessor in *The American Evasion of Philosophy*, one must not ignore the insufficiencies and inadequacies of James's approach.[4] As Cotkin correctly states:

> In presenting his melioristic attitude and his conception of the universe's immense possibility, he avoided some important political questions: What form should strenuous activism take? What does it mean to say that "Man engenders truth upon" the world? [...] Although intended to be anti-imperialist, the politics of pragmatism remains vague and unimpressive in various ways. Many analysts have noted that James's political theorizing was occasional at best and that its exposition was never sustained. (171)

[3] In this context, see Ross Posnock, "The Influence of William James on American Culture." in *The Cambridge Companion to William James*. Ed. Ruth Anna Putnam. New York: Cambridge UP, 1997. 322-42; and Nancy Fraser, "Another Pragmatism: Alain Locke, Critical 'Race' Theory, and the Politics of Culture." in *The Revival of Pragmatism: New Essays on Social Thought, Law, and Culture.* Ed. Morris Dickstein. Durham: Duke UP, 1998. 157-75. For a discussion of the question of pragmatism and race, see Bill E. Lawson and Donald F. Koch (Eds.) *Pragmatism and the Problem of Race.* Bloomington and Indianapolis: Indiana UP, 2004; Eddie S. Glaude, Jr. *In a Shade of Blue: Pragmatism and the Politics of Black America.* Chicago: U of Chicago P, 2007; Walton M. Muyumba. *The Shadow and the Act: Black Intellectual Practice, Jazz Improvisation, and Philosophical Pragmatism.* Chicago: U of Chicago P, 2009; and Chad Kautzer and Eduardo Mendieta (Eds.). *Pragmatism, Nation, and Race: Community in the Age of Empire.* Bloomington and Indianapolis: Indiana UP, 2010.

[4] For a critique of James's political theorizing and public philosophizing, see Bruce Kuklick. *A History of Philosophy in America, 1720-2000.* Oxford: Clarendon P, 2001. 167-71.

With regard to James's stance as a public philosopher, the first lecture of *A Pluralistic Universe*, one of his late texts, is particularly illuminating. He declares that "the over-technicality and consequent dreariness of the younger disciples [of philosophy] at our american [sic] universities is appalling" (637). Philosophy, to the late James, is "a discipline of such universal human interest" that it would be truly "fatal [for it] to lose connexion with the open air of human nature" (ibid.). James continues by underscoring that "[w]ith this exclusion of the open air all true perspective gets lost, extremes and oddities count as much as sanities, and command the same attention" (ibid. 638). It goes without saying that these sentences are to be understood as a vehement critique of abstract, technical, purely speculative, and unworldly philosophy which has completely lost contact with the problems of men in the Deweyan sense. One of James's primary concerns in *A Pluralistic Universe* is a critique of what he calls a philosophy of the absolute (or absolute idealism). Expanding on the crucial differences between this philosophy of the absolute, in its monistic form ('the all-form'), and his own radical empiricism, in its pluralistic form ('the each-form'), he unequivocally states that the latter understanding of philosophy is dominated by the notion of worldliness:

> It surely is a merit in a philosophy to make the very life we lead seem real and earnest. Pluralism, in exorcising the absolute, exorcises the great de-realizer of the only life we are at home in, and thus redeems the nature of reality from essential foreignness. Every end, reason, motive, object of desire or aversion, ground of sorrow or joy that we feel is in the world of finite multifariousness, for only in that world does anything really happen, only there do events come to pass. (*A Pluralistic Universe* 652)

A discussion of the worldliness of the Jamesian understanding of pragmatism cannot ignore his aversion to Hegelian idealism. James's severe critique of Hegel's monistic and absolute idealism is a main part of *A Pluralistic Universe*. In Lecture III ("Hegel and His Method"), James criticizes various aspects of Hegel's thought such as, for instance, his vocabulary and habits of speech, his dialectical method, his coercive logic, and his tendency to see opposition, friction, resistance, and struggle in a non-empirical light. James's main focus, however, rests on Hegel's concept of truth, his notion of totality, and his striving to establish a closed system. It is interesting to see that James uses Hegel's concept of truth in order to once more underscore the difference between pluralistic empiricism, in its radical version, and rationalism as absolute and monistic idealism. Whereas James vehemently argues for a pragmatist pluralization of truth, Hegel holds that it is possible and desirable to attain *the* final and eternal truth:

> Hegel was dominated by the notion of a truth that should prove incontrovertible, binding on every one, and certain, which should be *the* truth, one, indivisible, eternal, objective, and necessary, to which all our particular thinking must lead as to its consummation. This is the dogmatic ideal, the postulate, uncriticized, undoubted, and unchallenged, of all rationalizers in philosophy. (*A Pluralistic Universe* 675)

In the context of his discussion of Hegel's method of double negation, James convincingly demonstrates that the conception of a final truth ought to be considered together with the notion of a closed system. Hegelian totality, notoriously attacked by poststructuralists, deconstructionists and others since the 1970s, can only be grasped, as James shows, when seen in connection with the German idealist's notion of truth:

> That one and only whole, with all its parts involved in it, negating and making one another impossible if abstracted and taken singly, but necessitating and holding one another in place if the whole of them be taken integrally, is the literal ideal sought after; it is the very diagram and picture of that notion of *the* truth with no outlying alternative, to which nothing can be added, nor from it anything withdrawn, and all variations from which are absurd, which so dominates the human imagination. (*A Pluralistic Universe* 676)

James's pragmatism, with its stress on pluralism, novelty, particularity, finite immediate experiences, fallibilism, meliorism, contingency, non-systematicity, and non-teleology, is interested in precisely those 'outlying alternatives' or 'variations,' i.e. it seeks to underline the crucial nature of that which refuses to be subsumed under the absolute idea or rigid conception of totality (think of Adorno's negative dialectics in this context). Absolutism as a rationalist conception, going from wholes to parts, assumes those wholes to be self-sufficing; moreover, it defines the absolute as the ideally perfect whole. James views absolutism as utterly incapable of providing us with the necessary tools in our confrontation with the messy world of everyday life. Conceptual abstraction cannot represent the complexity of man's continuous flux of experiences, nor can it depict a reality governed by contingent changes (and the unpredictably creative work of strong poets). Additionally, in contrast to radical empiricism it does not let one grasp the full implications of the idea that it is not only things which can be directly experienced but also the relations between those things. As a radical empiricist, James's contention is that there is no need to look for a transempirical, i.e. metaphysical, way of connecting things and parts.

Pluralism, as James contends in *Some Problems of Philosophy*, "protests against working our ideas in a vacuum made of conceptual abstractions. Some parts of our world, it admits, cannot exist out of their wholes; but others, it says, can" (1053). Furthermore, he argues that the belief "in the genuineness of each particular moment in which we feel the squeeze of this world's life, as we actually do work here, or work is done upon us, is an Eden from which rationalists seek in vain to expel us, now that we have criticized their state of mind" (ibid. 1039). It is in this world of practice ('as we actually do work here') that the postmetaphysical theorist comes to understand two things. First, the potential of the world's partial stories and the overflowing nature of immediate experience in its depth and richness; and second, the worldly (antifoundationalist) theorist realizes that his work would remain incomplete without consequences in the world of practice. Let me repeat the obvious here: James's turn to practice makes philosophy pragmatic; he reminds us that philosophy is a practice. It is something we do which has consequences in the world of practice. It either makes a difference or it is not philosophy. What this also signifies is that James's texts illuminate the possibility and desirability of consequences of theory in history. In one of the most famous passages of *Pragmatism*, James stresses that the pragmatic method ought to be regarded as an "*attitude of looking away from first things, principles, 'categories,' supposed necessities; and of looking towards last things, fruits, consequences, facts*" (29; emphasis in original). The pragmatist, in other words, "turns away from abstraction and insufficiency, from verbal solutions, from bad *a priori* reasons, from fixed principles, closed systems, and pretended absolutes and origins. He turns towards concreteness and adequacy, towards facts, towards action and towards power" (ibid. 27; emphasis in original). John J. Stuhr comments on the question of practical consequences in James's pragmatism as follows:

> [J]ust as philosophical problems have practical origins, so too philosophical theories and positions have practical consequences – consequences in practice. But pragmatists do not simply claim that a given philosophy has practical consequences. They make practice central in a more far-reaching and important way: for pragmatists, the practical consequences of a philosophy constitute the meaning of that philosophy. The meaning of a philosophy is to be found in its practical consequences; these consequences are that philosophy's practical meaning – and, as James observed, for us there is no meaning other than practical meaning. (35)

I have interpreted the Jamesian notion of the malleable character of the world as an invitation to interpret the world's partial stories, that is, to actively engage in the actual world of practice (there is no other). Referring to Marx's *Theses on Feuerbach*, Frank Lentricchia summarizes the main idea of his "The Return of William James" as follows:

> [I]ndependently of Marx, and as the founding gesture of his work, James makes the point of the most famous of Marx's theses on Feuerbach – that philosophy should be trying to change, not interpret the world – but James in effect out-Marxes Marx by saying that all the interpretive efforts of philosophy are always simultaneously efforts to work upon and work over things as they are. All intellectuals play social roles, whether they like it or not, James believed, because interpretation is always a form of intervention, a factor in social change or in social conservation. The recurring double point of James's pragmatism is that all theory is practice (situated intellectual involvement with real local effects) and that all practices are not equally worthy. (6)

Lentricchia is right in calling James's pragmatism a "philosophy of consequences" and in drawing attention to "the action of changing-by-interpreting the world's various texts, verbal and otherwise" (7). As Lentricchia shows, James's worldly pragmatism does indeed seem incompatible with the new pragmatism as proposed by Fish, Michaels, Knapp and others in the 1980s. Theory as practice, here the practice of interpreting the world's partial stories, ought to lead to the achievement of emancipatory goals. One of the primary tasks of a leftist brand of neopragmatism is to suggest that the notion of worldliness cannot be grasped in its complexity without an understanding of the idea of theory as practice, that is, without realizing that our theoretical ideas should have consequences in the messy world of everyday life. What our discussion of James's worldly pragmatism has illustrated is that this idea of the consequences of theory in history goes hand in hand with a stress on the importance of fallible, revisable, heuristic, and tentative theories which critique the notion of grand theory, but which at the same time do not subscribe to the general, or radical, resistance to theory.

James and the Idea of a Postmetaphysical Literary Culture

James never intended to present an elaborate and sophisticated pragmatist political theory. Rather, he desired that his public philosophy become an influential part of the public conversation and thereby strengthen the community. In his discussion of ethics in "The Moral Philosopher and the Moral Life," James not only maintains that no ethical philosophy in the traditional, dogmatic, and *a priori* sense is possible, but he also claims that in some rare cases (public) conversation might be shaped by the revolutionary thought or action of what we would call today a strong poet in the Bloomian or Rortyan sense. He writes:

> Every now and then, however, someone is born with the right to be original, and his revolutionary thought or action may bear prosperous fruit. He may replace old 'laws of nature' by better ones; he may, by breaking old moral rules in a certain place, bring in a total condition of things more ideal than would have followed had the rules been kept. (258)

Undoubtedly, one might argue that these sentences can be applied to James himself. As a public philosopher he was at the same time a (romantic) strong poet, offering creative and innovative redescriptions and, within the framework of his worldly pragmatism, never forgetting about the "howling mob of desires" (ibid. 255) shaping our ideals, judgments, and decisions.

The complexity of the relationship of individual and community is of course central to the thought of all classical pragmatists. Charlene Haddock Seigfried points out that in James's modification of the Darwinian model of evolution it becomes obvious that the individual doubly depends on his or her community:

> Social relationships are the only means for the transmission of the cultural heritage that provides the intellectual tools necessary for the creative spontaneity that defines human beings, and the community is the only means to test the wider validity and worth of the individual's contributions to organizing experience and enacting values. (95)

While it is impossible to fully appreciate James's brand of pragmatism without paying attention to the crucial role of the community in his texts, it is interesting to see him, together with Emerson and Whitman, as a strong poet who prepared the establishment of a postmetaphysical literary or poeticized culture. The idea of a post-Philosophical culture already preoccupied Richard Rorty in his introduction to *The Linguistic Turn* (1967). It was central to many of the essays collected in *Consequences of Pragmatism* (1982), and it played a decisive role in the last chapter ("Philosophy without Mirrors") of *Philosophy and the Mirror of Nature* (1979). In its most fully developed form the idea of a post-Philosophical culture as poeticized culture is one of the primary aspects of Rorty's *Contingency, Irony, and Solidarity*. In all of these texts Rorty underscores the fact that he has no use for a traditional understanding of philosophy. In his opinion, "[i]nteresting philosophy is rarely an examination of the pros and cons of a thesis. Usually it is, implicitly or explicitly, a contest between an entrenched vocabulary which has become a nuisance and a half-formed new vocabulary which vaguely promises great things" (9). He describes his own way of doing philosophy when he summarizes the new method as follows:

> The method is to redescribe lots and lots of things in new ways, until you have created a pattern of linguistic behavior which will tempt the rising generation to adopt it, thereby causing them to look for appropriate new forms of nonlinguistic behavior, for example, the adoption of new scientific equipment or new social institutions. (ibid.)

The radical antifoundationalist and anti-Platonist Rorty redescribes the notion of philosophy as a foundational discipline, and this redescription directs attention to the idea of a postmetaphysical literary culture.[5] Rorty's antifoundationalism should be seen as an important part of the attempt to de-divinize the world. We should no longer rely on and believe in foundations, we should no longer worship anything, we should face the consequences of secularization, and we should finally realize that our self, our language, and our community are governed by contingency. Rorty's ideal liberal democracy, and culture, would no longer need any foundations, "it would be one which was enlightened, secular, through and through. It would be one in which no trace of divinity remained, either in the form of a divinized world or a divinized self. Such a culture would have no room for the notion that there are nonhuman forces to which human beings should be responsible" (*Contingency* 45). In his description of an ideal poeticized culture most of the crucial elements of his neopragmatist thinking come together: his antifoundationalism and antiessentialism, Davidsonian and late-Wittgensteinian nominalism, Hegelian historicism, Darwinian naturalism, Nietzschean and Proustian perspectivism, as well as his Freudian conception of the human self.

In one of his last pieces, "Philosophy as a Transitional Genre," Rorty advances an argument which is central to his thought: "It is that the intellectuals of the West have, since the Renaissance, progressed through three stages: they have hoped for redemption first from God, then from

[5] For a detailed discussion of the Rortyan notion of a literary or poeticized culture, see Ulf Schulenberg, "From Redescription to Writing: Rorty, Barthes, and the Idea of a Literary Culture." *New Literary History 38* (2007): 371-85.

philosophy, and now from literature" (8). According to Rorty, we live in a (not fully realized) literary culture. The transition from a philosophical to a literary culture began with Hegel. It was with Hegel that philosophy reached its most ambitious and presumptuous form which almost instantly turned into its dialectical opposite, that is, the Hegelian system eventually turned out to be a kind of utterly unironical self-consuming artifact. Hegel's system was serious in its desire to depict things as they really were and it sought to fit everything into a single context. This also signifies, of course, that it pretended to represent the totality. Rorty contends:

> Since Hegel's time, the intellectuals have been losing faith in philosophy. This amounts to losing faith in the idea that redemption can come in the form of true beliefs. In the literary culture that has been emerging during the last two hundred years, the question "Is it true?" has yielded to the question "What's new?" ("Philosophy" 9)[6]

In today's literary culture, philosophy and religion have become marginal; they appear as only optional literary genres.

For our present purposes it suffices to recognize that an essay like James's "Great Men and their Environment" can be interpreted as illustrating the power of the strong poet in the Bloomian and Rortyan sense. Following James, the mutations of societies are primarily due to the acts of (creative and innovative) individuals. These individuals often appear as an example which others strive to imitate. In *Pragmatism*, James speaks of "men of radical idiosyncrasy" with a "strong temperamental vision" (9). The genius of these individuals, whom we interpret as strong poets, "was so adapted to the receptivities of the moment, or whose accidental position of authority was so critical that they became ferments, initiators of movement, setters of precedent or fashion, centers of corruption, or destroyers of other persons, whose gifts, had they had free play, would have led society in another direction" ("Great Men" 227).

This passage beautifully elucidates the potential power James grants to the extraordinary individual. Well aware of the potential dangers of aggression, corruption, or destruction in connection with the reign of the strong individual or poet, James also puts a particularly strong emphasis

[6] One should also think of Rorty's notions of sentimental storytelling and sentimental education in this context; see Rorty's *Achieving Our Country: Leftist Thought in Twentieth-Century America.* Cambridge: Harvard UP, 1998 and his "Human Rights, Rationality, and Sentimentality." *Truth and Progress: Philosophical Papers,* Vol. 3. New York: Cambridge UP, 1998. 167-85.

on the fermentative influence of the new genius. He or she proves to be capable of causing changes in the direction of social evolution. His or her contingent *gestalt* switches have a profound impact on the development of the community. In "Great Men and their Environment," James draws attention to the aforementioned relation between the individual and the community when he famously formulates as follows: "The community stagnates without the impulse of the individual. The impulse dies away without the sympathy of the community" (232). A certain genius may of course eventually turn out to be incompatible with his or her surroundings, with no possibility of influencing and creatively changing them, but this only means, if we follow James, that this community is still under the influence of some previous poet or redescriber. There are two things I want to underline with regard to James's essay. First, his strong emphasis on "the vital importance of individual initiative" ("Great Men" 245). Second, his wish that the energy and creativity of the individual ought to form and change the world of practice. The strong poet in the Jamesian sense is not an anemic and unworldly man of abstraction or speculation. He does suggest new forms of abstraction, yet his main concern is the seemingly spontaneous offer of a new way of thinking (and speaking), and thus of coping with daily practice. The Jamesian genius seems to propose the following: "Try to think of things in this radically new and at first surprising way, and find out whether it is not only stimulating and exciting but also useful for you in your continuous attempt to cope with the messy world of practice." The next passage sounds almost Rortyan in its explanation of the strong poet's desire to make it new:

> Instead of thoughts of concrete things patiently following one another in a beaten track of habitual suggestion, we have the most abrupt cross-cuts and transitions from one idea to another, the most rarefied abstractions and discriminations, the most unheard-of combinations of elements, the subtlest associations of analogy; in a word, we seem suddenly introduced into a seething caldron of ideas, where everything is fizzling and bobbing about in a state of bewildering activity, where partnerships can be joined or loosened in an instant, treadmill routine is unknown, and the unexpected seems the only law. According to the idiosyncrasy of the individual, the scintillations will have one character or another. They will be sallies of wit and humor; they will be flashes of poetry and eloquence; they will be constructions of dramatic fiction or of mechanical device, logical or philosophic abstractions, business projects, or scientific hypotheses, with trains of experimental consequences based thereon; they will be musical sounds, or images of plastic beauty or picturesqueness, or visions of moral harmony. ("Great Men" 248)

James's pluralism urges one to understand that the world of practice and the world of poetry do not necessarily have to be mutually exclusive, that is, the 'flashes of poetry and eloquence,' going back to the idiosyncratic vocabulary of the genius or strong poet, may cause contingent changes in the world of practice. To put this somewhat differently, we might be shocked and disoriented in our first confrontation with this new set of metaphors, this new way of speaking, but eventually we might find out, surprisingly enough, that it helps us cope with the multitudinous, messy, and tangled world of everyday life. Clearly, the above quotation, with its emphasis on 'the most unheard-of combinations of elements, the subtlest associations of analogy,' 'the seething caldron of ideas,' and 'the state of bewildering activity' where 'the unexpected seems the only law,' depicts the exact opposite of the world described by absolute idealists, monists, or rationalists as metaphysicians (or vulgar materialists, for that matter). This, I believe, is a description of a literary or poeticized culture, a pluralistic world governed by novelty, contingency, and the desire for constant redescriptions – namely, a world in which man no longer sees the necessity of looking for the certainty, reliability, purity, and profundity of what would be more than another human invention.

Conclusion

Throughout *The American Evasion of Philosophy*, Cornel West directs his readers' attention to the productive tension between pragmatism's insights and blindnesses, its obvious strengths and its no less obvious weaknesses. Although West realizes the plurality of possible pragmatisms, he maintains that this heterogeneity must not prevent one from seeing that pragmatism always aims at expanding (creative) democracy and enriching individuality. He interprets pragmatism as a future-oriented instrumentalism which uses thought as a weapon for more effective action and vocabularies as tools for coping with the world. In the introduction to his book, West stresses the Americanness of pragmatism when he writes:

> I understand American pragmatism as a specific historical and cultural product of American civilization, a particular set of social practices that articulate certain American desires, values, and responses and that are elaborated in institutional apparatuses principally controlled by a significant slice of the American middle class. (4f.)

In West's view, the American evasion of philosophy, that is, the pragmatists' radical critique and evasion of epistemology-centered philosophy, has led to a profound change in the conception of philosophy. Because of this evasion, philosophy has slowly but steadily turned into a kind of cultural criticism in which the meaning of America is continually questioned and debated. What this means is that this swerve from epistemology or abstract pure philosophy in general has led not to a radical dismissal of philosophy but to its reconception as a form of cultural criticism which is politically engaged and which, at least in its Westian version, can be understood as a kind of American leftist critique.[7]

Following West, getting rid of all the misjudgments, myths, distortions, and stereotypes surrounding pragmatism would finally enable one to appreciate that this way of thinking can be seen "as a component of a new and novel form of indigenous American oppositional thought and action" (8). It is precisely the development of such an oppositional American cultural criticism that West sees as his task in *The American Evasion of Philosophy* and other texts (mainly of the 1980s). In this article, I have argued that one might interpret James's worldly pragmatism as a precursor of this Westian oppositional cultural criticism. James, of course, was not a political radical, but rather a middle-class (progressive) liberal and a vehement anti-imperialist who in his old age at least temporarily showed a certain penchant for anarchistic ideas. However, his significance for a contemporary leftist version of neopragmatism becomes obvious in the following quotation from *The American Evasion of Philosophy* where West elaborates on the crucial nature of the notion of struggle for his prophetic pragmatism: "Human struggle sits at the center of prophetic pragmatism, a struggle guided by a democratic and libertarian vision, sustained by moral courage and existential integrity, and tempered by the recognition of human finitude and frailty" (229). In spite of West's aforementioned critique of James's political position, this sentence can be seen as describing a crucial parallel between these two pragmatists.

There is, however, not only the public philosopher William James, but also the creative redescriber who focused on "the world's poem" (James, *Pragmatism* 122). One could interpret this tension between the worldly pragmatist and public philosopher, on the one hand, and the strong poet who helped prepare the establishment of a postmetaphysical

[7] For a detailed discussion of West's version of neopragmatism, and of his development from leftism to left-liberal progressivism, see the chapter "Love and Resistance: Cornel West's Prophetic Pragmatism as Oppositional Cultural Criticism," in Ulf Schulenberg. *Lovers and Knowers: Moments of the American Cultural Left*. Heidelberg: Winter, 2007. 187-221.

literary or poeticized culture, on the other, by means of a Rortyan public-private split. However, one can also simply argue that this tension calls attention to the complexity of what could be termed a leftist romanticism. As such, James, Rorty, and West, despite the obvious differences between their versions of pragmatism, should be regarded as crucial parts of a tradition of leftist romanticism. Narrating the story of this kind of romanticism is still a desideratum.[8] The story of the poets, the philosophers, and the pragmatists waits to be told and retold anew.

[8] For a discussion of the relationship between pragmatism and romanticism, see Nancy Fraser, "Solidarity or Singularity? Richard Rorty between Romanticism and Technocracy." *Reading Rorty*. Ed. Alan Malachowski. Oxford: Basil Blackwell, 1990. 303-21; Russell B. Goodman. *American Philosophy and the Romantic Tradition*. New York: Cambridge UP, 1990; Kathleen M. Wheeler. *Romanticism, Pragmatism, and Deconstruction.* Oxford: Basil Blackwell, 1993; and Ulf Schulenberg, "'Becoming the Poets of Our Own Lives:' Pragmatism and Romanticism." *Arbeiten aus Anglistik und Amerikanistik* 34.2 (2009): 293-314. It is interesting to note that Ralph Barton Perry confirms our idea that James's thinking was governed by a tension between the poles of worldliness and romanticism. He writes: "It is characteristic of individualism that it should be divisible into two divergent motives which create a tension even when they do not break into open antagonism. There is the motive of self-assertion, and the motive of sympathy: the expression of one's own individuality, and the appreciation of the individuality of others. In the case of James both motives were native and strong. There is, therefore, an oscillation between the ethics of conciliation, peace, and social utility, and the ethics of aggression, militancy, and romanticism. His literary enthusiasm followed these motives – now the one and now the other" (226).

Works Cited

Bauerlein, Mark. *The Pragmatic Mind: Explorations in the Psychology of Belief*. Durham: Duke UP, 1997.

Cotkin, George. *William James, Public Philosopher*. Baltimore: Johns Hopkins UP, 1990.

Dickstein, Morris. "Introduction: Pragmatism Then and Now." *The Revival of Pragmatism: New Essays on Social Thought, Law, and Culture*. Ed. Morris Dickstein. Durham: Duke UP, 1998. 1-18.

Fish, Stanley. *The Trouble with Principle*. Cambridge: Harvard UP, 1999.

Gunn, Giles. *Thinking Across the American Grain: Ideology, Intellect, and the New Pragmatism*. Chicago and London: U of Chicago P, 1992.

James, William. *A Pluralistic Universe*. *William James, Writings 1902-1910*. Ed. Bruce Kuklick. New York: The Library of America, 1987. 625-819.

—. "A World of Pure Experience." *Pragmatism and Other Writings*. Edited and with an Introduction by Giles Gunn. New York: Penguin, 2000. 314-336.

—. "Great Men and their Environment." *The Will to Believe and Other Essays in Popular Philosophy*. New York: Dover Publications, 1956. 216-254.

—. *Pragmatism and Other Writings*. Ed. Giles Gunn. New York: Penguin, 2000.

—. "Preface to *The Will to Believe*." *Pragmatism and Other Writings*. Ed. Giles Gunn. New York: Penguin, 2000. 193-197.

—. "On a Certain Blindness in Human Beings." *Pragmatism and Other Writings*. Ed. Giles Gunn. New York: Penguin, 2000. 267-285.

—. *Some Problems of Philosophy*. *William James, Writings 1902-1910*. Ed. Bruce Kuklick. New York: The Library of America, 1987. 979-1106.

—. "The Moral Philosopher and the Moral Life." *Pragmatism and Other Writings*. Ed. Giles Gunn. New York: Penguin, 2000. 242-263.

Lentricchia, Frank. "The Return of William James." *Cultural Critique* 4 (1986): 5-31.

Perry, Ralph Barton. *The Thought and Character of William James*. 1948. Nashville: Vanderbilt UP, 1996.

Rorty, Richard. *Contingency, Irony, and Solidarity*. New York: Cambridge UP, 1989.

—. "Philosophy as a Transitional Genre." *Pragmatism, Critique, Judgment: Essays for Richard J. Bernstein*. Eds. Seyla Benhabib and Nancy Fraser. Cambridge: MIT P, 2004. 3-28.

Seigfried, Charlene Haddock. "James: Sympathetic Apprehension of the Point of View of the Other." *Classical American Pragmatism: Its Contemporary Vitality*. Eds. Sandra B. Rosenthal, Carl R. Hausman, and Douglas R. Anderson. Urbana and Chicago: U of Illinois P, 1999. 85-98.

Stuhr, John J. "William James's Pragmatism: Purpose, Practice, and Pluralism." *Classical American Pragmatism: Its Contemporary Vitality*. Eds. Sandra B. Rosenthal, Carl R. Hausman, and Douglas R. Anderson. Urbana and Chicago: U of Illinois P, 1999. 31-44.

West, Cornel. *The American Evasion of Philosophy: A Genealogy of Pragmatism*. Madison: U of Wisconsin P, 1989.

PRAGMATISM AND CULTURAL POLITICS

Verification and the Public Philosopher: George Orwell and William James

Patricia Rae

> True ideas are those that we can assimilate, validate, corroborate and verify. False ideas are those that we can not. [...] Woe to him whose beliefs play fast and loose with the order which realities follow in his experience. (James, *P* 92, 94)

> [H]owever much you deny the truth, the truth goes on existing, as it were, behind your back, and you consequently can't violate it in ways that impair military efficiency. (Orwell, "Looking Back on the Spanish War" XIII, 505)

Given the opportunity to address the subject of William James and modernist literature, I'll begin by confronting what Charles Altieri perceived as a limitation in my own earlier work on this subject, and, indeed, in all of the efforts to explore that connection during the hey-day of Rortyian "neo-pragmatism" in the 1990s. In my 1997 book, *The Practical Muse*, I explored the affinity between James's program for pragmatist truth-making and the practice of several modernist poets, notably T. E. Hulme, Ezra Pound, and Wallace Stevens.[1] My argument was that modernist poems, like James's pragmatist "truths," are often "tensional" structures, holding in balance what James, in *The Will to Believe,* called the "passion for simplification" and its rival "passion for distinguishing" (*WB* 66). Both structures – the modernist poems and the pragmatist "truths" – invite us to glimpse provisional patterns in the cindery "flux" of experience, but also to test and, if necessary, *revise* those abstractions, against the "flux." Their visual analogues are something like the Vorticist paintings of Wyndham Lewis and David Bomberg. "God-like lines are not for us," said Lewis, but, rather, a powerful but remote *suggestion of finality,* or an *elementary*

[1] I supplemented this with an essay, "Bloody Battle-Flags and Cloudy Days: The Experience of Metaphor in Pound and Stevens," in which I targeted Marjorie Perloff's categorical distinction between the traditions of American modernist poetry shaped by Stevens and Pound. The two poets, I suggested, were alike in more ways than they were different, a point James's pragmatism, with its deliberate disruption of certain binary oppositions, helps us to understand.

organization of a dark insect swarming, like the passing of a cloud's shadow or the path of a wind" (*PM* 101; my italics). Pragmatist modernism, to quote Lewis again, catches *"clearness and logic in the midst of contradictions"* (Lewis, "Vortex," 2; my italics). The function of these provisional truths in modernist poetry is, as it is of James's truths, to *help us along* with the practical business of living. James likens a truth to a "blaze" in the forest that will help us find our way ("Philosophical Conceptions and Practical Results," 185). Pound writes that a poem is an equation for building "bridges and devices" (*Selected Prose,* 332). Stevens idealizes the "virile poet," whose work will "help people to live their lives" (*Necessary Angel,* 30).

Another term for this practice of holding up provisional truths against reality's "flux" is verification. "Truth," says James, "is simply a collective name for verification-processes" (*P* 98). "Any idea that helps us to *deal*, whether practically or intellectually, with reality or its belongings, that doesn't entangle our progress in frustrations, that *fits*, in fact, and adapts our life to reality's whole setting, will agree sufficiently to meet the requirement. It will hold true of that reality" (*P* 97). In my book, I stressed that James's commitment to verification was what differentiated his version of pragmatism from some others, such as the exuberant "fiction-making" of Friedrich Nietzsche and Hans Vaihinger or, later, the "neo-pragmatism" of Richard Rorty.

While I will stand by my claim about the tensional structure of modernist poems, and by a conviction about the deep correspondences between the poets' reasoning about truth and James's, I must concede now that the writers I discussed in *The Practical Muse* don't press as *hard* into the flux as James would have recommended. Wallace Stevens is a case in point. However beautifully he emulates pragmatism in the structures of his poetry, however eloquently he writes about the poet's duty to confront the "alien, point-blank, green and actual Guatemala," or about the "events […] [that lie] beyond our power to tranquillize [sic!] them in the mind" (*NA* 22), the truth is that we encounter very few strong references to the "actual world" in his poetry. Alan Filreis's analyses of Stevens's poetry notwithstanding,[2] we really do have to look very hard to see evidence of the grim poverty of the Depression or of World War I, or of the brutalities of imperialism, or the hardening of nationalism, or the emergence of totalitarian states across the globe. The "virile poet" may exercise his reader's minds by throwing out hypotheses or presenting "true" metaphors,[3] but we receive little guidance from the

[2] See Filreis, *Wallace Stevens and the Actual World.*
[3] See my "Bloody Battle-flags and Cloudy Days."

"virile poet" on these pressing issues. What I'd like to propose is that we may find an even more satisfactory exemplar of Jamesian pragmatism in one of the great writers of modernist *prose,* a writer who had much in common with Stevens and other modernist poets, but whose engagement with the "actual world" is undisputed: George Orwell.

The affinity between James and Orwell is by no means obvious. The quintessentially American Harvard professor and famous optimist seems a very long way away, culturally, from the quintessentially English ex-Imperial policeman, sometimes tramp, and author of the most famous literary dystopia in English. And yet Orwell's habits of thought are strikingly similar to those of James: anti-intellectualist, deconstructive, relentlessly focused on the empirical flux and attentive to the consequences of our provisional "truths." My plan is to explore a series of important points of correspondence between the two writers, an exercise I hope will not only consolidate Orwell's status as a "Jamesian modernist," but also illuminate Jamesian pragmatism itself, in ways pertinent to the twenty-first century, which has not shed the sort of trouble Orwell confronted seven decades ago.

One similarity between James and Orwell that *does* come fairly quickly to mind is their prominence as "public philosophers."[4] In George Cotkin's definition, "to be a public philosopher [means] accepting responsibility for addressing public problems and for applying insights gained from one's technical work to public issues" (Cotkin 4). James and Orwell came to the task from very different backgrounds (the most notable being that James was formally educated and lived an academic life, where Orwell was and did not) but the fact remains that both made a point of speaking out on issues of social and political importance. They resemble one another, too, in the ways in which they are susceptible to misinterpretation by dogmatists in political argument. As Cotkin has explained in the case of James, and as both John Rodden and Christopher Hitchens have observed about Orwell, these are figures that activists and ideologues – whether imperialists or anti-imperialists, jingoists or anti-war protestors, capitalists or socialists – want desperately to claim for their own side. The fact is, however, that what both James and Orwell have to offer is not so much dogma on any particular political issue as a

[4] George Cotkin has written a fine book on the subject of James's role as "public philosopher." John Rodden describes Orwell as "perhaps the leading twentieth-century exemplar of the public intellectual" (93). Christopher Hitchens has done much to publicize Orwell's relevance to contemporary issues. Currently, an "Orwell Prize" is granted annually to the best political writing of the year in Britain, a signal of his enduring importance to the public sphere.

method,[5] a method that serves the second in these binaries more than the first, but that is meant to improve the discourse of all sides and, above all, the interactions between them.

"Unstiffening" Categories

In one of the most engaging passages in *Pragmatism,* we learn that pragmatism is a woman. One of her key functions as such, James says, is to "unstiffen" the rigid binary categories governing thought (P, 38, 73). She is a "mediator" and "reconciler." She is open-minded and "widens the field of search for God." Ironically, given how well they qualify to be Stevens's "virile poets," James and Orwell fit this profile. They are especially bent on disrupting those classifications that divide human beings: the us/them binaries that drive imperialism, nationalism, and war.

Many of Orwell's most important insights were forged through his experience of fighting Fascism in the Spanish Civil War. Early in 1937, he fought as a volunteer in defense of the Spanish Republic with the far-left militia POUM. On his return to England in June of that year, he was anxious to write about the war, but not about the anti-fascist cause *per se.* Rather, he was anxious to talk about the extraordinary propaganda war he had seen sparked by the civil one. The latter, he came to appreciate, was a context where what James called "*rationalism*" (*PU* 24-26), the "dogmatic rigoristic temper" (*P* 73), or "*vicious intellectualism*" (*PU* 150; my italics) prevailed. That is to say, it was one where the categories the antagonists used to represent one another were fixed and mutually exclusive, brooking no impurity or cross-fertilization. What James called the "disposition to see everything as yes or no, as black or white," or the "incapacity for discrimination of intermediate shades" (*PU* 159),[6] was abundantly evident in discourse like that of the famous questionnaire, *Authors Take Sides on the Spanish War,* which circulated amongst writers in Britain shortly after Orwell's return home:

[5] Pragmatism claims "no dogmas, and no doctrines save its method" (*P* 32). As Cotkin points out, "the anarchistic edge of James's early metaphysics would always prevent him from embracing any easily definable political attitude" (17). Rodden traces many instances of Orwell's appropriation by both left-wing and right-wing thinkers, as does Hitchens. The "anarchistic" or "perverse" character of both writers' thought produced tensions in their relationships with progressive thinkers.

[6] Or to think in "only in the most violent extremes" (*PU* 159), or "brook […] no degrees" (*P* 73).

"Are you for or against the legal Government and the People of Republican Spain?" it asked, "Are you for, or against, Franco and Fascism? […] [I]t is impossible any longer to take no side" (Cunard et al., June, 1937). In countless posters, the battle was a Manichean allegory between the heroic dragon-slayers of the Republic and Fascist monsters drawn straight from the surrealist imagination. The intellectualist character of anti-fascist discourse became even more apparent to Orwell when the Communist Party, who maintained increasing control over policy on the Government side, began to encounter dissension in the Republican ranks. Orwell's POUM militia, along with the anarchist CNT, rejected the Soviet strategy of deferring social revolution so as to maintain Popular Front allies. The Communist response to this independence of thought, as Orwell recounts it, was to demonize the dissenters, to accuse them of betraying their own side and crossing over to the enemy camp.[7] The message of the crackdown was unequivocal: you are either with us, or you are against us. In James's terms, there prevailed a spirit of "*vicious intellectualism*:" either the absolute whole is there, or there is absolutely nothing (*PU* 158). Eight years later, with many more encounters with this black and white sort of thinking under his belt, Orwell offers the term "nationalism" to describe it:

> By "nationalism" I mean first of all the habit of assuming that human beings can be classified like insects and that whole blocks of millions or tens of millions of people can be confidently labeled "good" or "bad." But secondly—and this is much more important—I mean the habit of identifying oneself with a single nation or other unit, placing it beyond good and evil and recognizing no other duty than that of advancing its interests. (Orwell, "Notes on Nationalism" XVII, 141)

Orwell objected strenuously to this way of thinking. In his 1937 essay "Spilling the Spanish Beans," for example, he directly confronts the logic that says "XY has been heard to speak favorably of world-revolution; therefore he is a Trotskyist; therefore he is a Fascist … [in the pay of Franco or Hitler]" (XI, 45). This is what motivates his work as

7 "In Spain, everyone whose opinions are to the Left of those of the Communist Party is sooner or later discovered to be a Trotskyist, or at least, a traitor" ("Spilling the Spanish Beans" XI, 45). Notice also Orwell's observation in Appendix I (formerly chapter V) of *Homage to Catalonia*: "The people who wrote / pamphlets against us and vilified us in the newspapers all remained safe at home, or at worst in the newspaper offices of Valencia, hundreds of miles from the bullets and the mud" (V, 208). This distance from the muddy truth of experience is consistent with the abstract rationalism James eviscerates in *Pragmatism.*

a "contrarian." He is fully committed to the point that one can criticize one's own side from within, without giving up membership in it. On this point, James would have strongly endorsed him. Membership in one category, James writes, is not an exclusive thing: "the same part may figure in many different systems, as a man may hold various offices and belong to several clubs" (*P* 64). The world consists of "innumerable little hangings-together" (*P* 64). Things may be "partly joined and partly disjoined" (*P* 74). Pragmatist descriptions will flex and adjust to accommodate these multiple affiliations.

Orwell was a Jamesian pragmatist, then, in placing a premium on the practice of "unstiffening" political categories, in light of the evidence of "experience." For him, evidence of the continuity between things trumps abstract distinctions every time. Another way of describing this strain in his work is to say he is interested in (indeed, almost obsessed with) identifying "strange bedfellows:" that is, for pointing out how self-identified enemies actually *resemble one another*. He likes to point out how their similarities qualify them for "membership" in a different category altogether. The propensity for pointing out such things is what commentators have called the "perverse" or "persistently oppositional [...] turn of [Orwell's] thinking" (Cain 115): his habit of "telling people what they did not want to hear" (Cain 115, 117). Here again his comments on anti-fascist discourse are revealing. The Republican side's caricature of the Fascist "monster," the Communist Party's intolerance for criticism from within, the willingness of the anti-fascist movement to exploit atrocity propaganda and to "play fast and loose" with facts, caused Orwell on more than one occasion to remark that the *anti-fascist* side is beginning to resemble its enemy. By way of explanation for this morphing of a group into its opposite, he invokes the famous adage from Nietzsche: "He who fights too long against dragons becomes a dragon himself: and if thou gaze too long into the abyss, the abyss will gaze into thee" (Orwell XI 166-67).[8]

What is becoming visible to Orwell here, and what continues to interest him as mid-twentieth century history unfolds, is a version of the dialectical process described by Hegel, in which things come to resemble their nominal opposites, regrouping into new, more inclusive, classifications. And here it is notable that James, in the *Essays on Radical Empiricism,* explicitly endorses Hegel's dialectical processes as a fact of the "empirical flux of things" (*ERE* 163). Though James was antipathetic to the more abstract dimensions of Hegel's thought, his pragmatist's ongoing process of making, unmaking, and re-making the

[8] Cf. Orwell XI 113.

truth in some ways mirrors the dialectical processes Hegel envisions. Orwell finds the related process of classifying and reclassifying political opponents irresistible: he points out the affinities between anti-fascists and fascists in Spain, between allied capitalists and Fascists during World War II, between capitalist and communist managers during the Cold War. Indeed, there is a very close connection between Orwell's interest in exploring the "strange bedfellows" phenomenon and his curious turn, in the last few years of his life, from documentary writing towards allegory. Allegorical images (Nietzsche's dragons, his own pigs) enable a writer to focus a critique on categories of things that encompass nominal opposites. With them, he may satirize, in a single target, *both* sides in a bitter dispute.

A "Transcendent Reality"

The second point of correspondence between James and Orwell clarifies the rationale behind their commitment to verification. It concerns the matter of why a pragmatist should be accountable to a "transcendent reality" at all, if "truth" is as wedded to "satisfaction" as he believes it to be.

The fact that a pragmatist approach to truth-making includes attentiveness to "facts" transcending the truth-maker was not at all obvious to James's first readers. Indeed, we owe one of James's most illuminating texts, *The Meaning of Truth*, to the need he felt to clarify this very point. Subtitled *A Sequel to Pragmatism,* this book is all about refuting "the slanderous charge that [...] [pragmatists] deny real existence" (*MT* xv), *"that we are persons who think that by saying whatever you find it pleasant to say and calling it truth you fulfill every pragmatistic requirement"* (*P* 104; my italics). Critics suspicious of pragmatism have been arguing that, if we accept pragmatism's conflation of truth with what is "good" or "satisfying" in the way of our thinking,[9] we cannot also be realists in epistemology.[10] Reality, quite simply, will have to be *whatever it would advance our interests for it to be.* The indifference to unmediated "fact" is reinforced by the fact that

[9] As James does when he says in *Pragmatism* that "[t]he true is the name of whatever proves itself to be good [or "satisfactory"] in the way of belief" (*P* 37), or in *The Meaning of Truth* when he asserts that "the truth of our beliefs consists in general in their giving satisfaction" (*MT* 190).

[10] See the "fourth misunderstanding" discussed in "The Pragmatist Account of Truth," in *MT* 190.

there is, quite simply, no unmediated perception of reality; there is therefore no meaningful standard against which we could be held accountable.

James offers two very clear points in response to this "slanderous" mischaracterization of his pragmatist view of truth. The first is that what he has been calling "satisfaction" *includes* "truth-satisfaction," that is, a sense of the fittedness between representation and fact. Compared with the satisfaction that comes with "the inherent relation to reality of a belief," he says, "all other[s] [...] are the hollowest humbug" (*MT* 194). His second point is that the critic of pragmatism who denies its commitment to verification is ignoring a fundamental difference between "realities" and "beliefs." "Realities are not *true,*" he notes, "they *are*; and beliefs are true *of* them" (*MT* 196). "[I]n the anti-pragmatist mind the two notions sometimes swap their attributes" (*MT* 196), such that the need to establish a "satisfactory" belief translates into an authorization to equate "reality" with something "satisfactory." The only truth important for pragmatism is that a belief *will be* satisfactory *if* it has some *inherent relation* to reality. Quite clearly, then, as Cotkin puts it, "The brunt of the will to believe was not a right to deceive, a right to make-believe, or a right to believe in anything one wanted for whatever narrow purposes," as some of James's critics, in his time as well as ours, have claimed" (81). The pragmatist "is willing to treat our satisfactions as possibly really true guides to 'reality,' not as guides solely true for *us*" (*MT* 192).

Orwell's reflections on the propaganda war over Spain closely replicate this argument. The civil war, he writes in his 1942 essay, "Looking Back on the Spanish War," has been the occasion for an unprecedented degree of self-interested bias and distortion in truth-making. He wrings his hands at the cynicism of those entrusted with reporting on the war:

> [I]n Spain, for the first time I saw newspaper reports which did not bear any relation to the facts, not even the relationship which is implied in an ordinary lie. I saw great battles reported where there had been no fighting, and complete silence where hundreds of men had been killed. I saw troops who had fought bravely denounced as cowards and traitors, and others who had never seen a shot fired hailed as the heroes of imaginary victories; and I saw newspapers in London retailing these lies and eager intellectuals building emotional superstructures over events that had never happened. I saw, in fact, history being written not in terms of what happened but of what ought to have happened according to various 'party lines.' (XIII, 503)

The situation Orwell describes here is what James would have called a "playing fast and loose" with truth. To use a phrase coined later by

Richard Rorty, it was a "floating, ungrounded conversation" (*Consequences of Pragmatism* 174). Satisfaction trumps reality to an extraordinary degree, without any empirical "checks."[11] Orwell responds to the picture with horror, but not for the simple reason that all the warring representations are biased. In his memoir of fighting in the war, *Homage to Catalonia,* he has admitted to an (inevitable) bias in his own account, but this has not replaced a concern with attending to experience and establishing the truth so far as this is possible. "Like everyone who was in Barcelona at the time," he writes, "I saw only what was happening in my immediate neighborhood, *but I saw and heard quite enough to be able to contradict many of the lies that have been circulated*" (VI, 131; my italics). His position here is strikingly reminiscent of James's warning to potential critics of his ongoing commitment to verification: "Please observe, now, that when as empiricists we give up the doctrine of objective certitude, we do not thereby give up the quest or hope of truth itself" (*WB*, 17).

What truly upsets Orwell, as it would have James, is the fact that "the very concept of objective truth is fading out of the world" ("Looking Back on the Spanish War," XIII, 504). In Orwell's analysis of the war, it is very clear that behind the exaggerated tales of atrocities and malfeasance, from both sides, certain transcendent facts present themselves. "The main issues," he argues, "were what [the Spanish government] said they were" –contradiction to the "pure fantasy" of the war propagated by the Fascists (XIII, 503). "Unfortunately," he writes, "the truth about atrocities" – the "behavior of the Japanese in China" and the "long tale of Fascist outrages in Europe" – "is far worse than that they are lied about and made into propaganda. *The truth is that they happen.* [...] *They happened even though Lord Halifax said they happened*" (XIII, 500; my italics). It is the decent man's duty to accept this and respond appropriately. And this means not sliding into a pacifism born of radical skepticism (as he himself had, briefly, on returning disillusioned from Spain), but taking up arms to put an end to them. What becomes very clear with this episode is that Orwell is a pragmatist and a realist: he believes in a transcendent reality and will adjust his truths to honor what appears to be incontrovertible evidence about it. As Orwell's critique of totalitarianism grows during the 1940s, he will make it clear that holding firm in this belief about objective realities outside the bounds of propaganda is crucial for resisting totalitarianism. It is in his discussion of the issue that we see his first

11 By contrast, Orwell, like James, would have wanted to see experience "boil over" and change the Manichean binaries governing the discourse on the war.

references to the figure of Big Brother: "More frightening than bombs," he says, is the prospect of a world where "If the Leader says of such and such an event, 'It never happened'—well, it never happened," or where "[I]f he says that two and two are five – well, two and two are five."[12] It is crucial for all citizens everywhere to remember that "however much [we may] deny the truth, the truth goes on existing, as it were, behind your back […]." Failing to do that will, quite frankly, "impair military efficiency" (XIII, 505).

The "Stream of Experience"

The final point of correspondence I'd like to explore between Orwell and James is their sense of the *sort* of evidence involved in the "verification procedure" itself: *what factors*, exactly, the pragmatist is obligated to take into account.[13] In a move of incalculable importance to modernist writers in English, James represents the process of truth-making as a plunging forth of provisional truths into the "stream of experience" (*P* 69), or "the flux of our sensations" (*P* 110). "[T]he whole coil and ball of truth, as it rolls up, is the product of a double influence. Truths emerge from facts; but they dip forward into facts again and add to them; which facts again create or reveal new truth (the word is indifferent) and so on indefinitely" (*P* 101). This picture of the truth-making process attests to the *flexibility* of pragmatism's concepts, theories, and representations and to their *performative* power.

But also of great interest is all that is implied by the liquid substance into which the pragmatist "dips" his truths (or that "boils over" (*P* 100) sometimes, causing him to correct them.) Four things, it seems to me, are important about this substance, for both James and Orwell, the Jamesian modernist.

The first is that it is a blend of objective and subjective elements, a perceptual field in which the thing perceived and the emotional response to the thing remain undivided. James also uses the image of a panorama in which foreground and background commingle (*ERE* 18). The world of

[12] Convincing Winston to attest to this proposition is one of the goals of his torture at the hands of O'Brien. See Orwell IX, 262.

[13] A strong connection with the modernist literary tradition generally will be apparent here, for the "stream of consciousness" is of course one of the formative concepts in the history of modernist prose writing. Orwell was deeply inspired by James Joyce's experiments in the method.

theory – of abstract ideas not directly experienced – remains outside of this blended reality, like the oxygen outside the stream.

The second important thing about the stream is its inclusiveness. When the pragmatist – or "radical empiricist" – tests his truths, it is with a view to leaving nothing out: no "affectional fact," nor transitional perception, no emotion or reason, no ignominious attitude or motive, nothing the reporter would prefer to censor or forget. It is a policy of full-disclosure. It demands the exploration and revelation of one's authentic, "fundamental" self.[14]

The third salient feature of this liquid "flux" is that it is *interpenetrated,* by which I mean: of a complexity elusive to the formulations of the intellect. Here it is important to recall James's endorsement, in *A Pluralistic Universe,* of Henri Bergson's account of the liquid flux (*PU* 227–64). The key point of Bergson's metaphor of an "interpenetrated flux" is that it *blends* elements *the intellect* sees as incompatible. Attending to this realm, says James, to this "world of concrete personal experiences" is "*like putting muddiest confusion in face of clearest thought*" (*PU* 245). It confronts us with what may be messy, "*muddy, painful, and perplexed* [...]" (*P* 14). This helps to explain the connection between this picture of pragmatist truth-making and the "perverse" approach to categories and classifications I was discussing earlier. For establishing contact with it may mean grasping the sometimes *paradoxical* combinations of feeling in our experience. It may require our recognizing that "both honesty and dishonesty, courage and cowardice, stupidity and insight" (*PU* 248) may be operating in ourselves or others at the same time. The notion of an interpenetrated flux allows, too, for the extraordinary possibility that we may in many ways be the opposite of what we are. Plunging forward into it may mean grasping that "each of us actually *is* his own other," a "trick which logic tells us can't be done" (*PU* 247).[15] In Bergson's account, and by extension in James's, grasping the paradoxes of experience will require calling upon the faculty of "intuition," not intellect. It will involve experiencing "the expanding center of a human character" (*PU* 247) from within.[16]

The final crucial feature of the liquid flux against which the pragmatist checks his truths – for Bergson and James, and also for Orwell – is that it includes *memory.* As the pragmatist plunges forward

[14] The notion of the "fundamental self" comes from Bergson. For a vivid account of this entity, see the *Introduction to Metaphysics,* 6-37.

[15] See *PU* 247 also for a list of the questions Bergsonism allows us to answer.

[16] Orwell will implicitly pursue this notion in references to Taoist philosophy.

into new experiences, he remains cognizant of "previous truths" (*P* 98). "We plunge forward into the field of fresh experience with the beliefs our ancestors and we have made already" (*P* 114f.). The pragmatist is responsive to new experience, but never "capricious" (*P* 98). As James puts it, he must "derange common sense and previous belief as little as possible" (*P* 98).

Orwell famously boasted about himself that he had a capacity for "facing unpleasant facts" (XCIII, 316). Indeed he did, and in doing so he exemplified everything James was looking for in the "verifying" pragmatist, or "radical" empiricist. His interest in attending to the stream of experience is evident in some experimental moments in his early fiction[17] but it is especially clear in his documentary writings, including *The Road to Wigan Pier* (1937) and *Homage to Catalonia* (1938). As James and Bergson conceive it the "stream" of experience blends objective and subjective elements; it does not divide matters into things and what those things are "of" (*ERE*, 15). Orwell's documentaries documenting his investigations into the execrable living conditions of Britain's northern miners, as well as his experiences with POUM in Spain, unabashedly mingle subjective responses with objective facts (often over the protests of leftist critics, who favored a more "objective" (or "socialist realist") sort of literature. They also honor the principle of inclusivity, making no effort to whitewash the dirty truth about how he sometimes feels about his allies. We learn about his revulsion at the "smell" of poverty, and at the way his fellow militiamen defile the property of a fascist landowner with their excrement (leaving him in "sneaking sympathy" with his nominal enemy.) What he has to say about his own feelings is often politically incorrect, but he reminds us of the practical purpose of acknowledging it: if we do not know ourselves *from within,* and the cultural differences dividing us from those with whom we are united in our political activities, we stand to lose to enemy forces who may understand our inner workings better than we do.

It is in connection with this imperative that Orwell is committed to understanding the *interpenetrated* quality of the "stream" of experience. He wants us to grasp the paradoxical blends of attributes within ourselves that evade logical analysis. The political activism of the 1930s saw him confronting awkward complexes of feeling towards those whose causes he shared. In *The Road to Wigan Pier,* he admits to a sense of physical revulsion from the victims of poverty whose story he tells (V, 5, 14, 55f.). In *Homage to Catalonia,* he admits to feeling alienated from

[17] See for example *A Clergyman's Daughter* (III, 151-84) where Orwell writes in obvious imitation of Joyce's *Ulysses.*

fellow militiamen in Spain who defile a fascist estate, and admits a secret sympathy with the fascist landowner (VI, 54). During the 1940s, he often conjoins his analyses of the uncompromising binaries of nationalism with Jamesian reflections on the ways "each of us actually *is* his own other" (*PU* 247). Nationalism is a form of power-hunger made all the worse by "*self-deception*" (XVII, 142). "Unshakably certain of being in the right," the nationalist "persuades himself that his own side is strongest, "even when the facts are overwhelmingly against him" (XVII, 142). The cure for this is to face the facts, which can mean recognizing one's own complicity in the problem: one's own propensity, perhaps, for clinging to "irrational belief[s]'" (XVII, 70) about others. Orwell develops this theme, targeting numerous guilty parties, in two important 1945 essays, "Anti-Semitism in Britain" and "Notes on Nationalism."

Attending to such tough truths about our inner selves goes with a willingness to speak that truth. The project of overthrowing falsifying clichés, and of laboring at sincere self-representation, is the subject of numerous essays in Orwell's last decade, including "New Words" (1940), "Inside the Whale" (1940) and "Politics and the English Language" (1945). All of these, in affirming the importance of attending to "the stream of nameless things" (XIII, 129) within, read like manifestos of a Jamesian or Bergsonian literary modernism. A recognizable pragmatist modernism thus becomes a strategy for fighting political correctness, the strictures of totalitarianism, and many variations of nationalism.[18]

There is ample evidence, finally, of Orwell's commitment to the view that truth-making should be respectful of "previous belief" and not "derange" it unnecessarily. The best of this is found in his criticism of others who are not so scrupulous, whose interpretations of reality change on a dime. He was suspicious of many British recruiters for the Spanish Republican cause, for example, because they seemed to have discarded the theory "War is hell" for the theory "War is glorious" "without any intervening stage" (XIII, 499). He was equally appalled later, when he saw many loyal Communists unapologetically changing their position on Fascism, with the Hitler-Stalin pact, and again, when that pact fell apart and the Russians rejoined the allied side. "The mutability of the past"

[18] Cf. also his comments on the anti-fascists who criticize anti-Semitism: "What vitiates nearly all that is written about anti-Semitism is the assumption in the writer's mind that *he himself* is immune to it. 'Since I know that anti-Semitism is irrational,' he argues, 'it follows that I do not share it.' He thus fails to start his investigation in the one place where he could get hold of some reliable evidence—that is, in his own mind" ("Anti-Semitism in Britain" XVII, 70).

(IX, 28) was one of the sacred principles of Ingsoc (the Party of Big Brother) in *Nineteen Eighty-Four.*

The Battle against "Bigness"

I began by suggesting that Orwell may be a better example of a Jamesian modernist than Hulme, Pound, or Stevens because he did more than they did to plunge flexible truths into the actual world. I hope my remarks have clarified the kind of verification procedure he shared with James, and his very similar rationale for pursuing it. His program for "help[ing] people live their lives" was coextensive with it. We are now in a position also, I think, to grasp the very strong connection between the work of the late nineteenth-century American optimist and what I have called the most famous literary dystopia of the twentieth century, *Nineteen Eighty-Four*. For Orwell's Oceania is a world where the prevailing standards for truth-making are everything Jamesian pragmatism repudiates. Big Brother and the Party inculcate an unthinking nationalism in their citizens. "Newspeak," their official language, reinforces this by reducing thought to crude, categorical binaries. Big Brother is the incarnation of the leader who disregards "transcendent reality" and insists his subjects do the same: he will have citizens tortured to accept the proposition "two plus two make five."[19] The successful party members known to Orwell's hero, Winston Smith, know nothing of their fluid inner selves; they function as automatons, performing physical calisthenics and spouting the "duckspeak" (IX, 57) of their leaders; they are in no way crafters of sincere self-expression. Finally, they must be capricious, for they are to have no access to memory; when the Party suddenly changes its official version of history, they dutifully flush the old one down the "memory hole," out of reach, along with the fluid, private selves they have renounced.

Jamesian pragmatism is present in the Orwellian nightmare for being so absent. Only Winston Smith, whose subject position we, as readers, occupy, attempts to do things differently, and Orwell offers us some hope that his strategies, which in many ways resemble those of pragmatist modernism,[20] hold the key to preventing this kind of

[19] See Orwell IX, 262.

[20] Winston's diary writing, his obsession with a hard coral paperweight, and his fascination with the fragments of history in Mr. Charrington's junk shop can all be linked to the practices of modernist poets, especially T.S. Eliot. See Rae, "Mr. Charrington's Junk Shop."

totalitarian specter from prevailing forever. A full account of those strategies is the topic of another paper, but the basics are not difficult to see. Reject reflex-speech. Keep a diary. Remember, and be faithful to, what you have seen with your own eyes. Don't use the mediated nature of all truth to be an excuse for being accountable to nothing. Oceania is an allegorical signifier for the "totalitarian" tendencies Orwell saw springing up everywhere, for a number of countries and institutions that would be exceedingly uncomfortable with being grouped in the same category. Orwell asks us to consider whether one individual, by rejecting reflex-speech, scribbling in his diary, crediting what he has seen with his own eyes, remaining stubbornly true to his memory, may hold the clue to stopping totalitarianism in its tracks. Here one last word from James, from an 1899 letter to Mrs. Henry Whitman, will seem hauntingly and usefully proleptic both of Orwell's dystopia and of the determination fueling all his writing about how to live in the world:

> I am against bigness and greatness in all their forms. [...] The bigger the unit you deal with, the hollower, the more brutal, the more mendacious is the life displayed. So I am against all big organizations as such, national ones first and foremost [...] and in favor of the eternal forces of truth which always work in the individual [...]. (*The Letters of William James* vol. 2, 90)

James's declaration points to a major way in which both public philosophers speak to the twenty-first century. "Bigness and greatness" have many new incarnations. A "verifying" pragmatism, with all the strategies we have reviewed here, remains a powerful way to resist them.

Works Cited

Altieri, Charles. "Practical Sense – Impractical Objects: Why Neo-Pragmatism Cannot Sustain an Aesthetics." *REAL: Yearbook of Research in English and American Literature.* Eds. Winfried Fluck et al. Tübingen: Gunter Narr, 1999. 113-36.

Bergson, Henri. *An Introduction to Metaphysics.* Tr. T.E. Hulme. Intr. John Mullarkey. London: Palgrave and Macmillan, 2007.

Cain, William E. "Orwell's Perversity: An Approach to the Collected Essays." *Bloom's Modern Critical Views.* Ed. Harold Bloom. New York: Chelsea House, 2007. 115-132.

Cotkin, George. *William James, Public Philosopher.* New York: Johns Hopkins UP, 1990.

Cunard, Nancy, et al. *Authors Take Sides on the Spanish War.* London: Left Review, 1937.

Filreis, Alan. *Wallace Stevens and the Actual World.* Princeton: Princeton UP, 1991.

Hitchens, Christopher. *Orwell's Victory.* London: Allen Lane, 2002.

James, William. *A Pluralistic Universe* (PU). Ed. Ralph Barton Perry. New York: E.F. Dutton, 1971.

—. *Essays in Radical Empiricism* (ERE). Ed. Ralph Barton Perry. New York: E.F. Dutton, 1971.

—. "Philosophical Conceptions and Practical Results." *The Heart of William James.* Ed. Robert Richardson. Cambridge, MA: Harvard UP, 2010.

—. *Pragmatism* (P). Edited by Bruce Kuklick. Indianapolis: Hackett, 1981.

—. *Psychology: The Briefer Course* (PBC). Edited by Gordon Allport. Notre Dame: U of Notre Dame P, 1985.

—. *The Letters of William James.* Ed. Henry James. London: Longman's, 1920.

—. *The Meaning of Truth* (MT). Mineola and New York: Dover, 2002.

—. *The Will to Believe and Other Essays in Popular Philosophy* (WB). New York: Dover, 1956.

Lewis, Wyndham. "A Review of Contemporary Art." *Blast II.* London, 1915; rpt. Santa Barbara California, Black Sparrow Press, 1981. 39-40.

—. "Wyndham Lewis Vortex No. 1." in *Blast*. London, 1914; rpt. Santa Barbara California: Black Sparrow Press, 1981.

Orwell, George. *The Complete Works of George Orwell.* Ed. Peter Davison. London: Secker and Warburg, 1998. 20 vols. *(References to this work will appear in parentheses with the relevant volume number in Roman numerals.)*

Pound, Ezra. *Selected Prose: 1909-1965.* Ed. William Cookson. London: Faber & Faber, 1973.

Rae, Patricia. *The Practical Muse*. Louisburg: Bucknell UP, 1997.

—. "Bloody Battle-Flags and Cloudy Days: The Experience of Metaphor in Pound and Stevens." *The Wallace Stevens Journal* 26.2 (2002): 143-59.

—. "Mr. Charrington's Junk Shop: T. S. Eliot and Modernist Poetics in *Nineteen Eighty-Four*." *Twentieth Century Literature* 43.2 (1997): 196-220.

Rodden, John. *The Politics of Literary Reputation: The Making and Claiming of 'St. George' Orwell.* Oxford: Oxford UP, 1989.

Rorty, Richard. *Consequences of Pragmatism.* Minneapolis: U of Minnesota P, 1982.

Stevens, Wallace. *The Collected Poems.* New York: Vintage, 1990.

—. *The Necessary Angel: Essays on Reality and Imagination.* London: Faber and Faber, 1984.

Negating Domination: Pragmatism, Pluralism, Power

Miriam Strube

> "Ideals ought to aim at the *transformation of reality* – no less!"
> William James

In 2007, Nobel prize winner James Watson, who helped discover the double helix structure of DNA, noted in a speech that he was "inherently gloomy about the prospect of Africa" because "all our social policies are based on the fact that their intelligence is the same as ours – whereas all the testing says not really" (Moya and Markus 16). He added that while many have a natural desire to believe that all human beings should be equal, "people who have to deal with black employees find this not true" (ibid.).

Not many agree with the outlandish assertion of this accomplished scientist. On the contrary, explicit versions of the notion that race no longer matters (at least in the same way), that the US has become a post-race, post-ethnic nation have been seriously and scholarly discussed since David Hollinger's book *Postethnic America* was published in 1995. Moreover, ever since Obama was elected president of the United States, headlines heralded the emergence of a new era: "Race Is History."

I find both of these positions deeply troubling, as one is an expression of essentialism and the other one of color-blindness. But how can we theorize race and ethnicity in a more sophisticated way? As I argue, pragmatism can be – and indeed has been – important and productive for so-called race theories. Admittedly, in their writings, classical pragmatists did not pay much attention to race. Moreover, most studies of this distinctly American philosophy have almost entirely ignored African-American thinkers, thus comporting with the widespread exclusion of African Americans from American culture and the omission of blackness from definitions of Americanness. However, as I want to show, black pragmatists are an important part of and add a significant dimension to pragmatist thinking, namely the dimension of domination, or more specifically racial domination and empowerment. My title, "Negating Domination," thus is meant to be read on two levels, one when looking at pragmatism as a tool to criticize racial inequality, and the second – rather implicit – one negating the domination of a mostly white historiography of pragmatism leaving out important thinkers.

As is widely known, William James claimed that the pragmatic attitude is one of "looking away from first things [...] and of looking toward last things, fruits, consequences" (*What Pragmatism Means* 32). I thus want to outline four pragmatist revisions: Alain Locke's and W.E.B. Du Bois's critical pragmatism of the early to mid-twentieth-century New Negro Movement, Cornel West's prophetic pragmatism as described in his 1989 book *The Evasion of Philosophy*, and finally Paula Moya's race theory as laid out in her works *Learning from Experience* and her co-edited anthology *Doing Race: 21 Essays for the 21 Century*. This anthology was published in 2010 and does not reference classical or black pragmatists, but it can be seen as a continuation of the tradition I am sketching. When reading these theories as pragmatic, I particularly pay attention to aspects of pluralism, the means of critical intelligence and social action, the role of experience, the procedural nature of knowledge and the self as well as the fallibility but usefulness of truth claims.

Alain Locke: From James's Pluralism to Cultural Pluralism

Alain Locke, arguably the most important African American philosopher of the twentieth century, has been widely neglected; he is even curiously missing (and I mean completely absent) in Cornel West's broad view of the pragmatist tradition.[1] Fortunately, in recent years his philosophy has gained more attention, particularly in the works of Leonard Harris and Johnny Washington.[2]

Locke studied at Harvard and in 1917 received his doctorate in philosophy. At Harvard he also met James, whom he revered, loudly applauding James's success at dethroning absolutism with value relativism and pluralism. Pluralism, indeed, is one of James's central concerns. It involves the orientation of accepting that the universe is not a closed system, and neither is a human life. Possibilities abound as, in

1 See Cornel West's *The Evasion of Philosophy: A Genealogy of Pragmatism* (1989).

2 See both volumes Harris has edited: *The Philosophy of Alain Locke* (1989) and *The Critical Pragmatism of Alain Locke* (1999), which includes excellent articles by Nancy Fraser and Judith Green, as well as Johnny Washington's *Alain Locke and Philosophy: A Quest for Cultural Pluralism* (1986) and *A Journey Into the Philosophy of Alain Locke* (1994).

James's words, "[a]bsolute insulation, irreducible pluralism, is the law" (*Pragmatism* 20). James continuously associates pluralism with pragmatism. For example, in his lecture "The One and the Many" James emphasizes: "Pragmatism, pending the final empirical ascertainment of just what the balance of union and disunion among things may be, must obviously range herself upon the pluralistic side" (ibid. 72). And in *A Pluralistic Universe*, his most extended statement of his pluralism, he states:

> Things are 'with' one another in many ways, but nothing includes everything, or dominates over everything. The word 'and' trails along after every sentence. Something always escapes. 'Ever not quite' has to be said of the best attempts made anywhere in the universe at attaining all-inclusiveness. (321–322)

James engages the problem of pluralism to vanquish "monism," developing pragmatism as a hermeneutic device for the pluriverse he is trying to stage. But he does not engage pluralism to vindicate cultural diversity, it took his students – most notably Randolph Bourne, Horace Kallen, and Alain Locke – to do so.

Alain Locke indeed absorbs James's pluralism. But in good pragmatist fashion, he revises it in his own way. Locke believed such a revision necessary, firstly when claiming that pragmatism, as a philosophical movement, had itself become a conservative dogma by the late 1930s and, secondly, when criticizing that it failed to recognize its own ethnocentrism (cf. Hutchinson 17). While not engaging in a systematic critique of James, he often referenced James's arguments as sufficient warrant for rejecting absolutism, universalism, and dogmatism. He then ensued to develop his own theory, insisting on imperatives of tolerance, reciprocity, and parity as conditions for the possibility of the peaceful coexistence of cultures. Locke explicitly rejects the conception of philosophy as a value-free striving, as a merely textual "sphere of intellectual dialogue over universalizable principles of rationality, knowledge and nature or a domain of discourse that is or should be unconcerned with the human condition" (ibid. 20). Accordingly, he rejects what he calls value anarchism, that is, the view that facts, preferences, terms and relations are to be recognized as coequal factors shaping human experience; a position, by the way, he normally attributes to James (cf. Harris, *Critical Pragmatism* 32).

With his philosophy, Locke wants to overcome "provincial limitations" and "dogmatic bias," while going beyond those with his "value pluralism" and relativism. To him, cultural relativism includes tolerance as an everyday habit, contrasting it to a democratic liberalism in which tolerance exists primarily as a value. In his essay "Pluralism and Intellectual Democracy," Locke introduces three principles. The first is the principle of *cultural equivalence*. According to Locke, there are differences between racial groups or cultures, yet you can find "functional similarities" (here and in the following Locke 443f.) or equivalences, which help to discern "culture-cognates" underneath superficial difference. He calls his second principle *cultural reciprocity*, pointing to – in current jargon – the hybridity of culture. He concludes:

> By a general recognition of the reciprocal character of all contacts between cultures and of the fact that all modern cultures are highly composite ones, would invalidate the lump estimating of cultures in terms of generalized, *en bloc* assumptions of superiority and inferiority. (443)

His third principle is the principle of *limited cultural convertibility*. Locke claims that cultural elements are widely interchangeable. Yet, at the same time these elements can be "so separable" that the "organic selectivity and assimilative capacity of a borrowing culture becomes a limiting criterion for cultural exchange." Furthermore, he sees a problem in what he calls "pressure acculturation" and "stock procedure of groups with traditions of culture 'superiority' and dominance" as they hinder "natural trends of cultural selectivity." In other words, while he sees cultural exchange he also argues that due to hegemonic structures there is a clear limit to this exchange. Locke therefore concludes that in looking for cultural agreement on a world-scale, people have to be satisfied with the "agreement of the common-denominator type and with 'unity in diversity' discovered in the search for unities of the functional rather than a content character, and therefore of a pragmatic rather than a content character." Thus, according to Locke, we can and should be satisfied with accepting a unity in diversity, although it is 'only' a unity on a functional level.

Such a perspective – looking for cultural agreement – has led to harsh criticism. Indeed, Locke has not only been criticized as an assimilationist, but also as an idealist and aristocratic elitist. One can find episodes in Locke's prolific and long-lasting history of writing or isolated statements to support attributing to him most of these traits. However, some of these tensions can be resolved if seen in the context of pragmatism and not simply in the cultural context of the Harlem Renaissance, as discussions of the Harlem Renaissance have seen a strong – unresolved – tension. For example, an aesthetic elitism has been put in opposition to politics. Moreover, for example in Gates's assimilationist version of the Harlem Renaissance, even the cultural pluralist Locke is accused of promoting an image of the New Negro who was just like every other American:

> If the New Negroes of the Harlem Renaissance sought to erase their received racist image in the Western Imagination, they also erased their racial selves, imitating those they least resembled in demonstrating the full intellectual potential of the black mind. (Gates n.p.)

In contrast to such a reductionist perspective, as becomes clear from his pragmatism, Locke actually provides an example of an effective rapprochement between a life committed to studying epistemology or metaphysics *and* the social reality of racism, producing a new conception of the relationship between social change and aesthetics, particularly for a multiracial and pluralist democracy.

Du Bois: The Continuities of Art and Life

Within the context of the Harlem Renaissance, Locke is not the only one adopting pragmatist thinking. In a similar vein to Locke, Du Bois cherished and absorbed James's philosophy. While a student at Harvard University, Du Bois later wrote, he was a "devoted follower of James at the time he was developing his pragmatic philosophy" and he credited James with converting him from "the sterilities of scholastic philosophy to realist pragmatism" (Kloppenberg 15). In his own pragmatist adaptation of James's philosophy, DuBois dialectically connects politics and aesthetics. Increasingly, Du Bois regards the emergence of exceptional black men as proof that "down among the mass, ten times their number with equal ability could be discovered and developed," if effort was exerted (*Dusk of Dawn* 218). Thus, it is important to point out that Du Bois turns his earlier elitism toward possibility, and by 1940 he even turns against a previous strategy – the flight of class from mass. Now "mass and class must unite for the world's salvation" (ibid. 217).

Du Bois performs an analogous democratizing of the aesthetic. His autobiography states his aesthetic awakening as "the opportunity [...] of looking at the world as a man and not simply from a narrow racial and provincial outlook" (*Autobiography* 159). And in *The Souls of Black Folk*, he describes this relaxed attention to objects of beauty as a way of seeking "freedom for expansion and self-development (in a) higher individualism which the centres of culture protect" (*Writings* 437). Yet, Du Bois concurs that the creative impulse is freed only when poverty is abolished; when men no longer fear starvation or unemployment (*Writings* 1061). In such a world the individual has the opportunity to develop and broaden "feelings and emotions through sound and color, line and form." Deriving a "higher individualism" from the practice of aesthetic contemplation, Du Bois avoids the segregation of essentialism (which makes identity prior to practice) and embraces democratic openness. To him (as to Locke) conceptions of both individual and group identity are a perpetual *becoming*, not simply a *being*.

After 1896, Du Bois's most persistent effort to place aesthetic experience at the center of ordinary black life occurs in his 1926 essay "Criteria of Negro Art." Here his emphasis has shifted from the early 1890's in two central ways: from the discontinuity to the continuities of art and life; and from art as a unique racial gift expressing an essence to art's ability to render racial identity irrelevant.[3] Regarding the latter he says:

> Just as soon as true Art emerges; just as soon as the black artist appears, racial categories destabilize: [S]omeone touches the race on the shoulder and says, "He did that because he was an American, not because he was a Negro." (*Writings* 1002)

However, with his pragmatism he wants to mediate between the aesthetic and the political, thereby moving beyond this polarizing and constricting dichotomy.

Du Bois's efforts to reconcile the aesthetic and political have long been noted but consistently dispersed as the effort of a self-confessed propagandist. Yet, as Ross Posnock convincingly shows in a close reading of the essay "Criteria of Negro Art," Du Bois boldly defamiliarizes the term propaganda (cf. 502). "Criteria of Negro Art" argues that beauty can redeem the stunted human condition under capitalism and renew democratic possibility. The essay revives Du Bois's effort to democratize access to cultural capital. The article is best known for one of Du Bois's often quoted but – as Posnock rightly claims – most misunderstood statements: "Thus all art is propaganda and ever must be, despite the wailing of the purists" (*Writings* 1000).

As Posnock points out readers at the time and since have isolated this sentence as proof that Du Bois had "retreated from the modernist aesthetic of the Harlem Renaissance toward a politicizing of art inspired

[3] Like Locke, Du Bois was James's student at Harvard. And also like Locke, he revered James. James was not only his favorite professor but also crucial in Du Bois's turn from philosophy to social science (cf. *Writings* 582).

by his enthusiastic visit to the Soviet Union in 1926" (Posnock 516).[4] But the article actually reveals a much more complex position. Far from propagating a vulgar Marxism, Du Bois conducts a pragmatist inquiry. From the essay's beginning, Du Bois insists on questioning a series of alleged binaries: truth and beauty, propaganda and art, politics and culture, aesthetic experience and American blacks. While his early lecture on the art galleries of Europe written in 1896 indeed urges African Americans to visit museums, now Du Bois enlarges his notion of beauty beyond distinct artifacts, a view *anticipating* Dewey's regret that art is regarded as the sole property of museums.[5] Such an aesthetic experience has heightened vitality; the effect on the psyche is to dissolve barriers of limiting prejudices and to expand sympathies. Accordingly, to pragmatists the aesthetic experience can be a powerful incentive to the destruction of social convention, and the creation of new forms of solidarity across traditional (including racial) boundaries.

While wanting to destruct limiting racist conventions, Du Bois refuses to hand out clear solutions. In a Deweyan fashion, he is more concerned to disclose the "turns and twists" of the "curious path" on which black Americans find themselves.[6] In doing so Du Bois – as Locke – exemplifies what Dewey calls a disciplined mind, namely one whose delight in the problematic is a sign of the scientific attitude, an attitude that makes productive use of doubt by converting it into operations of definite inquiry (cf. Posnock 510).

Cornel West: Prophetic Pragmatism

Like Locke and DuBois, Cornel West is concerned with the oppression of minorities and the means of overcoming that oppression. In *The Evasion of Philosophy*, he argues that pragmatism is a useful, yet not unproblematic tradition: "American pragmatism emerges with profound

[4] See also Posnock's thorough analysis in *Color and Culture* (2000).

[5] According to Dewey, art should be treated neither as a pleasure of the idle moment nor a means of pretentious display. On the contrary, art must become an acknowledged power in human association. As he claims in *Art as Experience*, aesthetic potential resides in "the sights that hold the crowd" (11): a fire engine rushing by, a machine digging up the earth, men working high above the ground, the grace of the ballplayer. When Dewey talks of experience, he differentiates between a simple experience and *an* experience. *An* experience is the process of *consciously* working with the elements involved in an interaction. To have *an* experience is to organize experience and derive meaning from it.

[6] See especially Dewey's *Quest for Certainty* (1960).

insights and myopic blindnesses, enabling strengths and debilitating weaknesses, all resulting from distinctive features of American civilization" (5). West repeatedly confronts both the mixed legacy of pragmatism and the challenge of postmodernism by proposing his own revision of pragmatism, which he calls "prophetic pragmatism."[7] With his version of pragmatism, West indeed readdresses Locke's wish to include questions of power and domination. In this process, four components are of the utmost importance for him: First of all, the African-American tradition of liberatory theology, and more generally the Christian heritage:

> My own version of prophetic pragmatism is situated within the Christian tradition. I am religious not simply for political aims, but also by personal commitment. To put it crudely, I find existential sustenance in many of the narratives in the biblical scriptures as interpreted by streams of Christian heritage; and I see political relevance in the biblical focus on the plight of the wretched of the earth. (170)

Secondly, he describes his pragmatism as a form of cultural criticism, and more specifically as a new kind of cultural criticism that, according to West, "must confront candidly the tragic sense" he finds in various thinkers in the pragmatic tradition. His prophetic pragmatism, he argues, "constitutes the best chance of promoting an Emersonian culture of creative democracy by means of critical intelligence and social action" (ibid. 150).

This aspect is closely connected to a third level, his emancipatory political project of securing a greater realization of democracy. The political core of West's pragmatism is an embrace of various social movements, while favoring a spiritual coalition involving these movements from "feminist, Chicano, black, socialist and left-liberal ones" (ibid. 170). He tries to unmask power structures and focuses on the everyday concerns of human beings, including the underserved and undervalued.

A final aspect of prophetic pragmatism, which is connected to his notion of the tragic, is the awareness of the presence of evil. This might not seem to be in accordance with James's description of the pragmatist as a "happy-go-lucky anarchist sort of creature" (James, "Pragmatism and Humanism" 377). However, West's notion of the tragic goes along with James's pragmatism as he does not see it as an invitation to concede

[7] Unfortunately, its vague character rather creates a sort of disorientation and dissatisfaction; see also Michael Quirk's convincing criticism in "Notes on Prophetic Pragmatism." *Cross Currents* 44.4 (1994): 535-539.

defeat but rather one to make people humble as they realize that even good intentions are not immune to failure.

Unfortunately, West does not offer a carefully argued version of his prophetic pragmatism. Furthermore, his pragmatism looks as if it were trying to propose too many things to too many people, and despite his concern with power he does not distinguish between the political movements but "writes as though they occupy a common egalitarian political space" (Headley 68). Nevertheless, for West – just as for James – "radical pluralism can be used as antidotes against the anti-empirical attitude that leads to the essentialization and exoticization of non-Western cultures" (Medina 139). Moreover, his prophetic pragmatism draws on the potentialities American pragmatism offers for radical political critique and it is an important and powerful call for philosophy to play its role in building a radical democracy in alliance with the world's underserved.

Paula Moya: Pragmatism and Race in the New Millennium

Like West, Paula Moya claims her work as a tool for progressive politics. Yet, she is more humble in her scope and often places the Chicana feminist at the center for broader and more general questions. Like African-American pragmatists, she grapples with the question of power, identity, knowledge, and race. In the introduction to the anthology *Doing Race*, which appeared in 2010, Moya and her co-editor Hazel Markus analyze eight common – and lacking – conversations about race, arguing for the need for "new and better conversations about race [... and] a way of *doing difference differently*" (4).

To do so, Moya establishes a connection of minority identity, experience, and the production of what she calls "objective" knowledge. Although Moya never explicitly references pragmatism, I would certainly place her in the pragmatic tradition in general and in the tradition of the critical pragmatism of black thinkers in particular. She herself calls her theory postpositivist realism, an approach responding to the "skepticism and constructivism in literary theory and cultural studies" (*Learning from Experience* 3).[8] As Moya's approach is multi-faceted, I want to single out three intersecting beliefs to sketch her approach: her notion a) of identity, b) of understanding and knowledge, and c) of race.

[8] With her approach Moya follows her mentor and dissertation advisor, Satya Mohanty, who has pointed to pragmatism as an influence.

a) According to Moya, all people are "'subjects-in-process' […] multiple and (to some degree) incoherent" (ibid. 71). However, she does not stop with this notion. One of Moya's main aims in her new book *Doing Race* is to affirm and further emphasize how identities are both real *and* constructed, that they can be politically and epistemically significant on the one hand, and non-essential, variable, and radically historical, on the other. Similarly, she claims in *Learning from Experience*:

> [Identities are] constructed because they are based on interpreted experience and on theories that explain the social and natural world, but they are also real because they refer outward to causally significant features in the world. Identities are thus context-specific ideological constructs, even though they may refer in non-arbitrary ways to verifiable characteristics such as skin color, physiognomy, anatomical sex, and socioeconomic status. (13)

Like James, Moya underscores the deep connection between epistemic and sociopolitical aspects of people's lives.

b) This notion is also important with respect to Moya's notion of understanding and knowledge. To Moya, understanding emerges from one's past and present experiences and interactions as interpreted in sociopolitical context. People generate knowledge dependent upon both historical and social locations and cognitive capacities (cf. ibid. 18). Nevertheless, she endorses a conception of objectivity, even if as an ideal of inquiry and not as a condition of absolute and achieved certainty. In *Reclaiming Identity*, she admits that the quest for knowledge is going to include errors but – in pragmatist fashion – that she does not "shy away from making truth claims" (13) despite acknowledging them to be open to revision on the basis of new or relevant information.[9] Redefining objectivity and truth as fallible, i.e. open to revision, allows Moya to theorize the production of objective knowledge as an ongoing, never-ending process of apprehending and interpreting the world. This concurs very much with

> James's radical fallibilism and pluralism which suggest that, far from being at odds with objectivity and truth, the openness to reinterpretation and renegotiation of our beliefs is in fact what makes it possible to improve their

[9] In James's approach, "truth is an instrument for getting us into satisfactory relation with experiences, an expedient in our way of thinking, a marrying function between old beliefs and new experiences, and something made rather than found" (Stuhr 2).

> objectivity, to correct their biases and mistakes, and to maintain their truth alive, that is, dynamic, adaptable, and integrated in our lives. (Medina 134)

c) Similarly, Moya looks at race as both true/real and constructed/dynamic. Though race is "a doing" – a dynamic system of "historically-derived and institutionalized ideas and practices," (*Doing Race* 42) Moya regards racial identities as significant exactly because they *refer* to the sociocultural construct of 'race.' Moreover, as she emphasizes, race is highly correlative to income level, social status, and economic opportunity in our society" (*Learning from Experience* 160). As a consequence, she argues that marginalized and oppressed groups engaging in oppositional struggles should be considered epistemically privileged because their specific experience of power relations might provide general information about the workings of power (cf. ibid. 90).

Furthermore, paying attention to one's own and others' particularity enriches society with a culturally particular behavioral and moral perceptiveness. Moya therefore advocates cross-cultural interaction. Optimistically, she concludes that multiculturalism practiced as an epistemic cooperation contributes to the moral and intellectual growth of all humans and nurtures the conditions that might lead to a better world.

Taken separately, Moya's ideas might not exactly be called original. However, taken together they do add up to an insightful position. To use the subtitle of James's famous book *Pragmatism*, she gives a new name for some old ways of thinking. And as her predecessors in the early twentieth century – when the 'melting pot' was the only celebrated model – she refuses a static norm which all Americans should aspire. These pragmatists all see "identity as more fluid and the United States as the product of a distinctive – and incessant – juxtaposition, jostling, and mixture of races, religions, ethnicities, and nationalities" (Kloppenberg 17).

Conclusion

It has often been claimed that James was a "radical individualist, with no interest in politics" (Miller 1). However, as Joshua Miller points out much of James's writing was at least implicitly related to politics[10] – and thus lends itself to political thinking. Despite his individualism, James also viewed people not only as connected to their communities but also

[10] James had "a Puritan commitment to moral action, i.e., to combating evil in order to reshape the world according to a vision of justice" (Miller 1).

as responsible and obliged to their fellow creatures (including those of future generations).

However, there is only a limited amount of options and actions a person can see and believe in. In his *Principles,* James settles the problem of multiplicity through an examination of the ways the self determines what is real. He arrives at the necessity of "interest" and "importance" in determining reality. That is, among the multiple possible realities, the self is involved in choosing the objects to which she will devote her belief. The organization of this chaos is achieved through selecting those objects which "strike a chord" with the individual psyche, those which "make a difference," are important, since pragmatists believe that "thinking begins with 'mental interests'" (Kloppenberg 8).

As seen, to pragmatists of color, questions of race, ethnicity and domination make a difference, a difference traditionally neglected by white pragmatists. Often, the idealist character of the classical (i.e. white) pragmatists have failed to give adequate weight to the 'hard facts' of power and domination in social life, assuming the unavoidable unfolding of an increasingly integrated world civilization, and emphasizing culture at the expense of political economy. The pragmatic revisions just outlined provide a glimpse of another pragmatism. Because they theorize race and racism, they link cultural issues directly to the problem of inequality; and they stress the centrality of power to the regulation of group differences in the United States. They pioneer an approach that takes domination seriously and examine how it helps to address conceptual problems that plague contemporary political life.

This includes, as Locke claims, looking for unities between diverse groups or cultures, unities of functional character. It includes Du Bois's democratic openness, approaching aesthetic experiences as a powerful enticement to the destruction of social convention, as well as the creation of new forms of solidarity across boundaries. It includes West's promotion of an Emersonian culture of creative democracy by means of critical intelligence and social action. It includes Moya's way of thinking difference differently, and treating identity as well as race as simultaneously real and constructed. These pragmatists of color embrace and put forth a democratic openness and show a way of treating both individual and group identity as a perpetual *becoming*.

The theories discussed above thus add an insightful perspective to *both* pragmatism and critical race theories and they form and create an important branch of pragmatism. In his incomplete last book, *Some Problems of Philosophy*, James concludes that "pluralism need not be supposed at the outset to stand for any particular kind or amount of disconnection between the many things which it assumes" (115). The key to James's assertion of pluralism is not a challenge to the possibility of connection, but a challenge to the denial of disconnection. In effect, for James, things (and we might put race and racialized selves or groups here) must be understood to be *both* connected and disconnected. The claim that all is one must be negated, just as the claim that everything is independent must be negated as well.

Works Cited

Dewey, John. *Art as Experience*. New York: Putnam's, 1980.
—. *Quest for Certainty: A Study of the Relation of Knowledge and Action*. New York: Putnam's, 1960.
Du Bois, William Edward Burghardt. *The Autobiography of W.E.B. DuBois: A Soliloquy on Viewing My Life from the Last Decade of Its First Century*. New York: International Publishers, 1968.
—. *Dusk of Dawn: An Essay Toward an Autobiography of a Race Concept*. Piscataway: Transaction Publishers, 2009.
—. *Writings*. New York: Library of America, 1986.
Gates, Henry Louis, Jr. "The New Negro and the Black Image: From Booker T. Washington to Alain Locke." National Humanities Center. 10 Mar. 2010 <http://nationalhumanitiescenter.org/tserve/freedom/1917beyond/essays/newnegro.htm>.
Harris, Leonard (ed.). *The Critical Pragmatism of Alain Locke: A Reader on Value Theory, Aesthetics, Community, Culture, Race, and Education*. Philadelphia: Temple U, 1999.
Headley, Clevis. "Cornel West on Prophesy, Pragmatism, and Philosophy: A Critical Evaluation of Prophetic Pragmatism." *Cornel West: A Critical Reader*. Ed. George Yancy. Malden: Blackwell, 2001. 59-82.
Hollinger, David. *Postethnic America: Beyond Multiculturalism*. 2nd. ed. New York: Basic Books, 2006.
Hutchinson, George. *The Harlem Renaissance in Black and White*. Cambridge, Mass.: Harvard UP, 1995.
James, William. *A Pluralistic Universe*. New York: Longmans, Green, 1909.
—. "Pragmatism and Humanism." *The Writings of William James*. Ed. John J. McDermott. Chicago: U of Chicago P, 1978. 376-389.
—. *Pragmatism: A New Name for Some Old Ways of Thinking*. New York: Prometheus, 1991.
—. *Some Problems of Philosophy: A Beginning of an Introduction to Philosophy*. London: Longmans, Green, 1916.
—. "What Pragmatism Means." *The Writings of William James*. Ed. John J. McDermott. Chicago: U of Chicago P, 1978. 389-390.
Kloppenberg, James. "James's Pragmatism and American Culture, 1907-2007." *100 Years of Pragmatism: William James's Revolutionary Philosophy*. Ed. John Stuhr. Bloomington: Indiana UP, 2010. 7-40.

Locke, Alain. "Cultural Pluralism." *American Philosophies: An Anthology*. Eds. Leonard Harris, Scott L. Pratt, Anne Waters. Malden: Blackwell, 2002. 433-453.

Medina, José. "James on Truth and Solidarity. The Epistemology of Diversity and the Politics of Specificity." *100 Years of Pragmatism: William James's Revolutionary Philosophy*. Ed. John Stuhr. Bloomington: Indiana UP, 2010. 124-143.

Miller, Joshua. *Democratic Temperament: The Legacy of William James*. Lawrence: UP of Kansas, 1997.

Moya, Paula and Hazel Rose Markus (eds.). *Doing Race: 21 Essays for the 21st Century*. New York: W.W. Norton & Company, 2010.

Moya, Paula. *Learning from Experience: Minority Identities, Multicultural Struggles*. Berkeley: U of California P, 2002.

—. "Introduction." *Reclaiming Identity: Realist Theory and the Predicament of Postmodernism.* Eds. Paula Moya and Michael Roy Hames-García. Berkeley: U of California P, 2000. 1-26.

Ross Posnock. *Color and Culture: Black Writers and the Making of the Modern Intellectual.* Cambridge: Harvard UP, 2000.

—. "The Distinction of Du Bois. Aesthetics, Pragmatism, Politics." *American Literary History* 7.3 (1995): 500-524.

Stuhr, John. "Introduction: 100 Years of Pragmatism." *100 Years of Pragmatism: William James's Revolutionary Philosophy*. Ed. John Stuhr. Bloomington: Indiana UP, 2010. 1-6.

Washington, Johnny. *A Journey Into the Philosophy of Alain Locke*. Westport, CT: Greenwood Publishing Group, 1994.

—. *Alain Locke and Philosophy: A Quest for Cultural Pluralism*. Greenwood Publishing Group, 1986.

West, Cornel. "On Prophetic Pragmatism." *The Cornel West Reader*. New York: Basic Civitas Books, 1999. 149-173.

—. *The Evasion of Philosophy. A Genealogy of Pragmatism*. Madison: U of Wisconsin P, 1989.

Writing the Me and Not-Me: Native American Literature and William James's Radical Empiricism

Georg Schiller

In her searing autobiography *Lakota Woman*, Mary Crow Dog describes how "white Indian-lovers" used to turn Lakota school children into "caricatures of white people" (30). She refers to a poster which she "found among [her] grandfather's stuff, given to him by the missionaries to tack up on his wall" (31). It is obvious that this poster's many rules and admonitions aim at a complete erasure of native cultures. The central exhortation, "Let Jesus save you," is followed by nine other commandments, which, among other things, implore the native reader to "come out of [his] blanket, cut [his] hair, and dress like a white man," to "speak the language of [his] white brother," to "learn the value of a hard-earned dollar," and to stop "[wasting] money on giveaways" or "[going] to Indian dances or to the medicine man" (31).

While such an obvious example of 'good intentions' gone awry may strike the contemporary reader as almost grotesque in its display of hegemonic ignorance, the question remains how non-natives can possibly understand major differences in the (traditional) lives of North American Indian cultures without appropriating them. How can they, for example, translate the mystic experience of a Sioux medicine man into their own cultural arena? How can they interpret the meaning of stories in an indigenous society whose ties to its oral tradition remain strong?

As I see it, this is precisely where William James's concept of radical empiricism may prove to be especially helpful. Since James's philosophically grounded psychological approach believes in a human subject who is constantly negotiating with his many interactive relations with a pluralistic universe, a special awareness of the necessity of cultural and epistemic tolerance goes hand in hand with it. Or, as James himself once suggested, "Radical empiricism [...] is fair to both the unity and the disconnection. It finds no reason for treating either as illusory" (*Radical Empiricism* 24).

At the same time, James's focus on the lived experience of the individual human subject as embedded in a constantly changing reality ties in with many aspects of indigenous knowledge. Indeed, the many correspondences between Native American thinking and American pragmatism are quite striking. In his foreword to Bruce Wilshire's inspiring work on *The Primal Roots of American Philosophy*, Edward Casey writes about "the return of the native in American philosophy" and suggests that American pragmatism "is original because it is aboriginal" (ix). In the same vein, Scott L. Pratt establishes "an additional perspective" to studies which deal exclusively with "many of the connections between classical pragmatism and the European philosophical tradition" (8).[1] In his book *Native Pragmatism: Rethinking the Roots of Philosophy*, Pratt presents "the principles of interaction, pluralism, community, and growth" as the "four commitments that characterize a common core of classical pragmatism" (20).[2] He shows that these principles create "a coherent philosophical ground in American thought whose genealogy can be traced from indigenous traditions of America, through other American traditions of resistance, and into classical pragmatism" (37). What makes Pratt's reconstruction of the Native origins of American pragmatism so convincing is the fact that he produces a "story of cross-cultural contact and learning," which does not "proceed unimpeded and unchallenged," but is "the story of a struggle among radically different people" (19).

Both Wilshire's groundbreaking work and Pratt's fascinating genealogy add further plausibility to my decision to use James's focus on lived experience as a bridge towards a better understanding of indigenous rituals and perspectives. James's writings provide us with descriptions and conceptualizations that are able to help us understand native otherness without reducing it to the familiar within European American philosophical frameworks. In what follows, I will discuss (from a non-native position) three integral cultural characteristics of many Indian nations in North America: the vision quest, the daily experience of a direct connectedness to one's environment, and the function of storytelling and kinship within native communities.

1 Pratt comments on various publications which tell the story of American intellectual negotiation with European philosophies. In his chapter "The Problem of Origins" (1-16), however, he pays special attention to Morton White's *Science and Sentiment in America: Philosophical Thought from Jonathan Edwards to John Dewey*. London: Oxford UP, 1972; and to H. S. Thayer's *Meaning and Action*. Indiana: Hackett Publishing, 1981.

2 In a footnote, Pratt informs the reader that he "will primarily consider the work of Peirce, James, and Dewey as representative of 'classical pragmatism'" (20).

The Vision Quest

John Fire Lame Deer, another famous Lakota Sioux, begins his autobiography with a description of his first vision quest at the age of sixteen. While waiting "all alone on [a] hilltop" (11), Lame Deer feels anxious and apprehensive, since it is uncertain whether he will have the experience of transcendence he is craving – an experience which is necessary for him to turn into a medicine man. The following lengthy quotation contains key sentences I have selected from Lame Deer's detailed narrative, which actually covers several pages:

> What if I failed, if I had no vision? […] 'You'll know it, if you get the power,' my Uncle Chest had told me. 'If you are not given it, you won't lie about it, you won't pretend.' […]
>
> I thought of my forefathers who had crouched on this hill before me, because the medicine men in my family had chosen this spot for a place of meditation and vision-seeking ever since the day they had crossed the Missouri to hunt buffalo in the White River country some two hundred years ago. […]
>
> Sounds came to me through the darkness: the cries of the wind, the whisper of trees, the voices of nature, animal sounds, the hooting of an owl. Suddenly I felt an overwhelming presence. Down there with me in my cramped hole was a big bird. The pit was only as wide as myself, and I was a skinny boy, but that huge bird was flying around me as if he had the whole sky to himself. I could hear his cries, sometimes near and sometimes far, far away. I felt feathers or a wing touching my back and head. This feeling was so overwhelming that it was just too much for me. […] I don't know what got into me, but I was no longer myself. I started to cry. Crying, even my voice was different. I sounded like an older man, I couldn't even recognize this strange voice. […] Still I felt the bird wings touching me. Slowly I perceived that a voice was trying to tell me something. It was a bird cry, but I tell you, I began to understand some of it. […]
>
> I heard a human voice too, strange and high-pitched, a voice which could not come from an ordinary, living being. All at once I was way up there with the birds. The hill with the vision pit was way above everything. I could look down even on the stars, and the moon was close to my left side. It seemed as though the earth and the stars were moving below me. […] I felt that these voices were good, and slowly my fear left me. I had lost all sense of time. I did not know whether it was day or night. I was asleep, yet wide awake. (13-16)

Asleep, yet wide awake; down in the vision pit, yet way above everything; listening to his own voice, yet unable to recognize it; aware of what is happening to him, yet no longer himself: the many contradictory expressions suggest that John Lame Deer must, indeed, have had some kind of liminal experience which he struggles to translate into language. It is hardly surprising that he remembers every detail so well; he is, after all, recalling an initiation ritual that is extremely important in his culture.

To a non-native, however, Lame Deer's description may come across as both confused and confusing. How can a human being change into a bird (to some extent, at least)? How can somebody's sense of selfhood first dissolve and then re-emerge? In other words, how can one gain hermeneutic access to descriptions of mystical experience in a religious context that is not one's own?

Here, I want to turn to William James's descriptions in the *Varieties of Religious Experience*. My reading of James will focus on his discussion of the dissolution of the self and his portrayal of the mystical experience as an *emotional* insight. James is helpful in this context because his reference to psychology in connection with mysticism does not, in his own words, "exclude the notion of the presence of the Deity altogether" (*Varieties* 242). James supplies a philosophically grounded psychological approach which does not rule out the possibility of divine intervention as the *cause* of the numinous experience. It keeps its status as a unique religious event in a different cultural context.

In Lecture XVI of *The Varieties of Religious Experience* (1902), James pays special attention to four typical characteristics of the mystical event: ineffability, noetic quality, transiency, and passivity.

The term *ineffability* is meant to circumscribe the fact that a mystical union has to be *felt* in order for it to gain authority for a person and that it cannot convincingly be conveyed by discourse. The *transient* mystical experience "resembles the knowledge given to us in sensations more than that given by conceptual thought" (James, *Varieties* 405). Accordingly, John Lame Deer confesses that he still "does not know what got into him." He is aware that he lacks linguistic categories which are able to capture what actually happened. Nevertheless, his experience carries with it the sense of illuminating authority without which it is impossible to become a medicine man. This is what James calls the *noetic quality* of mystical states; they are "revelations, full of significance and importance, all inarticulate though they remain" (ibid. 380-81). James's fourth characteristic – *passivity* – is meant to denote a pervading "sense of higher control" (ibid. 243) which impels the individual to take up "a helpless and sacrificial attitude" (ibid. 51) towards the divine. In other words, the desired communion cannot be forced into existence by an act of volition, "although the oncoming of mystical states may be facilitated by preliminary voluntary operations, as by fixing the attention, or going through certain bodily performances" (ibid. 381). This feature of mystical experience accounts for John Lame Deer's feeling of anxiety after he has been left alone on the hilltop. He knows that isolation and lack of food and water are necessary ritualistic preparations in order to bring about a successful vision-quest. Yet, this does not mean that he will eventually "get the power."

To these four characteristics of mysticism, I would like to add another feature: "self-dissolution," which is – as James explains in his next lecture – the "overcoming of all the usual barriers between the individual and the Absolute." What he calls "the great mystic achievement" (ibid. 419) involves the opening up of the boundaries of the self: "It is as if the opposites of the world, whose contradictoriness and conflict make all our difficulties and troubles, were melted into unity" (ibid. 388). And this does, indeed, correspond neatly with John Lame Deer's narrative. Lame Deer speaks of "an overwhelming presence." He mentions his sudden ability to understand the voice of nature, the cries of a bird. At the same time, his own voice seems to belong to somebody else. He is no longer himself and is, all at once, able to fly "up there with the birds" until he arrives at a cosmic vision "of the earth and the stars." Habitual differences, the common "opposites of the world," such as day and night, have been erased, as has the dualism of subject and object.

How can non-initiated readers, who are unlikely to be acquainted with numinous experiences, possibly comprehend this process of mystical self-dissolution? What are we to make of statements that gesture towards the elimination of subjectivity as we commonly know it? Again, William James can help us. His basic philosophical assumption that the reality of every individual develops out of a continuous flow of experiences supplies us with an explanation for the possibility of ego-transcendence. In this context, it is essential to keep in mind that, for James, the supposedly "external" world of relatively reliable relations and identities is not an ontological given. James uses the perception and construction of a sheet of paper as an example:

> [...] the paper seen and the seeing of it are only two names for one indivisible fact which, properly named, is *the datum, the phenomenon, or the experience*. [...] paper and mind are only two names that are given later to the one experience, when taken in a larger world of which it forms a part, its connections are traced in different directions. (*Essays in Philosophy* 75)

What is given is merely the indivisible experience which emerges without being separated into thing and thought, or, in other words, without being placed in an "outside" or an "inside." For James, these dichotomies are constructions which are used when pure experience is retrospectively situated in different contexts. In this way the simple datum "white/rectangular" suggests not only the specific object "a sheet of paper" – the "outside" – but also a consciousness as "container" of the experience – the "inside." Yet, for James, this is only a functional differentiation and not a real ontological split: "The attributes 'subject' and 'object,' 'represented' and 'representative,' 'thing' and 'thought' mean, then, a practical distinction of the utmost importance, but a distinction which is of a functional order only, and not at all ontological as understood by classical dualism" ("Notion of Consciousness" 194). Thus, what is commonly called "the self" is nothing other than an organizational principle of the stream of experience. It emerges when it is contrasted with a relatively stable, that is to say repetitive, set of patterns which may function as its "outside." In this way the stream of experience organizes itself and produces its own heterogeneity, its own differences. As Jonathan Levin puts it, "[t]here is no unified self in control of the process. Instead, there is only the unfolding process" (61). However, while, according to James, the inside/outside difference emerges in every individual stream, he also emphasizes that we all draw the corresponding line of division between the "me" and "not-me" in a different place:

> One great splitting of the universe into two halves is made by each of us; and for each us almost all the interest attaches to one of the halves; but we all draw the line of division between them in a different place. When I say that those names are 'me' and 'not-me' respectively, it will at once be seen what I mean. (*Principles* 278)

It is now fairly easy to understand how the mystical experience may come about: As soon as the ongoing flow of various impressions is no longer strictly differentiated into "inside" and "outside" – as soon as the me/not-me difference begins to blur temporarily – a gradual dissolution of the contours of the self as "ego," or "subject," sets in. John Lame Deer, for example, no longer knew if he was wide awake (i.e., perceiving his "outside") or asleep – that is to say "dreaming" (i.e., perceiving his "inside"). Bruce Wilshire calls this moment "the trance-like primal level in which the distinction between self and other is suspended." He continues, "[i]t is misleading to say I regard the other, or even it regards me. Perceived in its immediacy, regard or regarding floats between things, permeating the world-experienced" (36).

James's concept explains why the temporary deletion of Lame Deer's me/not-me difference does *not* lead to complete chaos: his stream of experience has erased only one possible differentiation while many others are still working perfectly well. In this way, the importance of dreams and visions in the life of Native American cultures can be described as the result of a specific organization of the stream of experience which places less emphasis on the me/not-me division than other cultures do. James helps us to understand Native American religious experience without denying its uniqueness. Of course, one may object that James's approach may also be used in order to account for similar mystic events in other cultures. Since he has situated the moment of pure experience "before" rationalization, cultural differences emerge "later" within the me/not-me matrix. However, the aim of my argument is merely to mediate between native and non-native perspectives. I am not suggesting that this approach must be restricted to cultural practices that have developed in North America.

Direct Connectedness

Adjustment to the physical and social environment as a result of a strong direct connection to it may be regarded as a "cornerstone of Native American moral philosophy and ethics" (Bunge 92). However, one has to keep in mind that this experience is not necessarily a mystical one, since it accompanies the daily life of many tribes. You do not have to be a medicine man to feel related to the plurality of life which surrounds you.

In order to illustrate and discuss this strong attachment from a Jamesian viewpoint I will examine a well-known poem by N. Scott Momaday, "The Delight Song of Tsoai-Talee." "Tsoai-Talee" is Momaday's Kiowa name. It means "Rock-tree-Boy" and links him with a place more commonly known as "Devils Tower," which is located in the Black Hills.[3] Hence, the speaker in the poem is closely associated with Momaday, the author.

> I am a feather on the bright sky
> I am the blue horse that runs in the plain
> I am the fish that rolls, shining, in the water
> I am the shadow that follows a child
> I am the evening light, the lustre of meadows
> I am an eagle playing with the wind
> I am a cluster of bright beads

[3] In Northeastern Wyoming. *Devils Tower* rises more than 1,000 feet above the surrounding area.

I am the farthest star
I am the cold of the dawn
I am the roaring of the rain
I am the glitter on the crust of the snow
I am the long track of the moon in a lake
I am a flame of four colors
I am a deer standing away in the dusk
I am a field of sumac and pomme blanche
I am an angle of geese in the winter sky
I am the hunger of a young wolf
I am the whole dream of these things

You see, I am alive, I am alive
I stand in good relation to the earth
I stand in good relation to the gods
I stand in good relation to all that is beautiful
I stand in good relation to the daughter of Tsen-tainte[4]
You see, I am alive, I am alive. (Bruchac 158)

When I read Momaday's text for the first time, I was impressed by the many beautiful images assembled here: images which refer to the five human senses,[5] to the various ways of *feeling* manifold realities; images which tend to suggest movement and transience. At the same time, however, I had difficulties with comments made by native interpreters who insist on the *non*-metaphoric quality of the poem. Lee Francis, for example, who is Laguna Pueblo, writes, "[w]hile many might think that the poem is an excellent crafting of metaphoric images, I would posit that Momaday is telling the hearer that he *is* 'a feather on the bright sky' and not simply that he is 'like' an 'eagle playing with the wind'" (175). Although Francis adds that "the poem works for both the native and non-native hearer" (ibid.), I wondered how I could possibly understand a song which, on the one hand, does not necessarily evoke the complete self-surrender of mystical union and, on the other hand, asks for a non-metaphoric interpretation.

Again, I turned to James's process universe in order to understand what at first sight seemed inexplicable. In James's cosmos, every individual "element" is always in transition, always in flux, always temporal. It is, rather, an *event* which is constantly turning into something else and, consequently, always *realized through its relation to something else*. Hence, the idea of a process universe is closely

4 Tsen-tainte was a famous Kiowa war-chief who lived in the 19th century.
5 Hearing = "the roaring of the rain," sight = "the glitter on the crust of snow," smell = "a field of sumac," touch = "the cold of the dawn," taste = "the pomme blanche" or prairie turnip [edible as a root vegetable].

associated with the idea of dynamic plurality. Jonathan Levin again sums up: "[…] individual and pluralistic forces are not so much opposed as mutually constitutive. The individual […] is a function of a pluralistic heterogeneity" (45). James prefers the term "totality" to the term "unity" when referring to the world, since he associates "unity" with "an abstract monism," whereas "totality" indicates, for him, both "acquaintance with reality's diversities" *and* "understanding of their connection" (*Pragmatism* 65).

However, this "understanding of connection" is not necessarily a cognitive act. It may be a specific way of *feeling* reality. Or, rather, as I have already suggested, cognition and feeling are two sides of the same coin: "pure experience." As a result, James emphasizes repeatedly that "any kind of relation experienced must be accounted as 'real' as anything else in the system" (*Empiricism* 22). A famous passage from "The Stream of Thought" underlines how lopsided language use has predisposed us to forget about the variations of rate, direction, and intensity in experience (see also *Empiricism* 34).

> We ought to say a feeling of *and*, and a feeling of *if*, a feeling of *but*, and a feeling of *by*, quite as readily as we say a feeling of *blue* or a feeling of *cold*. Yet we do not: so inveterate has our habit become of recognizing the existence of the substantive parts alone, that language almost refuses to lend itself to any other use. (*Principles* 238)[6]

In other words, the way we speak has lead to a conceptual bias and has seduced us into viewing the world as a box of monolithic building blocks. As long as we restrict ourselves to such a partial perspective it is, indeed, difficult to comprehend how a self can turn into a running horse or the roaring rain or the glittering snow. A is B: this equation must disturb the inhabitant of the building-block universe. However, as soon as we begin to shift our attention towards the experience of fluidity, of relatedness – what the concluding stanza in Momaday's song explicitly calls "standing in good relation to" – as soon as we read the ongoing repetition of the copula "am" as the expression of *transition in continuous heterogeneity*, it is no longer difficult to arrive at a non-figurative reading of the text. Indeed, the singer does *not* merely compare himself metaphorically to a deer in the dusk, as Lee Francis

[6] Joan Richardson reads this statement [i.e. "a feeling of *and*, and a feeling of *if*, a feeling of *but*, and a feeling of *by*"] as an example of James's notion of the unconscious and suggests that he understood it as "the chaos of feelings that have not yet found words" (111). In the context of my paper, this would suggest that what remains unconscious is highly culture-dependent.

proposes. Rather, he celebrates that he – as an event – is a function of pluralistic processes which constitute him and which he, in turn, also helps to constitute. To a certain extent, his self-in-transition *consists* of the experience of a deer in the dusk. This is what he feels: He feels his ongoing relation to a *totality* (which, of course, includes an implied reader).

In one of his repeated attempts at reminding us of the many ways in which "language works against our perception of the truth," James writes: "We name our thoughts simply, each after its thing, as if each knew its own thing and nothing else. What each really knows is clearly the thing it is named for, with dimly perhaps a thousand other things. It ought to be named after all of them, but it never is" (*Principles* 234). "To know one thing and nothing else" – this is precisely what Momaday tries to avoid. On the contrary, the jubilant singer in his poem celebrates his embeddedness, his awareness of being related to "a thousand other things." This is why he repeats several times that he feels "alive."

At the same time, Momaday's long enumeration creates a sense of place that emerges in the course of these multiple ongoing processes. His song suggests that indigenous experience of place can be understood as constituted by a sense of belonging to a plurality of relations and activities which establish a cultural matrix. In her discussion of Native American constructions of space, Katja Sarkowsky writes:

> If the construction of space is understood as a social practice, space and culture have to be seen as closely intertwined – space as cultural, culture as spatial. Thus, cultural dynamics and understandings of how space is produced have to be addressed […] not as absolute and pre-determined, but as a set of practices and cultural codes to which individuals and collectives refer. (46)

Sarkowsky's statement reveals the obvious parallels between Native American practices (i.e. convictions) and James's concept of pluralities in process. Both assume the existence of fluid subjectivities that come into being through a matrix of relations. Matrix and self are viewed as interdependent and in transition. Robert Bunge's description of the traditional Lakota kinship system exemplifies this notion:

> […] the Indian child grew up among many fathers and mothers in a village wherein everyone was related in some way. Since everyone in his small world was related, it was easy for the child to extend this notion of 'relatedness' beyond his village circle when he grew older […]. Later on, when the medicine man explained to him the 'relatedness' of all things in the universe, the child, now a man, was receptive to this idea because that was the way it was in his early life. (93)

The Lakota child grows up within a dynamic set of relations and recognizes the village as constituted by ongoing and interrelated activities. In other words, to him, place *is* transition in continuous heterogeneity. The village is *not* experienced as a static container inhabited by strangers who live in isolation from each other. Rather, the kinship system (and by implication the whole concept of relatedness) leads to the idea of an extended family and, hence, to the acceptance of a plurality of mutual responsibilities that continue beyond the village circle. In this context, however, storytelling (here represented by the medicine man who explains the universe) is an integral moment which further consolidates the feeling of connectedness.

Storytelling and Kinship

Leslie Marmon Silko (Laguna Pueblo) opens her novel *Ceremony* with an unidentified voice (the author's persona, perhaps), which addresses her listener-readers before the story begins. Obviously concerned about their attitude towards what will unfold before them on the next pages, this voice speaks about the status of stories: "They aren't just entertainment. Don't be fooled. They are all we have, you see, all we have to fight off illness and death. You don't have anything if you don't have the stories" (2). In addressing the audience directly Silko's "voice" uses a strategic device from oral tradition "by which storytellers engage their listener-participants with and into the stories" (Brill de Ramírez 133) and, simultaneously, reminds us of the immense cultural signifycance of American Indian storytelling: Native stories are able to "fight off illness and death." In other words, they may bring about very real, ontological consequences.

A comment made by the poet/storyteller Simon Ortiz (Acoma Pueblo) will help to further clarify how one can possibly understand the great effect of storytelling on Native American communities:

> The oral tradition of Native American people is based upon spoken language, but it is more than that too. Oral tradition is inclusive; it is the actions, behavior, relationships, practices throughout the whole social, economic, and spiritual life process of people. In this respect, the oral tradition is the consciousness of the people. […] Oral tradition evokes and expresses a belief system, and it is specific activity that confirms and conveys that belief. (7)

By implication, storytelling, as an integral and "specific activity" of this oral tradition, may be viewed as both a living archive of "actions, behavior, relationships, practices" and, at the same time, as the ongoing actualization/renewal/recreation of these life-giving processes within the community. In order to express the participatory impact of storytelling Brill de Ramírez calls it a "conversive" experience. The term "conversive" is meant to "[convey] both senses of conversion and conversation," the "transformative and intersubjective act of communication" (1).

A non-native listener will, perhaps, wonder to what extent storytelling may possibly work as a transformative/conversive force. In this context, it is helpful to keep in mind that for many Native American people "kinship" is not necessarily defined as an exclusively biological term. In his book on Lakota storytelling, for example, Julian Rice points out repeatedly that "real kinship" is defined by *behavior*: You "[recognize] relatives on the basis of their acts" (11). Hence, mutually supportive behavior (especially over a long period of time) may create kinship ties. On the other hand, somebody who harms you cannot be a true relative. The high status of intersubjective relationality explains why stories are so essential in Native American societies, for they "demonstrate the proper attitude and identity [...] *in action*" (Rice 17, emphasis mine). In times of crisis, they "communicate that others in the past have had similar troubles and have survived those hard times" (Brill de Ramírez 142). They "imprint survival powers" (ibid. 24).

In Silko's story "Storytelling," for instance, a woman walks to the river, where she meets Buffalo Man and runs away with him. Ten months later, she returns to her pueblo, where her husband, to his great consternation, sees that she has become the mother of "twin baby boys." The woman, however, decides to stay with her own family, while her husband leaves and moves back in with his mother (see *Storyteller* 94-98). In her reading of this story, Brill de Ramírez stresses "the importance of [the woman's] return to her family, to her community and tribe, and to her everyday responsibilities" (142) and underlines the story's celebration of "the value of fertility and sexual relations" within the Pueblo (141). It is also necessary, however, to call attention to the obvious serenity with which the woman watches her husband go away. The story shows how a crisis that could have lead to a major conflict can be solved without resorting to violence and without disturbing the social balance within the community. Everybody acts as an interconnected participant within a dynamic social matrix, which, nevertheless, grants relative freedom to individual tribal members. This is a story about relatedness, about social competence. Since it is a story *about* social competence, it may, actually, also *provide* listener-readers *with* social competence; as William James might have put it, "knowledge *about* a thing is knowledge of its relations" (*Principles* 250).

However, this is only one half of the story. Since kinship is largely defined by behavior, the act of storytelling in itself also enables the various participants to establish and enter into kinship relations. As part of an oral tradition and as a cooperative and mutually supportive process, storytelling informs tribal members *about* relatedness while it *establishes* relatedness. I would argue that it is this *double achievement* which turns this process into a regenerative force. This is why de Ramírez writes about storytelling as a transformative act. This is why the voice in Silko's *Ceremony* emphasizes that stories are more than mere "entertainment."

This is also why stories and storytelling are able to unfold mythological power: in the process of evoking the past and what is important to know about the past and the integral role of kinship relations, the traditional experience of relatedness re-emerges in the present. Thus, past and present are connected. This is an integral aspect of mythology: it "stresses the simultaneity of 'now' and 'time immemorial'" (Sarkowsky 55). Silko begins her story about the woman who meets Buffalo Man in this mythological vein, "You should understand / the way it was / back then, / because it is the same / even now" (*Storyteller* 94).

It is thus only logical that Native American authors insist on the continuing importance of oral traditions as specific ways of knowing the world. They do not regard a traditional story as mere fiction or as untrue. The complete opposite is the case: the fact that Native American people still work successfully with a story proves that it is true. James's philosophy, at least, ties in with Native American truth claims. He writes, "Truth *happens* to an idea. It *becomes* true, is *made* true by events. Its verity *is* in fact an event, a process: the process namely of its verifying itself, its veri-*fication*. Its validity is the process of its valid-*ation*" (*Pragmatism* 97). James wants us to understand that we cannot work meaningfully with truth concepts which locate truth in a realm beyond human capacity for experience: "Truth is made, just as health, wealth, and strength are made, in the course of experience" (*Pragmatism* 104). As a result, we accept as true that which turns out to be a reliable tool for navigating us through a complex pluralistic universe. Bruce Wilshire explains that James's truth concept "can only mean reliable situational orientations, transitions, guidances, fulfillments – answers to meaningful questions, implicit or manifest" (75). In this sense then, both natives and non-natives continuously keep testing "truth's cash value" (*Pragmatism* 97) – to use James's famous phrase. As long as the cash-value of Native American storytelling manifests itself in the naming and production of relatedness, it is most certainly true.

Works Cited

Brill de Ramírez, Susan Berry. *Contemporary American Indian Literatures & the Oral Tradition*. Tucson: The U of Arizona P, 1999.

Bruchac, Joseph (Ed.). *Songs from this Earth on Turtle's Back: Contemporary Indian Poetry*. New York: The Greenfield Review P, 1983.

Bunge, Robert. *An American Urphilosophie: An American Philosophy BP (Before Pragmatism)*. Lanham: UP of America, 1984.

Crow Dog, Mary and Richard Erdoes. *Lakota Woman*. New York: HarperPerennial, 1991.

Francis, Lee. "The Shadow Knows: A Native Philosophical Perspective on the Light and Dark Side of the Soul." *Ayaangwaamizin: The International Journal of Indigenous Philosophy* 2.2 (2000): 171-185.

James, William. *Essays in Philosophy*. Cambridge: Harvard UP, 1978.

—. *Essays in Radical Empiricism*. Cambridge: Harvard UP, 1976.

—. *Pragmatism*. Cambridge: Harvard UP, 1975.

—. "The Notion of Consciousness." *The Writings of William James*. Ed. John J. McDermott. Chicago: U of Chicago P, 1977. 184-194.

—. *The Principles of Psychology. Vol. I.* Cambridge: Harvard UP, 1981.

—. *The Varieties of Religious Experience*. New York: Penguin, 1982.

Lame Deer, John Fire, and Richard Erdoes. *Lame Deer: Seeker of Visions*. New York: Simon and Schuster, 1972.

Levin, Jonathan. *The Poetics of Transition*. Durham: Duke UP, 1999.

Ortiz, Simon J. *Woven Stone*. Tucson and London: The U of Arizona P, 1992.

Pratt, Scott L. *Native Pragmatism: Rethinking the Roots of American Philosophy*. Indianapolis: Indiana UP, 2002.

Rice, Julian. *Lakota Storytelling: Black Elk, Ella Deloria, and Frank Fools Crow*. New York, Bern, Frankfurt: Peter Lang, 1989.

Richardson, Joan. *A Natural History of Pragmatism: The Fact of Feeling from Jonathan Edwards to Gertrude Stein*. Cambridge: Cambridge UP, 2007.

Sarkowsky, Katja. *AlterNative Spaces: Constructions of Space in Native American and First Nations' Literatures*. Heidelberg: Winter, 2007.

Silko, Leslie Marmon. *Ceremony*. New York: Penguin, 1986.

—. *Storyteller*. New York: Arcade, 1981.

Wilshire, Bruce. *The Primal Roots of American Philosophy: Pragmatism, Phenomenology, and Native American Thought*. University Park: The Pennsylvania State UP, 2000.

CURRENT DEBATES IN POLITICS, ETHICS AND THE SCIENCES

The Audacity of Pragmatism: William James, Barack Obama, and the American Deliberative Tradition

Trygve Throntveit

I teach American history to college students, and in 2008, while planning my syllabus in the heat of an election summer I decided it could not hurt my enrollments to include a unit on Barack Obama. Succumbing to the contemporary rage for multimedia instruction, I went looking for a provocative image of the president to "break down" with my students, an artifact to examine from present and historical perspectives in hopes of illuminating the "Obama Phenomenon." I chose the cover of January 26, 2009 issue of *The New Yorker*, Drew Friedman's "The First:" A naturalistic portrait of a serious but not stoic Obama, mouth set, brow level, steely gaze fixed ahead and to the left, as if on a horizon not yet sharpened by the dawn reflected in his pupils. His look of total composure was oddly arresting – and made all the more so by the powdered wig, white cravat, and coat from George Washington's closet in which the artist had dressed him.

What to make of this portrait? I asked the class. Is Obama a new "Founder," poised to fulfill the creed of liberty and equality that Americans since the Revolution have embraced, yet too often betrayed? Or (I continued, arresting more than a few nodding heads) is this another ironic *New Yorker* cover, emphasizing the tawdry, disappointing reality behind some illusory dream or grave pretension? After all, irony sells. Vietnam, Watergate, Reaganomics, stalemated Wars on Poverty, Drugs, and Terror; such setbacks and scandals have ingrained a contempt for dupes and a fear of being duped that runs deep in the American psyche; a dupephobia reinforced by politicians, by our lazy (or crazy) fellow citizens, and by the secret knowledge of our personal failures to live up to the "American Creed" – whatever that is.

Ultimately, as good historians we agreed that we would have to go to the source and ask the artist. But our provisional hypothesis was that his message was not entirely, or even primarily, a dismal one. Certainly, it is impossible to ignore the incongruity, and dark irony, of dressing Obama – the nation's first black president – in the guise of a man who owned

African Americans as slaves. Then again, associating a Founding Father with a blackberry addict and admitted "tweeter" does evoke hopes of laying a new basis of national values for our modern age. Their merging into one likeness suggests that on this new basis something more radical than formal equality might be achieved; that perhaps Americans of all backgrounds will be equivalent not just in theory, or the eyes of the law, but in reality, in the eyes of each other. By shunning caricature for a realistic likeness (wig and cravat aside) the artist has interpreted his subject as genuine, suggesting on some level that what you see or hear might really be what you get. And if there is any message this ostensibly genuine Barack Obama has consistently delivered, it is that he wants to transcend irony. Not to ignore it, or wish away deception, disappointment, and unintended consequences; but to encourage our society to learn from the inevitable experience of failure without making inevitable failure itself the lesson.

In short, Obama is a pragmatist, in the richest sense of the word – the sense used by the American philosopher William James at the turn of the last century. James used "pragmatism" to describe an idealistic but critical attitude toward human endeavors. Pragmatism meant doing what worked, not what was easy; making informed decisions, not blind leaps of faith or fruitless compromises; judging ideas and acts by consequences, not ideological origins. Unfortunately, true pragmatism has long played a negligible role in American public life. The word's meaning has narrowed; the value of what it signifies has diminished. "Pragmatist" is an epithet of scorn among liberals enraged by Obama's modifications of many campaign positions. Meanwhile, conservatives, recalling Obama's promise of "pragmatic" rather than ideological governance, reproach him as a hypocrite for pursuing historically "liberal" courses on important issues. Apparently, neither group caught the uncannily pragmatist vision for a bipartisan politics Obama provided in his 2006 book *The Audacity of Hope*. "Genuine bipartisanship," he wrote, "assumes an honest give-and-take"; but it also assumes "that the quality of the compromise is measured by how well it serves some agreed-upon goal" (156).

According to this quite serviceable definition of pragmatist politics, Obama, in practice, is an imperfect pragmatist. But a Jamesian will tell you there is no other kind. Jamesian pragmatism combines an audacious "will to believe" with a humble skepticism, recognizing both human idealism and human fallibility as preconditions of an eternally improvable world (*Will to Believe* 1-31; *Pragmatism* 43-74, 239-301). In fact, it takes the same view of human progress Obama expressed with wonted eloquence the night he won the presidency. His improbable election, he asserted, was an answer for those who questioned the possibilities of America and the "power" of democracy, but that answer had none of the finality we often demand. "There will be setbacks and false starts," he warned. "This victory alone is not the change we seek; it is only the chance for us to make that change." In other words, the answer to the perennial question "Can we do better?" was not "Yes, we did," or even, "Yes, we most certainly will," but rather, as Obama repeated throughout his campaign and victory speech, "Yes, we *can*" ("Victory Speech").

Examining that message in historical perspective clarifies and enriches its meaning. America's neglected traditions of non-dogmatic idealism suggest ways to break the stranglehold of ideological politics, while revealing that the dark ironies of the nation's past can motivate rather than oppress thoughtful citizens – as Obama has insisted throughout his career in public life. Such examination will not permit predictions about the outcomes of Obama's policies or foretell the fate of his particular brand of liberalism. But it can give a clue to why many Americans remain alert to the audacity of his pragmatism.

Pragmatism: What It Means and What It Meant

Blogging in the spring of 2009, Robert Reich spoke for many on the left when he criticized Obama's tendency to describe his governance as "pragmatic." The term, as many erstwhile Obamians interpreted it, reduced their hero's vision of a sea change in American politics to safe navigation of its waters. As Reich bluntly put it, to tout the pragmatism of Obama's politics was "to rob it of its moral authority."[1] That assessment is ironic from the perspective of intellectual history. In the late nineteenth and early twentieth centuries, William James used "pragmatism" to describe a radical theory of knowledge that inspired a host of progressive reformers. These pragmatist progressives insisted that democracy was fundamentally a moral ideal, and that political practice be judged solely by the democratic goals it advanced.

Knowledge, James argued, arose from attempts to surmount problems impeding the achievement of goals. Truth measured how well an idea solved those problems while accommodating the rest of experience, both individual and social. Thus, the reflection and inquiry of an "intellectual

[1] Reich, Robert. "Obama and Pragmatism: Thinking Through Values." 5 May 2009. 27 Oct. 2011. <http://robertreich.org/post/257310346>.

republic," as James put it in "The Will to Believe," would best preserve "mental freedom" while advancing collective wisdom (*Will to Believe* 30).

Pragmatism had profound implications for ethics and politics. Like all forms of knowledge, moral knowledge evolved, as individuals tested ideals and values against experience. Only an "ethical republic," deliberating over the widest possible range of ideals and the demands they entailed, could determine truly social values—and even these would never be final, James wrote in 1891, "until the last man has had his experience and said his say" (*Will to Believe* 198, 184).[2]

Nevertheless, James emphasized three virtues vital to an ethical republic. First was experimentalism: the willingness to reflect critically on our values and actions in light of experience, and change them if necessary. Second was tolerance, understood to include empathy: the recognition that other people's values were facts of experience against which ours must be tested, and which we should try to understand. Third was "strenuosity," or moral courage, which demanded two things: commitment to ongoing reflection and deliberation, and acceptance that all moral choices sacrificed some values to realize others – ideally, those that preserved and expanded the membership of the ethical republic itself.

James, his philosophical ally John Dewey, and the pragmatist progressives considered this ethical orientation suited to the society and culture of the United States, a nation founded on the ideal of self-government through deliberative discourse. Their commitment to testing ideas against experience made them students of history, examining the best political practices of the past to determine which might be adapted to include more Americans in the democratic experiment of their day (Throntveit 26, 39, 43-44). Their purpose resembled Obama's as stated in the most systematic exposition of his political philosophy, *The Audacity of Hope*: to "excavate and build upon those shared understandings that pull us together as Americans" (13).

The specific "understandings" unearthed by Obama also echo those of the pragmatists, and get turned up from some of the same sites – the Constitution being one. In his 1914 book *Progressive Democracy*, James's student Herbert Croly described the Constitution as an instrument "wrought under the stress of historical vicissitudes" to satisfy "comparatively permanent but possibly changing social needs" (21). It

[2] The characterization of James's ethics in this and the following paragraph is distilled from my article "William James's Ethical Republic." *Journal of the History of Ideas* 72.2 (2011): 255-277.

was a mistake to treat it as a finished product. Rather, its value hinged on its "adaptability to new exigencies" and "power to survive the severest possible inquisition" (25). Happily, through the amendment process adaptability was built into the Constitution's structure, while public "inquisition" into its functioning and purpose was the mechanism of change.

Obama has expressed a similar view. The Constitution does not tell us what is "right," he wrote in *Audacity*, but fosters "a conversation, a 'deliberative democracy' [...]. [I]t challenges us to examine our motives and our interests constantly, and suggests that both our individual and collective judgments are at once legitimate and highly fallible" (110f.). In pragmatist terms, the Constitution sets parameters for an ongoing experiment in social organization. As the goals of the experiment change – often in response to its own results – the parameters should change too, along with our understandings of what they discourage and allow.

Such socio-political experimentalism dovetailed with the second virtue of pragmatist ethics: practicing and cultivating tolerance and empathy. Because we are social beings, the pragmatists argued, living virtuously requires familiarity with the needs and ideals of our fellows, in order to make choices that optimize everyone's opportunity for personal development. Self-government, which formalizes this process, should thus promote wide participation and a high level of formal tolerance permitting the airing of diverse views. But democratic participation meant more to the pragmatists than registering opinions: It meant deliberating over conflicting viewpoints to find, or create, common ground. To be successful, this process depended on citizens' willingness to treat alien views and values as important facts of their own social existence, surmounting what James diagnosed as our generic human "blindness" to the experiences of others (*Talks to Teachers* 229-264). This cosmopolitanism marked the thought and activism of progressive-era intellectuals including Jane Addams, Randolph Bourne, and W. E. B. Du Bois (Kloppenberg), who envisioned a society in which all members, as Du Bois wrote in his 1903 masterpiece *The Souls of Black Folk*, were "co-worker[s] in the kingdom of culture" (4).

Obama, too, has urged Americans to work toward cosmopolitanism, through genuine attempts to learn and care about their fellow citizens. Obama reminds white Americans of the universal lessons to be learned from the unique oppressions and triumphs of African Americans, while urging African Americans to see themselves as part of a larger community with related goals and grievances.

In both cases, the key is genuine conversation: *talking*, calmly but frankly, about Americans' "different stories" as well as their "common hopes" ("Speech on Race"). For Obama, the potential of deliberative discourse to open eyes, change minds, and continue the endless process of perfecting the Union is not a theory, but a fact demonstrated in his own personal experience as multiracial American, a community organizer, and a campaigner. In *Audacity* he described the satisfaction he derived from meeting voters of different backgrounds or political leanings and leaving with the feeling that "a relationship had been established between me and the people I'd met – nothing transformative, but perhaps enough to weaken some of our biases and reinforce some of our better impulses" (282).

Deliberation and Obligation

Of course, something "transformative" is exactly what America has needed at times, and perhaps needs now. With this in mind, many have criticized Obama for heeding rather than leading public opinion on certain vital issues. Certainly, if pragmatism means mere adaptation to prevailing thought and circumstances, even a "reforming" pragmatist can never be more than a political-ethical technician working to keep the machine running. A century ago Randolph Bourne accused fellow reformers Dewey, Croly, and Walter Lippmann of just such vulgar pragmatism when they supported intervention in World War I ("War and the Intellectuals"; "Twilight of Idols"). Pragmatists today are also confronted with what we might call "the Bourne Ultimatum:" *Act on your ideals, or forfeit them.* This ultimatum prompts a tough question for pragmatists: When does deliberation end, and action grounded in conviction begin?

James can help us answer this question. He provided his most eloquent defense of both strenuous morality *and* deliberative democracy in his 1897 oration honoring the Civil-War service of Col. Robert Gould Shaw and the Massachusetts Fifty-fourth, the U.S. Army's first black regiment since the Revolution. James recounted their tale as a lesson in the virtues democracy required, and the burden it placed on citizens to decide for themselves when the forms of democracy failed the ideal. By 1861, slavery had withstood several wretched lifetimes of deliberation. It took the "lonely courage" of Americans like Shaw and his regiment to act on the tragic conclusion that the tolerance long extended to the South must be sacrificed, to realize the ideal of tolerance in a nobler form. Yet there had been no formula for determining that the sacrifice was necessary. There never will be; as James put it, "Democracy is still upon its trial." Instead, James asserted, we must rely on two assiduously cultivated habits of "civic courage:" "disciplined good temper" toward those who adhere to democratic processes, and "fierce and merciless resentment" toward those who subvert them when the outcome is not what they wish (*Memories and Studies* 39, 42f.). The fact is, James stated bluntly in 1891, in every moral choice some ideal gets "butchered." In the ongoing campaign for the good the best we can do is support "the more inclusive side" (*Will to Believe* 202f., 205). *Sometimes* support demands measures more drastic than discussion, and the courage to take them. But such measures *always* entail great risk, with no certainty of righteousness, and no guarantee of reward.

Obama's views on the limits of deliberation resemble James's in content and inspiration. Many politicians have turned to the Civil War in their search for an American civic ethos. Few have done so as reflectively as Obama. The war that finally ended slavery, Obama wrote in *Audacity*, revealed that "it has not always been the pragmatist, the voice of reason, or the force of compromise, that has created the conditions for liberty" (116). But, he insisted, that does not mean ideas can effect change only through intransigence or coercion, or that commitment to "democratic deliberation" must compromise "commitment to the highest good" (112). In a society of conflicting perspectives and interests, a genuine intellectual exchange that promotes tolerance and facilitates cooperative action *is* the highest universal good. Moreover, zealous idealists have caused much misery and injustice. And as the Civil War demonstrated, even the noblest cause can exact "a terrible price" (117). "I'm left then with Lincoln," he concluded. Rather than lauding the Great Emancipator's clear-eyed view of justice, Obama emphasized the real Lincoln's conflicting attitudes toward slavery and race, his willingness to examine and change his ideas, and his courage to act on them when needed, despite inescapable doubts. For Obama, Lincoln's democratic heroism lay in "maintaining within himself the balance between two contradictory ideas – that we must talk and reach for common understandings, precisely because all of us are imperfect and can never act with the certainty that God is on our side; and yet at times we must act nonetheless, as if we are certain, protected from error only by providence" (116f.).

Obama's discussion of Lincoln's example for modern-day democrats also hints at his Jamesian views on religion in public life. Like the author of "The Will to Believe," Obama understands faith as a constructive response to the uncertainties of human endeavors and judgments, not a denial of them. He has often reminded religious and secular audiences that humility is a cardinal – if not *the* cardinal – tenet of the Christian faith. As a Christian politician mulling values-issues like abortion and gay marriage, Obama wrote in *Audacity*, "I must admit that I may have been infected with society's prejudices and [...] attributed them to God; that Jesus' call to love one another might demand a different conclusion" (265). Such doubts, far from being un-Christian, are reminders of one's humanity. Yet Obama's warning that today's verity of verities may prove tomorrow's vanity of vanities is not reserved for "values voters." He warns secular ironists that cynical assessments of faith's role in public life are frequently belied by the facts. Again like James, he insists that the power of faith in millions of lives is patent. It is thus self-defeating for secular progressives to shun attempts to reconcile religious faith with democratic pluralism. To reject the moral vocabulary through which so many Americans interpret their world is not just bad politics, however, but bad ethics. Poverty, racism, and other forms of social disfranchisement are problems with structural *and* moral roots. Solving them requires changes in policy as well as the "changes in hearts and minds" that moral appeals have effected throughout history (*Audacity* 253f., quoted 254).

For Obama, then, it is absurd to insist that self-governing citizens put aside their personal values in public-policy debates, for values – what values need promoting or protecting, and how – are what such debates are about (*Audacity* 64, 77, 83f.). Nevertheless, as the abortion debate makes especially clear, some values are irreconcilable – or at any rate cannot be reconciled in time to meet the exigencies of policymaking. In those cases we must recall the majesty of a deliberative system: the fact that discussion can *continue* and policies *change*, and that it is in the interest even of the losers – indeed, especially the losers – to keep discussion going. Deliberation depends for its regenerative power on people speaking their minds when their values are at stake. But values, religious or secular, are not scientific observations; they are expressions of faith. And as Obama noted in the abortion context, during his address at the 2009 Notre Dame commencement, "the ultimate irony of faith is that it necessarily admits doubt" ("Commencement Address").

Such doubt should check self-righteousness, encouraging persuasion through reason and, as Obama has put it, through the "charity, kindness, and service that moves hearts and minds." Cooperating to reduce unwanted pregnancies and care for living children, as he has urged "pro-choice" and "pro-life" advocates to do, will not end all conflict over abortion. But it might improve people's lives, move other hearts to help, and move minds closer together over time ("Commencement Address"). In short, whether we draw our truths from the shifting world of secular experience, or, as Obama wrote in *Audacity*, from the "Living Word" of scripture, there is virtue in remaining, as he put it, "continually open to new revelations" (265).

What Change?

If Obama's audacious pragmatism echoes prominent traditions from America's past, why does it come as a "revelation" (welcome or otherwise) to many Americans today? And what does it portend for American politics broadly viewed? Simply put, Obama has proposed a massive overhaul of our contemporary political culture, which has been corroding America's civic ties for decades. Beginning in the 1970s, increasingly vocal cultural conservatives pitted themselves against liberals, cultural minorities, and feminists who had also grown shriller in denouncing America's flaws. Contestants on all sides reduced one another and their positions to what Obama has aptly described as "caricatures" (*Audacity* 148). These conflicts were aggravated by politicians and strategists who cast them in the rhetoric of war and embraced a vicious attack politics. By the mid-1990s ideological extremists controlled the national machinery and message of both parties and their grip has proven hard to break.

"I had clung to the notion that politics could be different," Obama explained in *Audacity*, "and that the voters wanted something different." If offered a frank and civil alternative, he wagered, "the people's instincts for fair play and common sense would bring them around," and both "politics" and "policies" would change for the better (*Audacity* 22). Many have come around. But others could pay more attention to how Obama moderates his message of moderation. Deliberation, he has written, does not mean "getting chronically steamrolled" in the interest of appearing centrist (*Audacity* 157). It means approaching issues critically, empirically, and – to use his own surprisingly controversial term – with "empathy." Obama endorsed this pragmatist political ethic on May 1, 2009, when announcing Justice David H. Souter's retirement from the Supreme Court. "I will seek someone [to replace Souter] who understands that justice isn't about some abstract legal theory or footnote in a casebook," Obama declared. "It is also about how our laws affect the daily realities of people's lives [...]. I view that quality of empathy, of understanding and identifying with people's hopes and struggles, as an essential ingredient for arriving at just decisions and outcomes" ("Resignation of Justice Souter"). He reiterated this attitude when praising his nominee, Sonia Sotomayor, for treating precedent as but one of the repositories of social experience on which judges rely in making decisions that, intentions notwithstanding, often shape policy ("Choice of Sotomayor").

Taken at his word, Obama is attempting a difficult trick. He is trying to inspire, but to be frank; to be idealistic, but in a realistic way; to shape and adapt to circumstances, to lead and listen. Finally, he is trying to build such dual capacities into American government, and the capacity to appreciate them into an American culture trained to interpret subtlety as dishonesty.

Certain chronic pathologies of postwar American political culture seem to be against him. That culture trumpeted deliberative ideals, but accepted policies that too often skipped the deliberation: policies that sought to mask domestic conflicts with economic growth, and to overcome international differences through economic or military coercion. Indeed, modern American history can seem like one long lesson in irony. The rhetoric of democracy, freedom, and equality has been betrayed repeatedly by action – sometimes knowingly and cynically, sometimes unintentionally, despite genuine commitments.

So does that make the Obama phenomenon a farce? Fate's ironies are unavoidable. Like them or hate them, many of Obama's policies don't or won't work. None will be unmitigated successes. But Obama seems to know there will be disappointments, and to be trying to prepare Americans for them – not by eschewing lofty goals, but by explaining that pursuing them demands a certain stomach for failure and for changes of course. This chastened rather than churlish sense of irony explains the congruence of Obama's thinking with that of the pragmatists, and informs what could – *could* – prove his two lasting contributions to American politics and society.

The first is his promotion, at home, of a political culture that reflects his Constitutional theory: a culture in which "diffusion of power" forces us to look beyond our habitual interests and, in words John Dewey might have written, to "test our ideals, visions, and values against the realities of a common life" (*Audacity* 113). That pragmatist progressive ideal has inspired Obama's initiatives to distribute wealth more equally, regulate industries affecting vital public interests, and provide health care for all Americans. Whether he tackles issues like gun control, gay rights, and environmental degradation with the same vigor, and what will come of such efforts, remains to be seen.

Obama's second potentially lasting contribution is a similarly egalitarian and discursive approach to international affairs. Like no president since Woodrow Wilson, Obama has insisted on America's responsibility not just to subordinate narrow national interests to common international interests, but to let other peoples help determine what those interests are and how to pursue them. This is a matter of justice and prudence, he argued in *Audacity*, for the "painstaking process of building coalitions forces us to listen to other points of view and therefore to look before we leap" (366). The importance of deliberative diplomacy to all societies was the focus of Obama's major speech on foreign relations delivered in Cairo on June 4, 2009: "Given our interdependence," he declared, "any world order that elevates one nation or group of people over another will inevitably fail." That conviction led Croly, Dewey, and Lippmann to support intervention in World War I, in order to replace the balance of power with what Wilson called a "community of power" ("Conditions of Peace" 175) and to organize that community through a League of Nations with a deliberative structure resembling the United States' – an ideal that U.S. abstention from the League did much to destroy. Today, the same conviction drives Obama's outreach to Muslim nations, pursuit of nuclear disarmament, and repudiation of interrogation tactics condemned by the civilized world. Whether his Mideast and Asian policies prove inclusive and effective, or whether his handling of the wars he inherited improve or exacerbate those dismal situations, are among many open questions.

To the degree that Obamian pragmatism does come to characterize American politics, will it fulfill the Founders' vision? The pragmatic answer is yes and no. If that vision was one of freedom, there could be no greater fulfillment of it than to treat it as unfulfilled – to affirm our freedom to redefine freedom itself, try daily to make it a reality, and hope we succeed occasionally amidst our inevitable failures. As James wrote in 1899, we should be glad that any "newer and better equilibrium" we achieve for society will make no "*genuine vital difference*" to later generations, for the ideal of a free society is that its changes reflect the claims of its current members (*Talks to Teachers* 298). If those claims are better met, call it progress; but the next day might present new claims requiring choices for which all the progress in history offers no precedent. Then an open dialogue of ideals is our only guide, and mustering the civic courage to preserve and expand that dialogue is our clearest duty. For James, who saw such risky but reasoned choices as the ultimate moral acts, it was good that it should always be so. For Obama, it is a blessing that our system, at its best, reflects rather than resists that process. "That's the genius of America," he explained on election night 2008, upon becoming yet another "first" in a society defined by such innovations – "that America can change."

Works Cited

Bourne, Randolph. "Twilight of Idols." *Seven Arts* 2 (1917): 688-702.
—. "War and the Intellectuals." *Seven Arts* 2 (1917): 133-146.
Croly, Herbert. *Progressive Democracy*. New York: Macmillan, 1914.
Du Bois, W. E. B. *The Souls of Black Folk*. 3rd ed. Chicago: A. C. McClurg, 1903.
James, William. *Memories and Studies*. Ed. Henry James, Jr. New York: Henry Holt and Company. 1899.
—. *Pragmatism: A New Name for Some Old Ways of Thinking*. New York: Longmans, Green, 1907.
—. *Talks to Teachers on Psychology and to Students on Some of Life's Ideals*. New York: Longmans, Green, 1907.
—. *The Will to Believe and Other Essays in Popular Philosophy*. New York: Longmans, Green, 1897.
Kloppenberg, James T. "James's *Pragmatism* and American Culture, 1907-2007." *100 Years of Pragmatism: William James's Revolutionary Philosophy*. Ed. John J. Stuhr. Bloomington: Indiana UP, 2010. 7-40.
Obama, Barack. *The Audacity of Hope: Thoughts on Reclaiming the American Dream*. 2006. New York: Vintage Books, 2008.
—. "Barack Obama's Speech on Race [18 March 2008]." *The New York Times*. 18 Mar. 2008. 15 Jan. 2011. <http://www.nytimes.com/2008/03/18/us/politics/18text-obama.html>.
—. "Obama's Commencement Address at Notre Dame [17 May 2009]." *The New York Times*. 17 May 2009. 15 Jan. 2011. <http://www.nytimes.com/2009/05/17/us/politics/17text-obama.html>.
—. "Obama's Remarks on His Choice of Sotomayor [26 May 2009]." *The New York Times*. 26 May 2009. 15 Jan. 2011. <http://www.nytimes.com/2009/05/26/us/politics/26obama.sotomayor.text.html>.
—. "Obama's Remarks on the Resignation of Justice Souter [1 May 2009]." *The New York Times*. 1 May 2009. 15 Jan. 2011. <http://www.nytimes.com/2009/05/01/us/politics/01souter.text.html>.
—. "Obama's Speech in Cairo [4 June 2009]." *The New York Times*. 4 June 2009. 15 Jan. 2011. <http://www.nytimes.com/2009/06/04/us/politics/04obama.text.html>.
—. "Obama's Victory Speech [4 November 2008]." *The New York Times*. 5 Nov. 2008. 15 Jan. 2011. <http://www.nytimes.com/2008/11/04/us/politics/04text-obama.html>.

Reich, Robert. "Obama and Pragmatism: Thinking Through Values." *Robert Reich's Blog*. 5 May 2009. 15 Jan. 2011. <http://robertreich.blogspot.com/2009/05/obama-and-pragmatism-thinking-through.html>.

Throntveit, Trygve. "'Common Counsel': Woodrow Wilson's Pragmatic Progressivism." *Reconsidering Woodrow Wilson: Progressivism, Internationalism, War, and Peace*. Ed. John Milton Cooper, Jr. Washington and Baltimore: Woodrow Wilson Center P and The Johns Hopkins UP, 2008. 25-56.

Wilson, Woodrow. "Conditions of Peace (Address to the Senate) [22 January 1917]." *Selected Addresses and Papers of Woodrow Wilson*. Ed. Albert Bushnell Hart. New York: Modern Library, 1918. 172-179.

Jamesian Overbelief and the Therapy of Hope

Andrew Flescher

"The true survivor is the one who has finally learned that survival itself is beyond the point," the best-selling author and survivor of domestic violence, Hannah Nyala, once said. In this paper I want to explore not only the extent to which this thesis is true in the context of dire prognoses following illness or injury, but also whether its de-prioritization of the straightforward fact of survival in favor of emphasizing one's attitude towards surviving ironically leads to the best sorts of medical outcomes. In the process, I intend to connect hope to healing in a tangible way, distinguish genuine from false forms of hope, and, this distinction established, finally suggest realistic strategies for conceiving of hope as sound medical therapy. I maintain that hope, according to Jerome Groopman and others a virtue of healing, is, broadly construed, an example of Jamesian "overbelief," that is, a belief that is adopted without sufficient evidence but by virtue of whose adoption is made more likely to be true. This categorization in place, a question about hope, which is really a question about overbelief, arises: Does *believing* one's condition will improve, when the existing evidence does not suggest as much, itself con-stitute new evidence that needs to be taken into consideration? Does hoping make healing more likely? It does a great deal, I argue, and is in addition something worth pursuing for its own sake, so long as hope is understood as a subjective state which the hoper freely inhabits, rather than a set of expectations provided for the hoper by another party (even dear loved ones).

Romantic Love, Religious Faith, and Hope's Promise

In order to appreciate James's influence on the link that would medically be established a century later between belief and well-being one must first understand the epistemological dominance "evidentialism" had enjoyed through much of the modern era as well as the challenge to this standard view posed by the notion of overbelief. James's principal insight from "The Will to Believe" – "faith in a fact can help create that fact" (25) – flew in the face of Enlightenment epistemological orthodoxy by suggesting that belief in advance of a hypothesis actually creates evidence *in support* of that hypothesis. This was James's distinctive innovation in the burgeoning pragmatist movement: beliefs gained validity not on the basis of the set of known certainties in support of them, but in proportion to the positive effects that ensue following their introduction into the world by their holders. James argued that we have the right to harbor beliefs in unlikely propositions and even whole doubtful futures the actuality of which no one as of yet has the objective confirmation to refute. Thus characterized, "overbelief" is not delusion. The former imbues hope into the existing sphere of what is known, while the latter perniciously denies reality. Overbelief coheres with our excavation of the undiscovered universe, a process which delusion derails.

This is not to suggest that overbelief is without its risks. Imagining a hitherto unexperienced future, the overbeliever might fail to manage her expectations, or adversely impact others by not preparing for what is, if not inevitable, the most plausible unfolding of events. If hope is given a blank check, one risks being seduced by delusion, even though in themselves hope and delusion are very different things. Thus, it is important to bear in mind what one stands to gain by overbelieving. Doors close when another one opens. Beyond a certain threshold, the skeptic is inclined to press the believer to justify ignoring the predictive success of the thing in which the believer has claimed her right to believe, especially if she forgoes a real and significant good in favor of a fictitious or insignificant one. Fantasies that temporarily console often amount to costly distractions. In lieu of an airtight proof that something is *not* so, there are still reasons to be cautious to believing that it *could be* so.

James anticipates objections from the camp of skepticism by honing in on a specific sort of hoped-for good, namely a good (1) that is a *real* option for the one choosing it; (2) which *must* either be chosen or lost and (3) in which something very *significant*, indeed, life-altering, hangs in the balance. In James's parlance, "overbelieving" makes rational sense when the good to be gained is "live," "forced," and "momentous" (3). A flourishing romantic relationship between two individuals – this is to say the *fact* of whether the individuals relate to one another in a flourishing relationship – exemplifies just this sort of good on behalf of which it behooves one to overbelieve. The prospective relationship remains a real possibility for the two lovers; if it is not acted upon and subsequently nurtured it will dissipate; and it is plausibly the sort of relationship on which the rest of their lives could hang in the balance. In the case of a romantic relationship, the good to be gained depends on the attitude with which the good is pursued. What character will such a relationship take? On what do the traits by which it is to be characterized depend? Does it contain good-will? Trust? Love? Asks James:

> *Do you like me or not?* […] Whether you do or not depends, in countless instances, on whether I meet you half-way, am willing to assume that you must like me, and show you trust and expectation. The previous faith on my part in your liking's existence is in such cases what makes your liking come. But if I stand aloof, and refuse to budge an inch until I have objective evidence […] ten to one your liking never comes. How many women's hearts are vanquished by the mere sanguine insistence of some man that they *must* love him? (24)

In matters romantic, the "fact of the matter" is reliant on a *desire* for the fact to turn out to be true, a desire rendered moot without the desirer's displaying the additional risk to convert her desire into something actionable. Any insistence on evidence undermines the romantic objective. The very gesture of the request helps to ensure that that evidence will *not* be forthcoming, for it will be interpreted as a sign that one is not willing to back up the desired outcome with a faith in that outcome. And this brings us just to the point about certain sorts of outcomes we experience in the world: they in part *are*, already, substantively the faith that precipitates them. With regard to some things in this world, the most important things, faith in something *is* that something already, not entirely, but partially.

The good of romantic love is, for James, analogous to religious faith. Like trusting that the one you love loves you back, believing represents a subjective mental state that corresponds to a reality that transcends its subjectivity. With respect to those for whom religion is a "live" option to begin with, i.e., one for which my existing set of beliefs makes me eligible, the objective pay-off goes hand in hand with a subjective leap, so much so that vetoing faith in lieu of sufficient evidence becomes "illogical:"

> The more perfect and more eternal aspect of the universe is represented in our religions as having a personal form. The universe is no longer a mere *It* to us, but a *Thou* […] and any relation that may be possible from person to person might be possible here. For instance, although in one sense we are passive portions of the universe, in another we show a curious autonomy, as if we were small active centres on our own account. We feel, too, as if the appeal of religion to us were made to our own active good-will, as if evidence might be forever withheld from us unless we met the hypothesis half-way. (27-28)

With regard to this and similarly momentous relational states, ontological existence and human access to that existence are irretrievably intertwined. It is not merely that we have the right to believe in God or Nirvana; belief becomes the avenue for ascertaining these transcendent referents. In the case of love, religion, and other similar states that relational activities precipitate, truth-seeking is *ipso facto* passional. It involves a prior commitment to, not mere discovery of, beliefs in truths that, in turn, make other beliefs true. Hoping for the reality of a certain sort of relationship becomes a key feature of that relationship.

Despite James's insistence on the superfluity of evidence in advance of believing, it turns out that in the area of medicine it looks like there *is*, after all, evidence to support the hypothesis that overbelief helps to create a fact. The relation in question in the case of medicine occurs between a patient and a patient's well-being, where "well-being" often, but not always, pertains to bodily well-being. In patients who are afflicted with devastating diseases, many of whom are formally diagnosed as "terminal," the direst prognosis becomes less dire, the evidence suggests, when that prognosis is supplemented with hope. In what shortly follows, I will delve into the biology of how the act of hoping stimulates brain circuits that release hormones shown to have physiological benefits for the ailing patient. For now what is important to emphasize is that this finding, if true, calls attention to the critical but still underemphasized role of patient subjectivity in the patient-physician relationship. The convention is to see the patient as the *object* of a physician's attention, where the physician not only presents the patient with the options that are available, but, in effect, decides for the patient (or leads the patient to decide) which of these options make the most sense to pursue. In the conventional view, the physician sometimes becomes the patient's proxy, determining for her a path to well-being that should be hers alone to declare. Certainly a decision on which a physician weighs in, for example whether or not to administer the most aggressive regimen of chemotherapy, or whether an elderly patient ought to undergo a risky orthopedic surgery, is one that should also be significantly governed by the advice that is rendered. It bears noting, however, that the exact same treatments yield different outcomes depending on the extent to which the patient is involved in the decision making process. The data shows that a physician who promotes agency sees better results (cf. Snyder 259-261). A patient fares better when given the space within which to *choose* to hope.

This said, it follows that a medically therapeutic utilization of hope is volitional. It is not the static assertion of optimism. There is a balance to strike. The afflicted sufferer must tread between a Scylla of agency abdication – accepting another's vision of what is one's own well-being to determine – and a Charybdis of resignation, the premature denial of possibility of hope even in the face of the most restrictive sorts of situations (cf. Groopman 52-53). *Productive* hope, i.e., a hope that is medically "prescribable," represents a way of preserving control over one's life when it is precisely control that seems to be slipping away. This "way" is comprised of two aspects of how overbelief functions in a medical context. The first is reflected in the link between hope and good medical outcomes. The second, which is decisively Jamesian in character, moves from evidence to faith in lieu of evidence. These two aspects of overbelief, the pragmatic and the spiritual if you will, reinforce one another. Hope's immediate physiological benefits not only make the body better; they also propel a patient to a stable state of hopefulness, which, in turn, renews the positive thoughts that precipitate the body's organic, recuperative processes. Moreover, the pragmatic and spiritual aspects of hope, both of which are agency enhancing, combine to give warrant to discard, or at least sidestep, the conventional protocol that currently governs how physicians confer with their patients about what course of action to pursue in fighting serious disease by making the patient a more active participant in her own recovery.[1] Finally, in the instances in which dying does turn out to be the eventual outcome, I want to suggest, with James, that the right kind of hope makes dying better than it would have been without it.

[1] Eric Kodish and Stephen Post make the shrewd point that patient agency is also important because the physician does not always have every resource at her disposal to ignite hope within the patient. Spirituality is an example of a hope-promoting resource that is possibly outside the physician's purview, but which might have the best chance of being effectuated if the patient is encouraged to participate to a greater extent in her own recovery (by, perhaps, seeking resources within her community to help her through her ordeal). Kodish and Post lay the grounds for an "obligation" to promote hope for patients with cancer that should dovetail disclosure of all medical information based on a principle of "respect for the remarkable healing powers of the human spirit, responsibility for promoting the psychologic and physical health of patients, and humility in understanding the limitations of the clinician's ability to predict the future with certainty" (1821). See Eric Kodish and Stephen G. Post. "Oncology and Hope." *Journal of Clinical Oncology* 13.7 (1995): 1817-1822.

Some Evidence on Behalf of the Physiological Effects of Hope

The various ways in which hope improves the condition of an ailing patient is by now well-documented in the case of a number of medical diagnoses. Hopefulness about one's predicament dampens one's pain and amplifies one's immune response. It can reverse the irreversible in ways that are otherwise statistically inexplicable. How hope works at the physiological level, however, is just beginning to be understood.

One way in which hope concretely impacts well-being is with regard to the "placebo effect," the subjectively felt but also objectively measurable improvement in health attributable to inactive substances thought by the one ingesting them to be actual medicine. In a landmark study in 1998 on the effectiveness of medication for depression, Irving Kirsch and Guy Sapirstein of the University of Connecticut compared the improvements in 3,000 depressed individuals who were taking prescribed medications for their conditions with those taking placebos. They found that patients in the latter category, some suicidal, demonstrated improved conditions almost to the same degree as those on medication (75%). In a 2002 report that reanalyzed this data looking only at the highest doses of the medications that were prescribed, placebos were determined to be 82% as effective (cf. Kirsch, Moore, Scoboria, and Nicholls). The conclusion that is to be drawn from this investigation is not that antidepressants do not work – although their continued use may not be quite as supportable as was previously thought – but rather that placebos work about as well, without the expense and side-effects of their alternative.

Hope and Overbelief

Hope, then, is not a superstition or a magical healing potion but the genesis of a series of physiological interactions in the brain that mitigate almost intolerable symptoms caused by real diseases and injuries. Hope has a recuperative effect on musculoskeletal maladies, nerve damage and nervous system disorders, heart disease, autoimmune disorders, cancer, and a host of other conditions.[2] However, hope, I want to go on to suggest, also imbues the sufferer with a meaningfulness that is itself recuperative even when its direct impact on the body is minimal or absent. This is to say, hope furnishes its adherent with a new worldview, one in which the victim of a disease or injury is no longer bound by the typical criteria by which quality of life measurements are generally assessed.

[2] See especially Groopman, chapter 7.

Hope has a spiritual upside that complements its physiological one. It is here where James's notion of overbelief becomes critically relevant. Committing to a *future* for which one will work hard to realize, one improves one's lot here in the *present*. Hope is beneficial to the patient not only because of the physiological process it precipitates, but also because of the passional life with which it is at once, in the immediate, perpetuating. In this respect hope offers the self a way of living differently and better than the skeptic might not have thought possible. James's classical refutation of the skeptic, correspondingly, is significant because it confers upon the prospective hoper a certain freedom and purpose which would otherwise seem unavailable.

In "The Will to Believe" James emphasizes the usefulness of overbelief to the kinds of decisions that need to be made in the real world. What we know for certain admittedly represents the most secure sort of information upon which to base beliefs, but such information rarely amounts to the kinds of choices that make us happy, manifest our values, or develop our characters for the better:

> Objective evidence and certitude are doubtless very fine ideals to play with, but where on this moonlit and dream-visited planet are they found? I am, therefore, myself a complete empiricist so far as my theory of human knowledge goes. […] [W]e must go on experiencing and thinking over our experience, for only thus can our opinions grow more true; but to hold any one of them – I absolutely do not care which – as if it could be reinterpretable or corrigible, I believe to be a tremendously mistaken attitude, and I think that the whole history of philosophy will bear me out. […] Apart from abstract propositions of comparison (such as two and two are the same as four), propositions which tell us nothing by themselves about concrete reality, we find no proposition ever regarded by anyone as evidently certain that has not either been called a falsehood, or at least had its truth sincerely questioned by someone else. […] No concrete test of what is really true has ever been agreed upon. (14-15)

Objective certitude is simply not ascertainable with regard to decisions that take place in the real world, but by virtue of its elusiveness we should not, according to James, insist any less vociferously on the search for truth. It is virtually a criterion of the most important decisions in life that they are made on the basis of the decider's *not* having enough information at the outset of these decisions. Moreover, if this observation about "truth" holds for experiential knowledge in the present, then how much more it is plausible for states that pertain to the future. Short of denying that "two plus two equals four," or other comparable truisms the comprehension of which influence no real world outcomes, the one deciding what to believe, particularly when deciding about what to believe *will happen*, has no choice but to engage in passional decision-making.

It is thus a condition of gaining *new* truths, which include some of the most important truths, that one forego the skeptic's maxim of 'shunning error.' To remain cautious and "wait for more light" is to lose the thing one stands to gain. This is because waiting is not inaction but a different sort of action, one which in its conspicuous absence of conviction contravenes the arrival of the unlikely but desirable outcome. Not only is exercising the freedom to believe in an uncertainty therefore not absurd, *never* to so believe is tantamount to assuring that outcome's not coming to pass. As James notes, "if we believe that no bell in us tolls to let us know for certain when truth is in our grasp, then it seems a piece of idle fantastically to preach so solemnly our duty of waiting for the bell" (30). By implication, we should live our lives so as at least occasionally to have faith in the improbable; in not doing so the improbable becomes impossible. Emboldened by the confidence that we are not exploited in our embrace of the improbable, the door is now opened for experiencing what I above identify as the "deeper," or "spiritual" sense of hope: the passional claiming of jurisdiction over our destiny.

Hope is empowering because it allows its possessor to choose among viable courses of action (despite the panoply of options that no longer seem available), proactively anticipating trials that must soon be endured (cf. Groopman 199). It braces one for danger by safeguarding all that which *is* within one's control. More than an expectation of how successful a course of medical treatment will be, hope offers its possessor a mental freedom in general which continues to operate in the face of all potential outcomes, even death. Having established the *right* for one to believe, James illuminates for the one otherwise poised to despair the *dignity* of one's believing will. Hope assures that no matter what the prognosis, one lives and dies in this world on one's own terms, allows one to recognize rather than deny threats that are real, and furnishes its possessor with the courage to overcome a fear of the unknown. Spiritually, hope brings one back to the world by introducing avenues to find meaning in experiences that had previously seemed empty or unfruitful. Hope is not an escape. It aids one to manage reality. In hope, one learns to cope with that which one could formerly not accept. Finally, hope furnishes its possessor with humility, first in the form of a frank acknowledgement that however sure one is, one, in fact, does not know the future, and second in its implicit endorsement of human finitude, the acceptance of which goes hand in hand with the insight that whatever happens to us individually is not the most important thing. Hope, in this respect, puts our place within humanity in its proper context.

False Hope

Given this deeper sense of hope according to which it is not only reasonable, but also dignified to anticipate future betterment, the question naturally arises: in hope are we insulated from the bad? Is hope a catch-all remedy for any malady? Conversely, can the rhetoric of hope lead to the exploitation of a prospective hoper?

"He that lives on hope will die fasting," Benjamin Franklin once wrote. There are some who have rhetorically abused the notion of hope to shift the burden of healing entirely to the patient. For such thinkers, such as the surgeon Bernie Siegel, recuperation so rests in the purity of one's positive attitude that speculation about bad outcomes constitutes blasphemy. If one's cancer does not go into remission, it could only be a result of an insufficiently hopeful outlook. This sort of optimism is offensive to the patient who is doing all she can to cope with her affliction, and it deflects the urgent, time-sensitive measures that we all must often take in the face of a crisis. To read Siegel, one sometimes gets the impression that one's affliction should be seen as a "gift." The well-known author Barbara Ehrenreich recounts her encounter with Siegel and company after she herself was diagnosed with breast cancer. Seeking on-line support among fellow sufferers, Ehrenreich discovered to her dismay a surprising percentage of victims that had come to develop a love of their illness ("If I had to do it over, would I want breast cancer? Absolutely," said one. "I am happier now than I have ever been in my life," said another).[3] Of special concern to Ehrenreich was Siegel's well-known claim, first articulated in his best selling *Love, Medicine, and Miracles*, that cancer itself is something that arises from negative feelings. The implication is if one fails to hope, one brings about one's disease. By extension, one has the power, through hope, to undo that which one has brought upon oneself. Very quickly, the logic of such an analysis becomes a version of "blaming the victim." In such a view, the evil of cancer is understated, the subjective capacity to will cancer away is overstated, and in the meantime the precious time one has left is in danger of being squandered due to both false impressions. Clearly, hope ought not

[3] Ehrenreich, Barbara. *Welcome to Cancerland.* Nov. 2001. 7 Mar. 2011. <http://www.barbaraehrenreich.com/cancerland.htm>.

to replace criticism, sober reflection, and a realism that protects rather than spoils the resources one still does have at one's disposal.

How does this criticism square with the virtue of a subjectivity that is hypothesized to trump skepticism in "The Will to Believe"? Does not Ehrenreich's critique of Siegel – that it is well taken can be in no doubt – press us to consider the extent to which radical subjectivity is the equivalent of doubt issuing faith a blank check? Whether the case in point happens to be romantic love, religion, or hope about one's prognosis, one might be inclined to acknowledge a threshold beyond which faith overstays its welcome. Otherwise the Jamesian does not merely tolerate but gives safe haven to evils such as exploitation and domestic abuse within the context of a relationship, a religious cultishness that can result in mass suicide or even murder, or, in the case of medicine, the cruel abandonment to delusion in our worst moments. How do we know when to trust hope? That hope will not mislead?

Jerome Groopman has this to say about the distinction between true hope and the sort of daft rosiness that fails to recognize real threats and dangers: The former

> does not cast a veil over perception and thought. In this way, it is different from blind optimism: It brings reality into sharp focus. In the setting of illness, hope helps us weigh highly charged and often frightening information about the malady and its therapies. Hope incorporates fear in the process of rational deliberation and tempers it so we can think and choose without panic. (198-199)

Echoing James's justification for the right of one to believe without being accused of irrationality, Groopman calls our attention to the sobriety of hope. Hope invokes not a denial of but rather a working within a set of given facts. Unlike overbelief, the source of false hope is often external. In order to overbelieve one must take measure of all one knows about one's situation and subsequently assume the responsibility of resetting one's expectations. False hope, by contrast, represents the indulgent acceptance of a gift which the giver is not really in a position to bestow. False hope is a short cut. Genuine hope entails a leap of faith. It is an existential venture, not something one can be told to do by someone else.

Nor, furthermore, does hope succeed by *contradicting* a set of known facts. Hope represents a decision to embrace the possibly improbable, not a distortion of the probabilities. When in hope one chooses to fight on, one knows what the statistics say. An informed hoper builds into her psychological budget an awareness of death as the likely outcome. If she has been fully informed and chooses to fight death anyway, therefore, her decision cannot be dismissed as insane or absurd. The case of George Griffin, a seasoned pathologist Groopman discusses who had been diagnosed as terminal with stomach cancer, serves as a good example of the critical difference between the likelihood and certainty of a terminal prognosis. When he was practicing, Dr. Griffin had the reputation of a staunch realist. No one knew better than he did the odds against chemotherapy having a positive effect in a case of metastatic cancer as advanced as his. Groopman and the senior oncologists who had been called in to confer on Dr. Griffin's case concurred that aggressive treatment was tantamount to irresponsible "iatrogenic denial" (58-59). "He risked hastening his demise, or at least robbing himself of the last tranquil days at home with his wife, his children, his friends," writes Groopman. "What [Griffin's oncologist] termed 'madness' seemed rather a sad, self-defeating loss of judgment" (59-60). Yet, Griffin survived. No one can be sure what combination of a barrage of the most toxic chemotherapy, dumb luck, and positive thinking led to the staying of a disease diagnosed as fatal. However, that survival was known to be an improbability that was nevertheless possible, and not an outright impossibility, transformed a fight against a terminal disease into a meaningful endeavor regardless of its outcome. Had George Griffin died, he would have died on his terms, with dignity.

There is an inherent uncertainty in even the worst diseases. We are not merely justified in believing in the improbable, we *must* do so if we want to increase our chances. This is the lesson that Dr. Griffin brought to the very sick cancer patients he visited following his ordeal (78). Dr. Griffin's hope was not false because, once informed, he was permitted to govern the terms of his fate. False hope, by contrast, represents an abdication of agency in which one either forgoes or is stripped of one's ability to choose for oneself. What is at stake here is not the rudderless principle of autonomy for autonomy's sake, but the preservation of the right to form existential commitments to possible, if improbable, futures.

Conclusion

On April 3, 2009, The New York Times featured a front page exposé on a well-known palliative care physician, Dr. Desiree Pardi, who had recently succumbed to breast cancer after battling the disease for nearly eleven years. Pardi, a pillar in her field, was renowned for her compassionate demeanor but also for her tenacious ability to persuade patients with terminal diseases very near to the end of their lives to come to terms with their predicaments and stop battling death. The article, entitled "Helping Patients Face Death, She Fought to Live," reveals that when her time came to deal with metastatic cancer, Pardi rejected the wisdom she so often dispensed to her patients. But its point was not to brand Dr. Pardi a hypocrite but rather to convey the indispensible virtue of trust, and in particular of trusting the patient: trusting that *she* will know when to hope and what it is appropriate to hope for. As hope is about retaining meaningful control over one's future, it is ultimately not outcomes-based but decisions-based. Hope is a positive thing in one's life – it has a medical upside – because it envelops its possessor not as some foreign imposition from the outside but organically, from within. One hopes genuinely on one's own terms. One is persuaded to hope against the odds because, as James points out, one existentially summons the *will* to do so.

Keeping in mind this critical feature of hope – that it is the summoning of courage and resolve whose source is internal – one can begin to suggest practical recommendations for ensuring that hope is prescribed in a way that is medically sound. First, as hope is garnered existentially, it ought never to be foisted upon the prospective hoper as a mandate that emanates from some external source. The "cowboy" oncologist who under the pretext of leaving no stone unturned fails to respect a terminal patient's repeated attempts to express that she no longer wishes to have treatment prevents his patient from pursuing the goals she has deemed more pressing. A physician ought always to suggest further options, but never force those options on a patient once the patient has understood and considered them reflectively. Agency critically remains a necessary component of authentic hoping. Physicians, family members, friends, and other concerned parties can have faith in the future health of the ones they love, and they can of course do much good transferring their positivity by interacting with their loved ones, but hope itself cannot be transferred by a surrogate.[4] While hope can be communally expressed, it is individually engendered.

Second, hoping well involves an emphasis on the decision, and each successive moment of decision, not on the outcomes or expectations of

4 The reader will note that I have nowhere made an argument in favor of the causative or even correlational connection between what might loosely be termed "faith-healing" and patient well-being. In this paper I have restricted my discussion to the effect of hope on the hoper's own recovery from illness and injury. If there is an argument to be made about the effect of praying for a loved one on that loved one's improved health, I do not believe it is suggested in James or on the basis of an argument that proceeds from an analysis of overbelief. This is consistent with my assertion that hope is dependent on establishing agency.

outcomes to which these decisions correspond. When we hope we steel ourselves for realities over which we do not have full control and form the attitude that we will take our shot at overcoming them nonetheless. Construed in this way, hope's glory, if such is to be identified, is a subjective victory to be found in the brave decision to stay death, whether or not we live or die. Just as hope cannot be true if it is passively received, it cannot be false when it comes into being by virtue of the active decision of an informed and lucid patient.

Finally, hope involves the humility to accept that life is bigger than we are, that we are part of something larger, something redeeming if you will, that furnishes us with meaning even when the obvious pathways seem to lead to dead-ends. Humility, however, also refers to an ever-present uncertainty in medicine that leaves room for improbabilities, experimental strategies, and, on rare occasion, inexplicable miracles. As James reminds us, unless what one proposes to chase is the denial of two plus two equals four, nothing that has not yet occurred can *pejoratively* be labeled "absurd." Physicians ought never to deprive patients of the ability *to choose* to hope before the issue of their recovery is fully settled.

Responsible hopefulness sets the stage for deliberate living and converts the frequent capriciousness of the universe into a series of meaningful events. It is not a distraction that deflects attention away from terminal patients getting their affairs in order. To the contrary, hope imbues these activities with a sober clear-mindedness and determination and assures that we do not abdicate our values and ambitions during any phase of life. In this sense, there is yet a final benefit to hoping when the chips are down: hope links temporal stages of life and preserves the narrative continuity of our sense of where we are and where we are going. Here, the wisdom of the theologian Paul Tillich, quite sensitive to the importance of distinguishing genuine from foolish hope, seems apt:

> Where there is genuine hope, there that for which we hope already has some presence. In some way, the hoped for is at the same time here and not here. It is not yet fulfilled, and it may remain unfulfilled. But it is here, in the situation and in ourselves, as a power which drive those who hope into the future. There is a beginning here and now. And this beginning drives toward an end.

If hope is rooted in a reality, even if that reality is a faint possibility, then hopefulness itself is a state worth pursuing. And in this case it cannot be a mistake.

Works Cited

Amanzio, M., et al. "Response Variability to Analgesics: A Role for Non-Specific Activation of Endogenous Opiods." *Pain* 90 (2001): 205-215.

Ehrenreich, Barbara. *Welcome to Cancerland.* Nov. 2001. 7 Mar. 2011. <http://www.barbaraehrenreich.com/cancerland.htm>.

Groopman, Jerome. *The Anatomy of Hope: How People Prevail in the Face of Illness.* New York: Random House, 2004.

James, William. "The Will to Believe." *The Will to Believe and other Essays in Popular Philosophy.* New York: Dover Publications, 1956.

Kirsch, Irving, and Guy Sapirstein. "Listening to Prozac but Hearing Placebo: A Meta-Analysis of Antidepressant Medication." *Prevention and Treatment* 1.2 (1998): Article 0002a.

Kirsch, Irving, et al. "The Emperor's New Drugs: An Analysis of Antidepressant Medication Data Submitted to the U.S. Food and Drug Administration." *Prevention and Treatment* 5 (2002): Article 23.

Kodish, Eric, and Stephen G. Post. "Oncology and Hope." *Journal of Clinical Oncology* 13.7 (1995): 1817-1822.

Siegel, Bernie. *Love, Medicine and Miracles.* New York: Harper Paperbacks, 1990.

Snyder, C. R. "Hope Theory: Rainbows in the Mind." *Psychological Inquiry* 13.4 (2002): 259-261.

Taylor, Shelley E., et al. "Psychological Resources, Positive Illusions and Health." *American Psychologist* 55.1 (2000): 99-109.

Tillich, Paul. *The Right to Hope.* Nov. 1990. 7 Mar. 2011. <http://www.religion-online.org/showarticle.asp?title=62>.

Tindale, Hilary A., et al. "Optimism, Cynical Hostility, and the Incident Coronary Heart Disease and Mortality in the Women's Health Initiative." *Circulation* 120.8 (2009): 656-662.

Cultivating Wilderness: Pragmatism and Environmental Ethics

Robert Main

This paper approaches the connection between environmental ethics and philosophical naturalism from the perspective of an evolving pragmatism. Answering the central questions of both environmental ethics and philosophical naturalism, I argue, requires abandoning the traditional disjunction between the "natural" and the "artificial" (along with corollary disjunctions such as "nature" and "culture," "*physis*" and "*nomos*," etc.) in favor of a model that views human persons, their culture, practices and productions as "natural artifacts," continuous with the rest of "non-human" nature. This strategy, adopted by contemporary naturalists such as Marjorie Grene, Joseph Margolis and John McDowell can be seen to rest on key intuitions of the classical pragmatists, notably C.S. Peirce and Josiah Royce. The pragmatic model of nature I favor not only enables the development of an idiom that adequately handles both the physico-biological and culturo-intentional aspects of human being (the goal of present-day naturalisms) but also reveals a promising new strategy for addressing environmental ethics, one which shares insights with Deep and Social Ecology, and has already been employed (without the philosophical foundation I offer) by figures such as Wendell Berry, Courtney White and organizations like the Quivira Coalition. Bringing together these varied discussions reveals the interplay between the cultivation of wilderness to meet human demands and the cultivating work that nature itself plays in the development of human persons and communities. I take as my point of departure William James's essay "On a Certain Blindness in Human Beings," which, I believe, nicely captures traditional accounts of the 'value' of nature. I then proceed to outline a pragmatic model which evolves from that account and can be developed to aptly characterize the evolution of nature's value in contemporary contexts.

A New Blindness

In the dozen or so years that I have been away, moving from one city to another across the US and Europe, I have gained a better appreciation and even a love for the rural western town in which I grew up. Like all good things remembered (or mis-remembered) this affection for what was home grows in proportion to its now becoming less recognizably such, as it, like so many other towns in rural America, succumbs to larger forces of urban sprawl and cultural homogenization. The question raised by such process is, of course, whether or not this is a good thing, whether it lives up to the name 'development' which is so often used to refer to the shaping of wilderness to human need and desire.

My own experience here echoes that of William James, at least in terms of initial responses, as described in his paper "On a Certain Blindness in Human Beings." In his essay, James describes a visit he made to the rural mountains of North Carolina:

> Some years ago, while journeying in the mountains of North Carolina, I passed by a large number of 'coves,' as they call them there, or heads of small valleys between the hills, which had been newly cleared and planted. The impression on my mind was one of unmitigated squalor. The settler had in every case cut down the more manageable trees, and left their charred stumps standing. The larger trees he had girdled and killed, in order that their foliage should not cast a shade. He had then built a log cabin, plastering its chinks with clay, and had set up a tall zigzag rail fence around the scene of his havoc, to keep the pigs and cattle out. Finally, he had irregularly planted the intervals between the stumps and trees with Indian corn, which grew among the chips; and there he dwelt with his wife and babes—an axe, a gun, a few utensils, and some pigs and chickens feeding in the woods, being the sum total of his possessions. (231-2)

It is clear in this passage that James takes a dim view of the "cultivation" he sees on the squatter's farm, a sentiment which follows from his understanding of the value of nature. James betrays his prejudices, a romantic view in which nature is best left "natural," and valued as a source of sublime beauty or carefully and artistically molded into a New Englander's pastoral vision. James continues his account through an aesthetically-oriented discussion of the use of nature and the value of culture, descrying the work of the farmer as retrograde:

> The forest had been destroyed; and what had 'improved' it out of existence was hideous, a sort of ulcer, without a single element of artificial grace to make up for the loss of Nature's beauty. Ugly, indeed, seemed the life of the squatter, scudding, as the sailors say, under bare poles, beginning again away

> back where our first ancestors started, and by hardly a single item the better off for all the achievements of the intervening generations.
>
> Talk about going back to nature! I said to myself, oppressed by the dreariness, as I drove by. Talk of a country life for one's old age and for one's children! Never thus, with nothing but the bare ground and one's bare hands to fight the battle! Never, without the best spoils of culture woven in! The beauties and commodities gained by the centuries are sacred. They are our heritage and birthright. No modern person ought to be willing to live a day in such a state of rudimentariness and denudation. (232-233)

The crux of the story and the moral which James wishes to express in the piece comes immediately after this diatribe:

> Then I said to the mountaineer who was driving me, "What sort of people are they who have to make these new clearings ?" "All of us," he replied. "Why, we ain't happy here, unless we are getting one of these coves under cultivation." I instantly felt that I had been losing the whole inward significance of the situation. Because to me the clearings spoke of naught but denudation, I thought that to those whose sturdy arms and obedient axes had made them they could tell no other story. But, when *they* looked on the hideous stumps, what they thought of was personal victory. The chips, the girdled trees, and the vile split rails spoke of honest sweat, persistent toil and final reward. The cabin was a warrant of safety for self and wife and babes. In short, the clearing, which to me was a mere ugly picture on the retina, was to them a symbol redolent with moral memories and sang a very paean of duty, struggle, and success. I had been as blind to the peculiar ideality of their conditions as they certainly would also have been to the ideality of mine, had they had a peep at my strange indoor academic ways of life at Cambridge. (233-234)

James is here endorsing a sort of pluralism in aesthetic and ethical evaluation, the lesson being that the ideals pursued by actual persons are contingent, relative to disparate cultures and perspectives and that we would do well to recognize this fact and so overcome "a certain blindness" which afflicts most people. Although I confess that I would be hard-pressed to apply this lesson to my own experience of the sort of 'cultivation' currently underway in the American west, James's piece does offer a valuable insight into the multitude of ways in which nature and wilderness can be valued. More important for present purposes, however, is the conception of nature he employs, which is evident both in his initial, unreflective judgment of the farm as well as the position expressed by his guide. On this view, nature is that which is wholly independent of human influence or culture, and the latter are seen as artificial productions; James mourns the loss of nature's beauty "without a single element of *artificial* grace to make up" for it.

Traditionally, 'nature' has been viewed in one of two ways in Western culture: as a source of raw material for human practices and productions, something that can, and should, be improved through cultivation; or as an intrinsically valuable end in itself which we are obliged to preserve. Much of the contemporary debate within environmental ethics and ecology turns upon questions about the appropriate 'use' or 'non-use' of nature. In most accounts, as in James's own, there is no 'middle ground' between nature and artifice; this, I believe, is precisely the blindness we need to overcome today.

Between Nature and Artifice

The overriding question in both my own experience and James's is, of course, what is the good of or in nature? Ethical values, like all other 'meanings' which constitute and inform the world inhabited by human persons, are cultural constructs. To speak of the 'good' intrinsic to nature and which is independent of human culture is to fall prey to one of the most pernicious errors common to the entire history of philosophy: such a view leads either to a form of the naturalistic fallacy, confusing what is the case with what ought to be the case, or to an unjustified, anthropomorphic and hierarchical model of the world in which human beings and their interests are viewed as somehow more valuable than the non-human world. What is needed, I hold, is an account which reveals the continuity of the natural world with the cultural, a way to show how human persons and other cultural artifacts are themselves natural, while also revealing the meaningful and value-laden nature of nature itself. The primary difficulty faced by such a strategy, however, is how to extend our concept of nature so as to be continuous with culture when nature is, so often, taken to be that which is by definition *opposed* to culture.

I offer that our attempts at answering the question of the value of nature find an unlikely ally in contemporary discussions of philosophical naturalism. The connection I have in mind here is by no means a purely verbal product; I grant that the terms 'natural' and 'nature' have distinct meanings within those respective discourses. Nevertheless, certain disjunctions are common to both, and recent attempts to overcome them in one project can, I believe, be fruitfully applied to the other.

Philosophical naturalism is, among other things, concerned with the articulation of an idiom that captures intuitions and insights about the physical or biological world, i.e., 'nature' understood in contrast to human culture and cultural constructions, as well as the cultural world that enables and constitutes the existence of human persons, their practices, and meanings. Although there is nothing that approaches an orthodox description or even history of what can rightfully be gathered under the heading 'naturalism,' any attempt at its characterization must be able to define its central concept: the natural. Answering this demand is, of course, no simple task. Our inner mental lives, the meanings which inform our linguistic and artistic expressions, ethical values and the like have always been fundamental to human practices, but it remains unclear as to how, exactly, they might be fitted to a discourse that only makes reference to the 'natural' world. Typically, attempts to do so have been modeled after the natural sciences, the idea being that scientific investigation discloses a world that is not dependent upon any super- or preternatural elements or principles, and given its successes, appears to be a promising standard for any inquiry. Thus, a naturalist account following these lines grants a certain preeminence to the world as science reveals it; the cultural, the intentional and the normative are appropriate subjects of discussion only insofar as they are able to show themselves as proper objects of this scientific investigation. This line of thought is perhaps best exemplified in the work of W.V.O. Quine, Wilfrid Sellars, Jaegwon Kim and Daniel Dennett. On this account, the natural world is decidedly materialistic; it is characterized by being fixed, law-like and is that which is completely devoid of human or cultural influence. As such, human cultures, practices, norms and the like are artificial constructs that are best explained away if science is to progress.

In environmental philosophy we see a very similar disjunction between preservationist and developmental or use-oriented approaches to human interactions with nature. Each side of the debate in both contexts rests upon a similar value judgment: either nature is a 'good' only when left alone or its true good requires shaping by humans. The second of these has, I believe, the longer history. Religious and technological views tend to support the claim that nature is in need of improvement, that evolution or divine creation has made in humankind the highest form of nature and that humans know what's best for the realms of the natural world 'below' them. Opposed to this are the more recent preservationist movements and land ethics which view human interaction as a corruption and destruction of natural harmony and flourishing. Like the reductive accounts of philosophical naturalism sketched above, these views take the natural world, apart from human culture, to be more fundamental or 'real' and often see human uses of the natural world as a necessary evil at best. However, this view as well can be seen to be just as mythical as the one which takes a teleological view of nature in which humankind is seen as the goal or purpose of all other processes. This is because such preservationist approaches require a view of human being as somehow apart from nature, i.e., as decidedly unnatural. This, however, is an ultimately paradoxical view, as William Cronon notes:

> This, then, is the central paradox: wilderness embodies a dualistic vision in which the human is entirely outside the natural. If we allow ourselves to believe that nature, to be true, must also be wild, then our very presence in nature represents its fall. The place where we are is the place where nature is not. If this is so – if by definition wilderness leaves no place for human beings, save perhaps as contemplative sojourners enjoying their leisurely reverie in God's natural cathedral – then also by definition it can offer no solution to the environmental and other problems that confront us. To the extent that we celebrate wilderness as the measure with which we judge civilization, we reproduce the dualism that sets humanity and nature at opposite poles. We thereby leave ourselves little hope of discovering what an ethical, sustainable, *honorable* human place in nature might actually look like. (81)

What Cronon is saying is that it is not merely our 'animal' being and functions that make us part of nature, as reductive naturalisms would indicate; at least, we cannot hope to hold on to that notion and find our way out of the environmental mess we are currently faced with. For, to do so is both to deny the naturalness of our own capacities as human selves as well as to bar access to lines of development and inquiry that could help to rectify the problems which find their causes in unbridled faith in the progress of human invention and intervention.

There is, thankfully, a competing species of naturalism. This understanding of 'nature' replaces the contrast term 'artificial' with 'artifactual,' a term of art meant to imply the continuity between the natural and the cultural worlds. What distinguishes the artificial (as opposed to the artifactual) in this idiom is its conscious attempt to separate and distinguish itself from the natural, that is from the dynamic and interdependent relations that define organic complexity (and which can, I argue, include elements created by humans). This line of thought, advocated by Joseph Margolis, John McDowell and the classical pragmatists, takes the primary concern of philosophical naturalism to be the analysis of the human person.[1] What is needed, according to such accounts, is an idiom that shows how culture and human selves are natural.

[1] See, especially, Joseph Margolis, *The Arts and the Definition of the Human: Toward a Philosophical Anthropology*. Stanford: Stanford UP, 2009.

A New Naturalism

If human beings and their practices are seen as separate from nature, then the relationship between humans and the natural world will be one of conflict and any discussion of the 'good' of nature will continue to oscillate between the overly anthropocentric and the mystical. The lesson I find in philosophical naturalism, particularly as it is pursued by James and his fellow pragmatists, is that we must somehow fashion a view of the world and our place in it as an unbroken continuum, with human interests as actualized possibilities of the natural world which enable a reciprocal relationship that fosters the sustainable growth and flourishing of all involved.

There are two important ways in which these two discourses (philosophical naturalism and ecology) are linked. First, to talk of the good of nature is to raise a question of value that necessarily proceeds from an enculturated and enlanguaged (essentially, a human) perspective in which such values are made possible. As Darwin himself remarked in the concluding remarks to his *On the Origin of Species,* the "greatest difficulty which presents itself, when we are driven to the above conclusion on the origin of man [the theory of natural selection], is the high standard of intellectual power and of moral disposition which he has attained," (390). Put in other words, we can say that Darwin is here remarking on the fact that the central problem that faces any attempt at a naturalized model of the human self is how to account for an agent's acting on the basis of reasons. A model of the self which takes it to be just another object in 'nature' cannot account for an agent acting on reasons as *reasons*, but rather sees such as the mechanical operation of natural forces; 'ought' under such an account is reduced to 'is' and causal determinism threatens our intuitive distinctions regarding our own nature as persons. John McDowell offers a similar argument in his critique of any philosophical strategy that makes recourse to 'the Given:' "But it is one thing to be exempt from blame on the ground that the position we find ourselves in can be traced ultimately to brute force, it is quite another thing to have a justification. In effect, the idea of the Given offers exculpations where we wanted justifications" (8). The aim of the non-reductive naturalist, then, is to account for how human persons find themselves "already in the space of reasons" (McDowell's phrase, borrowed from Wilfrid Sellars), but in a manner that still allows for the constraint of such reasons by reality.

This is the point of McDowell's discussion of the 'second nature' of human persons. Only through the processes of acquiring a language and a tradition (i.e., acquiring a "second nature"), McDowell says, can a being come to engage with and act upon reasons. Nature, when viewed merely as a realm of law-like causal interactions, harbors no place for values or reasons and so to speak of its 'good' is a category mistake. However, in extending our conception of the natural world and including the development of reasoning and conceptual capacities within its sphere we gain a way to speak of the good in a manner that makes sense both of its human meaning and its aptness for discussing the non-human world.

Another way to put this point is to say that to understand nature, we must understand ourselves. The very idea of a non-human nature is itself a human construction. This is not to say that such only exists because we think it does. Rather, the importance of this observation lies in the corresponding recognition that our picture of non-human nature has its source in *human* nature. As Huw Price has argued, a naturalist characterization of the self and its function in inquiry is a necessary preliminary to the construction of a naturalist model of the objects of inquiry. Price roughly characterizes naturalism as the view that "natural science constrains philosophy," i.e., that the two disciplines cannot be separated and that "philosophy properly defers to science" (1). While this account may prove to be too limited (whether it is or not depends upon how broad a definition is granted to 'science'), it does lead Price to an illuminating and fruitful distinction. Price distinguishes between a commonly held popular version of naturalism (the reductive variety noted above) from a more fundamental and conceptually prior naturalism that avoids many of the objections raised by idealist or 'anti-naturalist' theorists.

The more common form of naturalism, according to Price, involves the position that reality consists solely of that which is the proper object of scientific investigation, and that "all genuine knowledge is scientific knowledge" (3). Due to its focus on the object of study and knowledge, Price labels this view "object naturalism." He contrasts this with what he terms "subject naturalism." This lesser-known version of naturalism takes as its primary focus the nature of human beings, that is, it begins "with what science tells us about ourselves" (4). Far from being just one among the set of all objects studied by science, Price argues, the human subject and its self-reflective relation to itself is a concern that inevitably precedes inquiry into the rest of the world. This is so, according to Price, because the position entailed by object naturalism must be "validated" from the position of subject naturalism; the problems addressed from the object naturalist perspective are, he argues, the products of the workings of human linguistic usage. The subject naturalist account begins with the view that language introduces the metaphysical and epistemological issues that object naturalism seeks to resolve. Thus, any account that object naturalism might seek to give must answer to the self-reflective concerns from which such problems originate. We need not follow Price in taking deficiencies or limitations of language to be solely responsible for our philosophical problems (as Ludwig Wittgenstein and Friedrich Nietzsche have sometimes been read as saying). However, his point regarding the dependence of a naturalist idiom on the understanding of what it is to be a human person (and the importance of language to this relation) is well-taken.

The second connection between philosophical and ecological naturalism is this: the very processes which lead to the emergence of selves can only be understood in connection to the "natural" environments which shape and are shaped by them. This is a point that is particularly clear in Wendell Berry's discussion of the relationship between local culture, land and language.

Despite his aversion to academic theorizing and his silence on classical philosophical themes and figures, in his description of local culture and its work Berry grasps and is able to convey in a palpable and eloquent way an aspect of life as it is actually lived which, I think, has for the most part eluded philosophers. Berry, a poet, novelist and essayist, but who would likely characterize himself as a farmer first and foremost, is often concerned with the description of the nature and importance of place, specifically in terms of what is captured by the loose term 'local.'

In one passage (in an essay titled "The Work of Local Culture"), Berry compares local culture with the process of soil-building as he observes it in an old bucket on his farm. The bucket, he says,

> is doing in a passive way what a human community must do actively and thoughtfully. A human community, too, must collect leaves and stories, and turn them to account. It must build soil, and build that memory of itself – in lore and story and song – that will be its culture. (154)

Berry's view, which courses through not only his essays, but his fiction and verse as well, is that the interaction of actual individuals in a specific locale (and here the individuality of both is of utmost importance) over generations (again, the time frame is crucial) cultivates a curious sort of knowledge – practical, small-scale, ill-suited to universalization and articulation in formal terms – which enables the joint transformation of persons and places into the world we know and inhabit. Owing to the transformative operations of each part of the relationship (i.e., the 'land' understood as the specific character and demands of nature as it is actually encountered, and the human persons who shape and are, in turn, shaped by it), this world is neither wholly 'natural' nor 'artificial,' if these terms are understood disjunctively.

Berry's insight is that, as is the case with all natural artifacts, rather than having a nature, local culture has a history – or, perhaps more precisely, *is* a history (its own). That is to say, local culture does not just develop on its own (at least beyond a minimal level) or appear ready-made as soon as two or more humans live together and come to some sort of agreement. Rather it is, as Berry's agricultural metaphors are meant to show, something that is cultivated in the fullest sense of the term. Like wild onions or grains, cultures (or proto-cultures) do grow in a limited fashion "in the wild," so to speak – that is, without concentrated or intentional nurturing. But their development occurs when such 'natural' growth is fostered by a community over time – often, and most fully, over generations. This takes place through the development and transmission of the narratives and stories that describe and form the history of the community, i.e., local culture. This process not only enables the evolution of the culture's history but also works to fix its reference, that is, what is being referred to (explicitly or implicitly) as the community or culture. Without such a local culture and its history, Berry says, the "very possibility of a practical connection between thought and the world is thus destroyed. Culture is driven into the mind, where it cannot be preserved" (*Standing by Words* 58). This is because,

> [i]ntelligence survives both by internal coherence and external pattern; it is both inside and outside the mind. People are born with and into intelligence. What is thought refers precisely to what is thought about. It is this outside intelligence that we are now ignoring and consequently destroying. (Ibid.)

In the case of actual individuals, this necessarily occurs within the space Berry describes as local culture. Berry stresses the importance of viewing the self not as an atomic individual, but as a function of several factors, including the local culture and environment to which the self belongs. According to Berry, the "correct formula" for human persons

> in fact, is more like this: mind = brain + body + world + local dwelling place + community + history. "History" here would mean not just documented events but the whole heritage of culture, language, memory, tools, and skills. Mind in this definition has become hard to locate in an organ, organism, or place. It has become an immaterial presence or possibility that is capable of being embodied and placed. (*Life is a Miracle* 49)

The pragmatic line I favor, drawn chiefly from C.S. Peirce, offers a strikingly similar account of intelligence, or Mind, with respect to the relationship between individuals and the (socially-constructed) worlds they inhabit. One of the key insights of the pragmatists, shared by Berry, is a way to view the natural world as already harboring the latent structures out of which human persons have constructed a space of reason, logic and meaning. This model, when developed along the lines Berry favors, offers us a way to address current environmental and ecological concerns without falling prey to the blindness which results from viewing nature and culture disjunctively. The remedy to this blindness is precisely the insight I locate in the classical pragmatists, C.S. Peirce in particular. Peirce's cosmology and metaphysics point to an ingenious strategy for overcoming the disjunctions currently stalemating both environmental ethics and contemporary philosophical naturalism. His model takes both nature and culture to be intertwined and leads to a view of human persons and their 'utterances' as 'natural artifacts.'

Humans as Natural Artifacts

Already in the late nineteenth century, Peirce saw that the progress of science had been hobbled by a stubborn insistence on reductionism and a mechanistic picture of the universe. What the scientific outlook needed, he argued, was a fresh perspective on the perennial question of how mind is related to matter. In our contemporary idiom, we might characterize Peirce's project, especially in his 1890s *Monist* papers, as both an attempt to free discussions of mind and culture from dualistic contexts as well as to extend the traditional scientific outlook to include non-mechanistic processes and the *sui generis* nature of the cultural and the intentional.

Peirce's metaphysics draws on both a Darwinian-styled model of chance-driven biology and a Hegelian-like account of the evolution of reason and culture, and on his account the human self emerges out of an interaction of these two processes. That is, Peirce synthesizes Darwinian and Hegelian evolutions because each is, taken alone, insufficient for describing both the natural world (conceived in terms that are independent of human thought and culture) as well as human institutions, practices and meanings which are of central concern for human persons. By drawing on a line of thought that is isomorphic to Hegel's own (although, according to Peirce, developed independently of any Hegelian influence) Peirce is pointing to the inadequacies of the Darwinian model in accounting for culture and its artifacts, notably human selves; these cannot be reduced to mere biology or the operation of chance which Peirce takes to be the governing process in natural selection.

However, in his frequent criticisms of Hegel's relation to science – a view he often contrasts with that of Darwin – Peirce is showing that biological development and the world revealed by the natural sciences themselves cannot be reduced to the evolution of culture, Mind or *Geist*. To employ this reductive strategy would indeed be overly anthropomorphic, and would ignore both the persistence of external reality and the limitations of actual humans.[2] It is only by viewing the self as the product of both operations working jointly that a full account of selfhood can be given. As such, the self is a cultural artifact, but Peirce's *synechism* (his doctrine of continuity) and evolutionary cosmology makes this the product of a natural process continuous with those studied by the natural sciences.

For Peirce, the evolution of human consciousness is enabled by and reciprocally dependent upon the evolution of *semiosis* in the form of language:

> [S]ince man can think only by means of words or other external symbols, words might turn round and say, You mean nothing which we have not taught you and then only so far as you address some word as the interpretant of your thought. In fact, therefore, men and words reciprocally educate each other; each increase of a man's information is at the same time the increase of a word's information and *vice versa.* (*Writings*, vol. 1, 496)

A self (as opposed to a human animal), then, is a sign and this sign is first produced by a community and only later appropriated, to an extent but never fully, by an individual. On this account, the self is actually *produced* (ontologically) by this process, making it an artifact arising from both 'natural' and cultural sources.

This leads Peirce to a characterization of selfhood that places particular emphasis on the community to which it belongs, much like Berry. In a short piece for the journal *The Open Court*, which was intended as a summary of Peirce's synechistic philosophy geared towards a popular audience, he makes this point clear and draws conclusions that may at first appear quite bizarre. The synechist, Peirce says, must never say,

[2] See Peirce's remarks in *Writings of Charles S. Peirce: Chronological Edition*. vol. 6, 180.

> "I am altogether myself, and not at all you." If you embrace synechism, you must abjure this metaphysics of wickedness. In the first place, your neighbors are, in a measure, yourself, and in far greater measure than, without deep studies in psychology, you would believe. Really, the selfhood you like to attribute to yourself is, for the most part, the vulgarest delusion of vanity. In the second place, all men who resemble you and are in analogous circumstances are, in a measure, yourself, though not quite in the same way in which your neighbors are you. (*Essential Peirce*, vol. 2, 2)

For Peirce, then, the self as sign and embodiment of ideas can only exist within a community of other selves. In other words, the model offered here takes the human person or self to be the product of the joint working of biological and cultural evolution. The self as sign is a cultural product, an artifact that cannot be explained in an idiom restricted to the world as revealed by the natural sciences.

What we arrive at, then, by drawing together these strands in philosophical naturalism, is a picture of human persons and their cultures that shows them to be continuous with the non-human world, shaped by and reciprocally shaping the local environments in which they emerge. Such an account shows how it is that human selves can be natural without reducing or eliminating the *sui generis* features that seem essential to their being *as* persons. This account also explains the intuitions put forth by McDowell and Price regarding the unique role of language in the construction of a world in which the very problematic of naturalism and the good of nature arises. Language becomes the primary means by which human beings actualize wholly natural possibilities and enable persons to view the world in terms of structures which feature normative evaluation. This pragmatic naturalism, in turn, offers a promising way to escape the dichotomy between the natural and the artificial, in a manner that enables a new approach to environmental problems. What this means for environmental ethics and policy is a middle way between preservation and used-based valuations of the natural world.

Cultivating Wilderness

The view I am sketching here is, of course, not radically unique; it shares several principle insights with several leading ecological and environmental theories, albeit with important differences. As with the 'Deep Ecology' of Arne Naess, it takes the recharacterization of the naturalness of the human self to be the first step in any suitable ecological philosophy.[3] However, it departs from Naess's view in the specifics of this recharacterization, as the latter tends to construe the self in a reductive manner. Moreover, this pragmatic account does not follow in the mystical or transcendental leanings promoted by many of Naess's followers.[4] The model I favor shares with Feminist Ecology the insight that our views of human persons and of nature are cultural constructs that have, too often, tended to pit each in opposition with the other, reinforcing trends of dominance and oppression.[5] However, I view these struggles as having a deeper foundation than the historical oppression of women leading to and being enabled by an oppression of nature. In this, the account I offer perhaps has the most in common with Social Ecology and Bioregionalism.[6] Both of these theories challenge dualistic views of the relationship between nature and culture, but in a way that does not lead to the reduction of one to the other. Moreover, both Social Ecology and Bioregionalism view the natural world pluralistically and emphasize relations (rather than entities), relying on localized, small-scale truths that arise from practice rather than seeking universal and changeless values to guide our interactions with the natural world. This, I believe, is precisely what the classical pragmatists had in mind in their reformulation of our concepts of mind and nature.

The way in which the view I offer differs most from these other theories, however, is in how it answers the question: How should we proceed? As I hinted at above, most environmental and ecological theories promote a strategy of 'minimum impact and use' and favor the preservation of 'wilderness.'[7] In my view, the very notion of wilderness serves only to reinforce the nature/artifice dichotomy that, as shown above, stalemates our attempts at a non-reductive naturalism capable of underwriting any practical response to the environmental problems we

[3] See: Arne Naess. *Ecology, Community and Lifestyle*. Cambridge: Cambridge UP, 1989; and "The Deep Ecological Movement: Some Philosophical Aspects." *Philosophical Inquiry* 8.1-2 (1986): 10-31.

[4] See, especially: Bill Devall and George Sessions. *Deep Ecology, Living as if Nature Mattered*. Salt Lake City: Peregrine Smith Books, 1985.

[5] See: Carolyn Merchant. *The Death of Nature: Women, Ecology, and the Scientific Revolution*. New York: Harper and Row Publishers, 1983.

[6] See: Murray Bookchin. *The Philosophy of Social Ecology: Essays on Dialectical Naturalism*. Toronto: Black Rose Books, 1990; and Kirkpatrick Sale. *Dweller in the Land, The Bioregional Vision*. San Francisco: Sierra Club Books, 1985.

[7] There are, of course, several noticeable exceptions to this generalization, including, notably, William Cronon, whose remarks on the dangers of the concept of "wilderness" are noted above.

currently face. What is needed is an approach based on the artifactual model I draw from the pragmatists and current philosophical naturalism.

When we look to nature in what might be called a "healthy" state, we see growth and change that is dynamic and emergent from interdependent and mutually beneficial relations. These latter features are the ones we have lost in the spread of strip malls and urban sprawl; such growth is, as has often been noted, more akin to cancer if we wish to stick with a biological metaphor. However, these features would be equally lost if we sought to impose stasis on (i.e., 'preserve') what we have come to view as nature in its wild form. I turn to the classical pragmatists in the way that I do because they, more than any other philosophical tradition, I believe, sought to take the lessons of growth in nature and apply them to the ways in which we view ourselves and our practices. Their doing so was largely motivated by a desire to better capture and describe those aspects of human being that seem *sui generis*, but their insistence on grounding such theorization in practical concerns points to a way in which we can carry on their project by reversing the order of their inquiry. The question then becomes: What can the development of nature in its human form offer to the continued growth and flourishing of non-human nature?

Despite first appearances, this is not as anthropocentric as it sounds. In fact, this line of thought moves beyond such distinctions. What has come to be seen as anthropocentric is, on such a model, recharacterized as the potentials of nature that are actualized in human thought and culture. Of course, these can be actualized in more or less beneficial ways, but that they can be corrupted does not count against their being 'natural.'

The shift I favor in practice is one away from models that focus on having a minimal impact on the natural world; even if it were possible to return to a way of life that would bring about the rejuvenation of 'pristine,' 'untouched,' or 'native' wilderness (something which, much as I hate to say it, I believe is not possible), it does not seem at all practical to hope for such. Multiple factors such as international economic practices by which over-industrialized nations have profited from the hegemonic treatment of the "developing world" have left these nations with little choice but to follow in the path laid out by superpowers just in order to "catch up." That this catching up process must be accelerated in order to be at all viable only intensifies the damage.

Moreover, given the steady increase in population, it seems unwise to promote a 'return to the land' movement; simple numbers would seem to prohibit our ability to live as, say, subsistence farmers. While certainly better than sprawling suburbs and strip malls, such an unbroken chain of small farmholds would likely prove too much for the limited resources of the world's landmasses. Given that cities such as Los Angeles and New York have, unlikely as it seems, proven to offer residents the lowest carbon footprint per capita, we must, I believe, turn to urban ways of living (Brown et al.). This, of course, involves development along human cultural lines and in the service of human interests. However, this need not take the form that it traditionally has. This new outlook focuses on ways to live which lead both to the sustainability of the 'natural' world, and the betterment of an ever-growing human population. For example, practices such as sustainable approaches to urban landscaping offer inhabitants both a higher quality of life and the ecosystems which they inhabit a diversified and functional health.

It seems that a very good case can be made that there is no part of the earth that remains in its "natural" state, completely free from human influence and the effects of human practices and technology. While it may be the case that, through careful stewardship and a global shift in thought and action, certain local environments could be returned to something more like they would be had they not been impacted by human artifice, the current rates of population expansion and resource usage and management certainly speak against the likelihood of any such approach succeeding. Consequently, we are faced with a situation in which there can be no practical distinction between the natural and the artificial. To proceed we require a way of seeing the world that recognizes the indissoluble interaction and interdependence that characterizes the world as we make it. Such a perspective is, I offer, found in the theoretical speculation described above. Furthermore, this theoretical discussion offers, in the spirit of the classical pragmatists I have drawn on, a framework for the practical methods which our current situation demands. In fact, something like what I have in mind has already been initiated with promising results.

The Quivera Coalition was formed to help navigate the often competing interests of environmentalists and ranchers in the American Southwest. Through a dialogue between these parties, the coalition was able to develop several practices related to the use and preservation of wilderness that go a great distance in providing for the needs and interests of both sides of equation. And, in turn, these practical solutions have generated new perspectives on the value that can be attributed to nature and our interactions with it. Some have taken to calling this the beginning of a 'new environmentalism' as it replaces traditional approaches which demand that we seek to minimize (or even eliminate, in certain contexts) our impact on the natural world, with a goal of finding ways to interact with nature that are mutually beneficial.

Courtney White, a leading member of the group describes the outcome of this dialogue as a fostering of 'working wilderness.' This apparently contradictory epithet captures perfectly the insight I wish to draw out of pragmatic philosophical naturalism. Working wilderness, as White describes it, involves "more stewardship, not less [...]. Stewardship [...] that is humble" (62). According to White, the central idea of this 'new environmentalism' is "a simple one: that before land can support a value, such as livestock grazing, hunting, recreation, or wildlife protection, it must be at least in proper functioning condition." (56)

One approach to the development of such a proper functioning condition involves grazing, traditionally a very destructive way of utilizing natural resources for human interests. Modified grazing techniques developed by the Quivera Coalition have not only allowed for sustainable approaches to the raising of livestock and the ranchers' livelihood, but have also proven beneficial to the land itself. 'Working wilderness' areas in the coalition have become significantly healthier than even the nature preserves which border them (Quivera Coalition).

This leaves us with two key lessons. First, as White says, we must ensure that the natural world is sustainable before it can support *any* value, be it use-based or preservationist. Determining just what such a sustainable condition looks like requires that we avoid initial descriptions framed in terms of the disjunction between the natural and the artificial, as such a distinction forces us to choose between two competing value sets in the very process of making the natural world capable of supporting value. The second lesson is that the practices which foster and enable such sustainability must be seen as leading to the reevaluation of those values, i.e., the 'good' of nature.

These two lessons also lead us back to James's point. James's piece reveals our blindness when it comes to competing values of nature (roughly, between use and preservation). The evolved pragmatism I am here endorsing seeks to reveal the blindness many of us suffer when it comes to the very nature of such values, the nature of nature itself, and what an appropriate response to our current environmental problems might be. On this view, wilderness becomes something that itself is and can be cultivated. That is, by way of this view we recognize that our concept of wilderness is artifactual; we cultivate this notion in the sense of allowing it to grow in beneficial ways and we in turn begin to see wilderness as something that itself can be cultivated, rather than merely developed or left alone.

Works Cited

Berry, Wendell. *Life is a Miracle: An Essay Against Modern Superstition*. Berkeley: Counterpoint, 1991.

—. *Standing by Words*. New York: North Point P, 1984.

—. "The Work of Local Culture." *What Are People For?* San Francisco: North Point P, 1990. 153-169.

Bookchin, Murray. *The Philosophy of Social Ecology: Essays on Dialectical Naturalism.* Toronto: Black Rose Books, 1990.

Brown, Marilyn A., Frank Southworth, and Andrea Sarzynski, "Shrinking the Carbon Footprint of Metropolitan America." *Blueprint for American Prosperity: Unleashing the Potential of a Metropolitan Nation*. Washington: Metropolitan Policy Program, Brookings Institution, 2008.

Cronon, William. "The Trouble with Wilderness or, Getting Back to the Wrong Nature," *Uncommon Ground: Rethinking the Human Place in Nature*. Ed. William Cronon. New York: Norton, 1996.

Darwin, Charles. *On the Origin of the Species.* Cambridge: Harvard UP, 1964.

Devall, Bill, and George Sessions. *Deep Ecology: Living as if Nature Mattered.* Salt Lake City: Peregrine Smith Books, 1985.

James, William. "On a Certain Blindness in Human Beings." *Talks to Teachers on Psychology: And to Students on Some of Life's Ideals.* New York: Henry Holt and Company, 1912. 152-173.

Margolis, Joseph. *The Arts and the Definition of the Human: Toward a Philosophical Anthropology.* Stanford: Stanford UP, 2009.

McDowell, John. *Mind and World*. Cambridge: Harvard UP, 1994.

Merchant, Carolyn. *The Death of Nature: Women, Ecology, and the Scientific Revolution.* New York: Harper and Row Publishers, 1983.

Naess, Arne. "The Deep Ecological Movement: Some Philosophical Aspects." *Philosophical Inquiry* 8.1-2 (1986): 10-31.

—. *Ecology, Community and Lifestyle*. Cambridge: Cambridge UP, 1989.

Peirce, Charles. *The Essential Peirce.* 2 vols., Eds. Nathan Houser, et al. Indianapolis: Indiana UP, 1992-1998.

—. Writings of Charles S. Peirce: *A Chronological Edition*. vols. 1-6. Eds. Max H. Fisch, et al. Indianapolis: Indiana UP, 1982-2000.

Price, Huw. "Naturalism Without Representationalism." *Naturalism in Question.* Eds. David Macarthur and Mario de Caro. Cambridge: Harvard UP, 2004. 71-88.

Sale, Kirkpatrick. *Dweller in the Land. The Bioregional Vision.* San Francisco: Sierra Club Books, 1985.

The Quivera Coalition. *Forging a West that Works: An Invitation to the Radical Center.* Santa Fe: The Quivera Coalition, 2003.

White, Courtney. "A New Environmentalism." *Forging a West that Works: An Invitation to the Radical Center.* Santa Fe: The Quivera Coalition, 2003. 53-70.

Transforming Main Issues of Philosophy of Science Pragmatically

Michael Anacker

The issue I would like to address in this article is the debate concerning scientific realism and instrumentalism and, specifically, one of the most prominent arguments within this debate: the thesis of the empirical underdetermination of theoretical frameworks.

My approach will be divided into four parts, beginning with a brief overview of scientific realism and instrumentalism – and of the problems these positions are facing. In a second step, I will take a closer look at the underdetermination-thesis and its role in the present debate. This analysis will show that much of the realism/antirealism-debate depends on a certain image of science, one which regards science as a syntactico-semantical construction with a historically contingent application in research which itself is more or less beyond the grasp of philosophical reflection. My third section offers a pragmatic conception of the foundations of the theoretical framework, suggested by C. I. Lewis's 1923 "A Pragmatic Conception of the Apriori," which remains very much at the core of Michael Friedman's argumentation in *Dynamics of Reason*. My fourth and last section will then, finally, take us to William James – to James as a philosopher and a psychologist, and especially to the James who – in his *Principles of Psychology* – spelled out the constitutional conditions of psychology as an experimental science in its own right in a given historical situation within a certain scientific environment. With this last section I hope to demonstrate that a pragmatic change of perspective not only allows us to see science as the practice of research but may also help us understand the dynamics of theoretical changes within the scientific deep-structure as part of a continuous process of empirical research of reality serving our purposes, needs, and interests. Realism and instrumentalism, then, are not points of view from the outside, but are integral features of this very process.

Realism vs. Instrumentalism

Stated briefly, scientific realism contends that our best confirmed theories describe, represent or explain the world as it really is. However, that does not mean that each and every issue postulated by a theory really exists. Scientific realism in its recent and most powerful version is more or less a thesis about the structure of scientific laws which claims that the structure of our best confirmed laws resembles the structure of the world.[1] Instrumentalism, on the other hand, assumes that hypotheses, theories, theoretical terms, and scientific laws are mere instruments or tools which we employ in order to categorize phenomena – and especially in order to categorize them to serve our technical and other purposes; van Fraassen, for instance, asks us to "withhold belief in anything that goes beyond the actual, observable phenomena, and to recognize no objective modality in nature" (202). Neither position questions our ability to observe phenomena, but what they do question is the status of the so-called 'unobservables,' such as theoretical terms and laws, and whether "what the theory says about *unobservable aspects of the world* is roughly right" (Psillos 306).[2]

A typical realist position against instrumentalism argues that if our best confirmed laws were only instruments that do not correspond to a reality which is basically independent of our epistemic goals, it would be a miracle that we are able to construct technical devices (and the like) that actually do work within the real world (cf. Putnam). The instrumentalist's reaction to this 'no miracles'-threat is called the 'pessimist induction,' whereby if the history of science tells us that all our former well-confirmed theories have turned out to be utterly wrong, there is no good reason to believe that our present theories are better off (Laudan 33). It is perfectly possible to fly to the moon on the basis of Newtonian mechanics, even though the theory of relativity tells us that Newtonian mechanics with its concepts of absolute space and time and forces must be wrong. Thus, in a way we are left with two no-miracles-arguments which oppose each other. While the realist claims that it would be a miracle if we were able to deal with the world with the help of our theories, if they were not literally true about this very world, the instru-

[1] Cf. Worral 117 for an epistemic version and Lyre 664 for an ontic version of this kind of realism.

[2] Of course, this is only a very rough and coarse sketch of these positions. Within the present debate you will find different and refined versions – but within the scope of this essay such an overview will suffice. For a more comprehensive overview and introduction to the debate on the different realisms and anti-realisms, see Brock and Mares.

mentalist claims that it would be a miracle if our present theories enjoyed a better fate than the old ones.

It is at this point that the thesis of underdetermination expediently enters the frame: "The central problem for realism is the problem of the *empirical underdetermination of theories by evidence*" (Brock and Mares 136).[3]

Underdetermination Thesis

In its most popular formulation, the thesis of underdetermination of the theoretical framework by empirical facts states that to every given theory that explains certain phenomena, we can find an empirical equivalent alternative theory that contradicts our theory in other respects.[4]

Usually this thesis is associated with the works of Pierre Duhem and Willard Van Orman Quine, and thus sometimes referred to as the Duhem-Quine-thesis.[5] Nevertheless, there are some major differences between Duhem's and Quine's versions. Duhem, for instance, makes it clear that underdetermination will arise as a serious problem if we ignore the metaphysical dimensions of our explanatory intentions. Explanations are not seen as falling under the scope of science, for as science itself is just a system of symbolic representations, the explanation of phenomena is the task of metaphysics (Duhem 29f.). Quine, on the other hand, thinks that underdetermination only presents a problem if we believe that there

[3] For a thorough discussion of the various implications of the underdetermination thesis, see Bonk.

[4] "Scientists invent hypotheses that talk of things beyond the reach of observation. The hypotheses are related to observation only by a kind of one-way implication; namely, the events we observe are what a belief in the hypotheses would have led us to expect. These observable consequences of the hypotheses do not, conversely, imply the hypotheses. Surely there are alternative hypothetical substructures that would surface in the same observable ways. Such is the doctrine that natural science is empirically under-determined; under-determined not just by past observation but by all observable events." (Quine 313)

[5] Cf. Grünbaum. According to Quine, there is a difference between the Duhem-Quine-thesis – which merely consists of holism – and the underdetermination thesis. Holism is seen as only exposing the interdependence of scientific statements whereas the underdetermination thesis raises questions about reference and truth claims (cf. Quine 313). However, as long as we believe that theories should be identified by their scope as theories about something, this difference does not matter because we always have to employ referential aspects in order to single out any theory.

are metaphysical dimensions to our explanatory enterprise and not just practical ones (328). Apart from these differences, there are important issues that both have in common, such as the idea that underdetermination is a consequence of the way scientific theories are established. Theories are sets of syntactically organized symbols in which laws, empirical hypotheses, auxiliary hypotheses, background knowledge, and so on are interwoven in a way that does not allow us to tell which of the single elements is responsible if your theory or hypothesis fails to pass an empirical test or experiment. In short, theories are always tested as a whole set and it is not even clear where this set begins or ends (Duhem 190). Thus, if your theory fails it is always possible to make some adjustments within your theoretical framework in order to save your theory. Another consequence is that it is also impossible to single out which part of the theory is related to which empirical fact, or, in other words, theories have their empirical content only as a whole.

Again, there are numerous problems arising from this thesis, such as asking what exactly should count as "empirical equivalent," what is the criterion for an adequate "alternative theory," and what does it mean that theory 1 and theory 2 contradict each other if we do not have the empirical grounds to establish this very contradiction (cf. Laudan and Leplin)?

But apart from these considerations, there is some *prima facie* plausibility that follows from the underdetermination thesis, even if it might be impossible to hold it in its strongest and most literal meaning. There is always an aspect of decision-making when we opt for one theory or another, and these decisions are neither grounded in empirical research, nor does it seem possible to establish their rationality on the basis of theoretical reasoning. If there is some truth to this, scientific realism and rationality face a serious threat. Moreover, it seems that quite frequently we can find a somewhat weaker, transient version of underdetermination as a constant companion of theoretical changes or paradigm changes within the history of science, for example in the change from Newtonian mechanics to the theory of relativity; this weaker version has been coined 'transient underdetermination' (Sklar 380f.).

Kyle Stanford, for example, contends that these transient forms of underdetermination lead us to the problem of ill-conceived alternatives, i.e. we can never be sure if we have considered all possible alternatives to our present theories, hence we cannot justify any claims that our present theories should be interpreted realistically.[6] Michael Friedman argues that due to transient underdetermination within a scientific crisis these radical changes or paradigm changes may even lead to a very strong form of incommensurability between the old and the new theory.

However, he also claims that this incommensurability is not a good sign for a holistic, purely symbolic view of scientific theories, but, on the contrary, it helps us to see a clear line between the *a priori* foundations of a science and its more empirical hypotheses.[7] If we reject Newtonian mechanics, there are some features we would not dismiss as wrong such as, for instance, calculus. Even though we might reject many of the empirical hypotheses which are formulated solely on the grounds of calculus, we would never go so far as to say that calculus is "false." We might say that it is inconvenient or not helpful – but not that it is false. Without calculus, Newtonian mechanics could not have been established, as it is a constitutional condition for Newtonian mechanics.[8] Following Immanuel Kant's understanding of constitutional conditions, conditions like calculus – without which we would not be able to construct an empirically testable theory like Newton's "Principia" – are valid *a priori* and are as such necessarily true. But how can a necessary truth become the object of a revolutionary change, as happens to be the case in a scientific crisis?

[6] "Little-noticed in the heated crossfire over empirical equivalents is the fact that even such a transient underdetermination predicament undermines our justification for believing present theories in general, so long as we have some reason to think that it is also *recurrent*: that is, that there is (probably) at least one such alternative available (and thus this transient predicament rearises) *whenever* we must decide whether to believe a given theory on the strength of a given body of evidence. [...] I am suggesting, that is, that any real threat from the problem of underdetermination comes [...] from ordinary theoretical alternatives of the garden variety scientific sort that we have nonetheless simply not yet managed to conceive in the first place. I will call this worry the *problem of unconceived alternatives.*" (Stanford 17f.; emphases in original)

[7] Cf. esp. Friedman 35f.

[8] "Newton's second law of motion (in only slightly anachronistic form) says that force equals mass times acceleration, where acceleration is the instantaneous rate of change of velocity (itself the instantaneous rate of change of position); so without the mathematics of the calculus (the mathematics of infinite limiting processes and instantaneous rates of change) this second law of motion could not even be formulated or written down, let alone function to describe empirical phenomena." (Friedman 35)

C. I. Lewis and the Pragmatic Conception of the *Apriori*

According to Lewis, the difficulty of understanding why something can be a necessary truth that enables us to develop a scientific research program while remaining at the same time a historically dependent idea that can be overcome, lies in the misconstruction of the *a priori* conditions themselves. *A priori* truths – like logical rules, mathematical formulas, and ontological agreements – are not necessary truths because they compel the mind to believe in them, but quite the opposite:

> What is *a priori* is necessary truth not because it compels the mind's acceptance, but precisely because it does not. It is given experience, brute fact, the *a posteriori* element in knowledge which the mind must accept willy-nilly. The *a priori* represents an attitude in some sense freely taken, a stipulation of the mind itself, and a stipulation which might be made in some other way if it suited our bent or need. Such truth is necessary as opposed to contingent, not as opposed to voluntary. And the *a priori* is independent of experience not because it prescribes a form which the data of sense must fit, or anticipates some pre-established harmony of experience with the mind, but precisely because it prescribes nothing to experience. That is *a priori* which is true, *no matter what*. What it anticipates is not the given, but our attitude toward it: it concerns the uncompelled initiative of mind [...], our categorical ways of acting. (169)

For Lewis, the *a priori* conditions for every scientific enterprise first of all represent our purposes, our intellectual and other interests, our needs, and our aims. The *a priori* conditions are necessary to prepare our scientific activities by preparing the field in which we can conduct our investigations. Because we cannot investigate reality as a whole, we could not even start to ask any questions at all without these *a priori* conditions which constitute the possibility of scientific research (Lewis 172f.). They allow us to categorically classify what kinds of entities we are looking for, what forms of methodological rules we should follow, and, perhaps most importantly, what we can regard as meaningful and what we should ignore. In this sense, constitutional conditions are necessary conditions.

But as soon as our interests, needs, and aims change – or our research turns out to be futile –, we may as well drop our *Aprioris*, our constitutional conditions, and look for others that serve our purposes better: "Yet it should be pointed out that such *a priori* laws are subject to abandonment if the structure which is built upon them does not succeed in simplifying our interpretation of phenomena" (174). For Lewis, the old constitutional conditions keep their status as necessary truths, they just become inconvenient, useless or misguiding.

What is important is that the constitutional conditions are not valuable for our epistemic goals because they are necessarily true, but rather they are valuable because without them we could not begin our research activities. Is necessary truth, then, a constitutional condition for constitutional conditions? If so, it is here where James becomes critically relevant.

James and the Constitution of Experimental Psychology

When James finally published his *Principles of Psychology* in 1890, he was well aware of the fact that he could not create psychology as a science out of nothing. Since the mid-1870s, he had been one of the most prominent and most frequent contributors to George Croom Roberts's *Mind* which was the forum for the discussions between empirical-minded proto-psychologists and the advocates of a transcendental, more Hegelian foundation of psychology. James was sure that it was necessary to stop all the "transcendental Ego business" (*Hegelisms* 186) – as he called it in one of his articles – in order to develop psychology as a science with a research program. In a letter to Roberts (on August 13, 1885), he wrote: "Why don't you have a special 'neo-hegelian department' in *Mind*, like the 'Children's department' or the 'Agriculture department' in our newspapers, which educated readers skip?" (*Correspondence* 62). Obviously, he did not hope for any help from philosophy.

In the chapter on the metaphysical aspects of psychology he states that a science is defined by its objects, by the entities which are the target of its research. According to James, the object of, and "first fact for," psychology is the "ongoing of thoughts," (219f.) and he gives a clear definition of what is meant by "thoughts" as the raw data of psychology (220). Therefore, following Lewis, we may say that this ontological agreement on the research object of psychology is the most prominent constitutional condition of this very science. Unfortunately, in this case we still would not know what to do with the thoughts or how to investigate them. Consequently, we have to look for something else.

In fact, James took the building blocks for the foundation of psychology from the – at that time extremely successful and broadly elaborated – field of sense-physiology. The working hypothesis on which he establishes all of his "Principles" is a correlation between physiological events and mental events. This correlation thesis is a *conditio sine qua non* for James's version of experimental psychology:

> *The immediate condition of a state of consciousness is an activity of some sort in the cerebral hemisphere.* [...] [T]he simple and radical conception dawns upon the mind that mental action may be uniformly and absolutely a function of brain-action, varying as the latter varies, and being to the brain-action as effect to cause. *This conception is the 'working hypothesis' which underlies all the 'physiological psychology' of recent years*, and it will be the working hypothesis of this book. (*Briefer Course* 12f.)

A perfect example for this working hypothesis, and how it is to be understood, is James's theory of memory:

> A simple scheme will now make the whole cause of memory plain. Let *n* be a past event; *o* its "setting" [...]; and *m* some present thought or fact which may appropriately become the occasion of its recall. Let the nerve centres, active in the thought of *m*, *n*, and *o*, be represented by M, N, and O, respectively; then the *existence* of the paths M – N and N – O will be the fact indicated by the phrase "retention of the event *n* in the memory," and the *excitement* of the brain along these paths will be the condition of the event *n*'s actual recall. The retention of *n*, it will be observed, is no mysterious storing up of an "idea" in an unconscious state. It is not a fact of the mental order at all. It is a purely physical phenomenon, a morphological feature, the presence of these "paths," namely in the finest recesses of the brain's tissue. The recall or recollection, on the other hand, is a *psycho-physical* phenomenon with both a bodily and a mental side. The bodily side is the functional excitement of the tracts and paths in question; the mental side is the conscious vision of the past occurrence, and the belief that we experienced it before. (*Principles* 616f.)

What is interesting here is not whether James's theory (which nowadays goes under the name of 'neuroplasticity') is correct. The only thing that is of interest for me here is the way in which James uses his correlation-thesis: It is not filled with empirical findings. James does not even offer a hint as to whether there is a certain psycho-physiological law that explains the correlation or what such a law could look like. His use of it is purely formal – as can well be seen from the diagram (fig. 1) that illustrates his theory (from *Principles* 617):

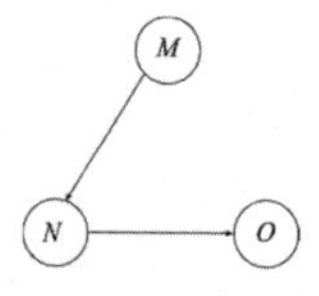

Figure 1

Obviously, this is not a naturalistic representation of the brain and its nerve centers or tissue, but a functional model at a very high level of abstraction in which the question of what could count as, for instance, the nerve center *M*, does not even arise.

Furthermore, if James's theory of memory fails, the correlation-thesis will still remain unrefuted. That is, the theory of memory is an empirical hypothesis that can be right or wrong, true or false, whereas the correlation-thesis gives a semantic framework, which in itself is neither true nor false, but gives meaning to various empirical hypotheses that can be formulated on its grounds. Therefore, what we are confronted with here is a formal constitutional condition that allows us to start a research program and that is based on a given historical scientific situation. But that is not all: According to James, the ultimate aim of psychology is to put this correlation-thesis to a test, to establish clear-cut laws explaining the correlation. However, this aim is not within the scope of the kind of psychology James is developing:

> This is no science, it is only the hope of a science. The matter of a science is with us. Something definite happens when to a certain brain-state a certain 'sciousness' corresponds. A genuine glimpse into what it is would be *the* scientific achievement, before which all past achievements would pale. But at present psychology is in the condition of physics before Galileo and the laws of motion, of chemistry before Lavoisier and the notion that mass is preserved in all reactions. The Galileo and Lavoisier of psychology will be famous men indeed when they come, as come they some day surely will, or past successes are no index to the future. When they do come, however, the necessities of the case will make them 'metaphysical.' Meanwhile the best way in which we can facilitate their advent is to understand how great is the darkness in which we grope, and never to forget that the natural-science assumptions with which we started are provisional and revisable things. (*Briefer Course* 401)

The important point is that James's idea of a fertile and successful science is that science begins with unquestioned *a priori* conditions which should be empiricized in the course of the research they initiated. At the beginning of this process of research they owe their meaning to their ability to start this process.[9] If the science in question is successful

[9] According to Richard Gale, James employs two different theories of meaning, a traditional empiricist theory, which is based on experienced sense data, and an operational one, which is teleological in nature. Both have to be combined in order to serve as a full-fledged account of meaning. In his terms the constitutional conditions only would have a pragmatic, operational meaning: they guide our actions but they lack any empirical content, that is, they owe their meaning to "operationalist or pragmatic empiricism" and not to "content empiricism" (152). Thus, it might be better to say that James's theory of meaning is not based on two

it will transform its constitutional conditions into empirical hypotheses and they will gain a glimpse of empirical meaning. At this instance, the former constitutional conditions become underdetermined, as there is a variety of possible answers to the questions our empirical hypotheses suggest. In order to choose one, we have to decide on new constitutional conditions and these, in turn, are dependent of our intellectual interests, purposes, and needs.

From this perspective, underdetermination is not an effect of the symbolic nature of theories but an important step within the scientific process: it is the result of successful research. What, then, happens to the realism/instrumentalism-debate? Within the scientific process it makes perfect sense to regard constitutional conditions as instruments and empirical hypotheses as something that aims to embrace real entities. Of course, we may fail to identify our different forms of hypotheses and we may also miss our aims with our hypotheses. But that is just the way experimental, empirical sciences are, for they develop and grow in the course of history; and in doing so, we develop, change, and transform our hypotheses and with them our needs and purposes. From outside of the scientific process there is simply no criterion to decide if something should count as 'real' or as a mere instrument. Thus, the philosophical debate as a meta-debate is utterly meaningless, for it only seemed to have a meaning as long as we have regarded science as a static set of theoretical sentences. If we choose to regard it as a dynamic process, we may have better questions to ask.

different conceptions of meaning but rather that it is evolutionary and dynamic throughout: It starts with an operational account which may be satisfied in the course of action it prepares, i.e. it gains empirical content, but this "empirical" satisfaction is only a stage within a wider range of actions; it is a preparation for new actions to follow.

Works Cited

Bonk, Thomas. *Underdetermination. An Essay on Evidence and the Limits of Natural Knowledge*. Dordrecht: Springer, 2008.

Brock, Stuart, and Edwin Mares. *Realism and Anti-Realism*. Montreal: McGill-Queen's UP, 2007.

Duhem, Pierre. *The Aim and Structure of Physical Theory*. Princeton: Princeton UP, 1954.

Friedman, Michael. *Dynamics of Reason. The 1999 Kant Lectures at Stanford University*. Stanford: CSLI Publications, 2001.

Gale, Richard M. *The Divided Self of William James*. Cambridge: Cambridge UP, 1999.

Grünbaum, Adolf. "The Falsifiability of Theories: Total or Partial? A Contemporary Evaluation of the Duhem-Quine-Thesis." *Synthese* 14.1 (1962): 17-33.

James, William. "On Some Hegelisms." *Mind* 7.26 (1882): 186-208.

—. *Psychology: Briefer Course. The Works of William James*. Vol. 14. Cambridge: CUP, 1984.

—. *The Correspondence of William James*. Ed. Ignas K. Skrupskelis and Elizabeth M. Berkeley. Vol. 6. Charlottesville: U of Virginia P, 1998.

—. *The Principles of Psychology. The Works of William James*. Vol. 8-10. Cambridge: Cambridge UP, 1981.

Laudan, Larry. "A Confutation of Convergent Realism." *Philosophy of Science* 48.1 (1981): 19-49.

Laudan, Larry, and Jarrett Leplin. "Empirical Equivalence and Underdetermination." *The Journal of Philosophy* 88.9 (1991): 449-72.

Lewis, Clarence Irving. "A Pragmatic Conception of the A Priori." *The Journal of Philosophy* 20.7 (1923): 169-177.

Lyre, Holger. "Holism and Structuralism in U(1) Gauge Theory." *Studies in History and Philosophy of Modern Physics* 35.1 (2004): 643-70.

Psillos, Stathis. "Scientific Realism and the 'Pessimistic Induction.'" *Philosophy of Science* 63 (Proceedings) (1996): S306-S314.

Putnam, Hilary. "Mathematics, Matter and Method." *Philosophical Papers* Vol. 1. Cambridge: Cambridge UP, 1975.

Quine, Willard Van Orman. "On Empirically Equivalent Systems of the World." *Erkenntnis* 9.1 (1975): 313-28.

Sklar, Lawrence. "Methodological Conservatism." *Philosophical Review* 84.3 (1975): 374-400.

Stanford, P. Kyle. *Exceeding Our Grasp. Science, History, and the Problem of Unconceived Alternatives*. Oxford: Oxford UP, 2006.

van Fraassen, Bas. *The Scientific Image*. Oxford: Oxford UP, 1980.

Worral, John. "Structural Realism: The Best of Both Worlds." *Dialectica* 43.1-2 (1989): 99-124.

List of Contributors

Michael Anacker

Michael Anacker, Associate Professor for philosophy and history of science at the Ruhr-University Bochum, studied philosophy, English literature, and history. He is author of *Interpretationale Erkenntnistheorie. Eine kritische Untersuchung im Ausgang von Quine und Davidson* (2005) and *Unterbestimmtheit und pragmatische Aprioris. Vom Tribunal der Erfahrung zum wissenschaftlichen Prozess* (2012). He has published on issues of epistemology and philosophy of science. His recent research focuses on the history of psychology, the history of verificationism, and a pragmatist model for the development of scientific theories as constitutional frameworks for research.

Andrew M. Flescher

Andrew M. Flescher is an Associate Professor of Preventive Medicine specializing in Religion, Ethics, and Medical Humanities at State University of New York, Stony Brook. There, he teaches ethics in the Medical School, co-directs and teaches in a Masters program in Medical Humanities, Compassionate Care, and Bioethics, serves on the Organ and Tissue Donor Council and on the University Hospital Ethics committee, and teaches courses in Philosophy and English. Dr. Flescher received his B.A. in Medieval and Renaissance Studies and History from Duke University (1991) and his M.A. (1995) and Ph.D. (2000) in Religious Studies from Brown University. He is the author of three books: *Heroes, Saints, and Ordinary Morality* (Georgetown University Press, 2003), *The Altruistic Species: Scientific, Philosophical, and Religious Perspectives of Human Benevolence*, co-authored with Daniel L. Worthen (Templeton Press, 2007) and most recently *Four Models of Moral Evil*, in print (Georgetown University Press). Dr. Flescher is currently one of the lead interviewers of first responders of September 11th, 2001, as a part of Dr. Benjamin Luft's World Trade Center Oral History Project.

Herwig Friedl

Herwig Friedl is Professor Emeritus of American Literature and History of Ideas at Heinrich-Heine-Universität Düsseldorf. He studied American and German Literatures and Philosophy at the University of Heidelberg and at Cornell; he was a Postdoctoral Fellow at Yale in 1973/4, a Visiting Professor at the University of New Mexico in 1984 and a Visiting Scholar at Harvard in 2002 and 2006. His book publications include a study of Henry James's aesthetic theory (1972) and – as editor – essay collections on E.L. Doctorow (1986), on Women Studies as Cultural Studies (2000), and on gender and conceptions of space (2006). His numerous essays focus on Transcendentalism, Pragmatism, Modernism (Gertrude Stein), and American thinking in an international context.

Kai-Michael Hingst
Kai-Michael Hingst graduated in law as well as in philosophy from Hamburg University. He is a lecturer for philosophy at Bucerius Law School, Hamburg, and a Hamburg based partner of White & Case LLP, an international law firm, having previously worked in Brussels, New York City and London. Kai-Michael Hingst has published books on *Perspektivismus und Pragmatismus. Ein Vergleich auf der Grundlage der Wahrheitsbegriffe von Nietzsche und James* (1998, Ph.D. thesis in philosophy) and *Die societas leonina in der europäischen Privatrechtsgeschichte* (2003, Ph.D. thesis in law) and co-edited *Pragmata. Festschrift für Klaus Oehler zum 80. Geburtstag*, 2008. He has written articles on William James, Nietzsche and O. W. Holmes as well as on various legal topics.

Heinz Ickstadt
Heinz Ickstadt, Professor Emeritus of North American Literature at the Kennedy Institute of North American Studies, Free University Berlin, since 1978; Prof. em. since 2003. Among his many publications are a history of the American novel in the twentieth century (*Der amerikanische Roman im 20. Jahrhundert: Transformation des Mimetischen* 1998), and essays on late nineteenth-century American literature and culture; on the fiction, poetry and painting of American modernism and postmodernism; on American fiction and poetry of the city as well as on the history and theory of American Studies. Some of these were collected in *Faces of Fiction: Essays on American Literature and Culture from the Jacksonian Period to Postmodernity* (2001). He also edited and co-edited several books on American literature and culture, and a bi-lingual anthology of American poetry from its beginnings to the present. He was president of the German Association of American Studies from 1990 until 1993, and president of the European Association of American Studies from 1996-2000.

Robert Main
Robert Main received his Ph.D. from Temple University in 2010. At Temple University he studied under the direction of Joseph Margolis. He is currently teaching at West Chester University of Pennsylvania.

Joseph Margolis
Joseph Margolis is currently Laura H. Carnell Professor of Philosophy at Temple University (Philadelphia, Pennsylvania). He has recently completed a trio of books on pragmatism and American philosophy in the second half of the 20th century, the third of which, *Pragmatism's Advantage*, was released 2010 by Stanford University Press. The final, fourth volume of the trio, *Pragmatism Ascendent: A Yard of Narrative, a Touch of Prophecy*, that will appear, with Stanford, in 2012 will place pragmatism within the Eurocentric tradition, with particular attention to Kant and Hegel.

Helmut Pape

Helmut Pape completed his Ph.D. in 1981 at the University of Hamburg with a thesis on the semiotics of C. S. Peirce. From 1985 to 1991 he worked as Assistant Professor at the University of Freiburg i.Br. In 1987, together with Günter Wohlfart, he founded the "Academie du Midi - Institute for Philosophy" which organized a series of 15 international philosophical symposia. From 1991 to 2000 he taught philosophy at the University of Hannover where he completed his "Habilitation" in 1994. In 2002 he became an extraordinary Professor at the University of Bamberg. From 2004 to 2005 he worked as a research fellow for practical philosophy at the FIPH (Hannover Research Institute for Philosophy). In 2003 he founded Vinosophia, which sells wines named after philosophers and their ideas. In 2006 and 2007 he worked for two terms as a professor for theoretical philosophy at the University of Darmstadt. From October 2009 to March 2010 he worked as a research fellow in the research group "Bildakt und Verkörperung" at Humboldt University. Helmut Pape has published about 30 books and 140 articles in various fields of philosophy ranging from pragmatism, philosophy of language, semiotics, philosophy of science and metaphysics to the ontology of visual properties.

Patricia Rae

Patricia Rae is Professor of English at Queen's University in Ontario. She is the author of *The Practical Muse: Pragmatist Poetics in Hulme, Pound and Stevens* (1997) and the editor of *Modernism and Mourning* (2007). She has published widely on modernist literature, in books such as *The Oxford Handbook of Elegy* (ed. Weisman) (2010), *Modernism* (ed. Liska and Eysteinsson) (2007) and *The Blackwell Companion to Modernist Literature and Culture* (ed. Norbrook and Dettmar), and in journals including *English Literary History*, *Comparative Literature*, *Twentieth Century Literature*, *Prose Studies*, *The Wallace Stevens Journal*, *Southern Review*, *The Journal of War and Culture Studies*, *Analecta Husserliana* and *English Studies in Canada*. Currently she is completing a book, *Modernist Orwell*, which explores George Orwell's relationship to literary modernism.

Joan Richardson

Joan Richardson is Professor of English, Comparative Literature, and American Studies at The Graduate Center, SUNY. Author of a two-volume critical biography of the poet Wallace Stevens, she coedited, with Frank Kermode, *Wallace Stevens: Collected Poetry and Prose* (Library of America, 1997). Her essays on Stevens, on Ralph Waldo Emerson, on Jonathan Edwards have been published in the *Wallace Stevens Journal*, in *Raritan*, and elsewhere, and essays on Alfred North Whitehead, William James, and pragmatism have appeared in the journals *Configurations* and *The Hopkins Review*. Review essays have appeared in *Bookforum* and other journals. Her study *A Natural History of Pragmatism: The Fact of Feeling from Jonathan Edwards to Gertrude Stein* was published by Cambridge University Press in 2007, and was nominated for the 2011 Grawemeyer Award in Religion. She is currently at work on another volume for Cambridge, *Pragmatism and American Culture* as well as a book-length study, *The Return of the Repressed: Stanley Cavell and Ralph*

Waldo Emerson. Joan Richardson has been the recipient of several awards and fellowships including a Woodrow Wilson Fellowship and a Senior Fellowship from the National Endowment for the Humanities. Her work reflects an abiding interest in the way that philosophy, natural history, and science intersect with literature.

Susanne Rohr
Susanne Rohr is Professor of American Studies at Hamburg University, Germany. She received her academic education at the John F. Kennedy Institute of the Free University Berlin and Cornell University, Ithaca, NY. From 1986-1994 Susanne Rohr was a member of the academic faculty at Stanford University, Study Center Berlin. As of October 2006 Susanne Rohr is full professor of American literature and culture and chair of American Studies at Hamburg University. She is the author of *Comedy – Avant-Garde – Scandal: Remembering the Holocaust after the End of History*, 2010 (together with Andrew S. Gross); *Die Wahrheit der Täuschung: Wirklichkeitskonstitution im amerikanischen Roman 1889-1989*, 2004 [True Deception: Reality Constitution in the American Novel 1889-1989]; and *Über die Schönheit des Findens. Die Binnenstruktur menschlichen Verstehens nach Charles S. Peirce: Abduktionslogik und Kreativität,* 1993. [On the Beauty of Discovery. The Internal Structure of Human Understanding According to Charles S. Peirce: Creativity and Logic of Abduction]. Susanne Rohr has also published numerous essays in the fields of literary and cultural theory, semiotics, American pragmatism, epistemology, and on a broad range of topics in American literature of the 19th and 20th centuries.

Georg Schiller
Georg Schiller is Associate Professor of American Studies at Heinrich Heine University in Düsseldorf. He studied Philosophy and American Literature at Düsseldorf University and at Duke University, North Carolina. His dissertation situates Gertrude Stein's aesthetic rendering of meaning-making processes in a pragmatist context. It was published as *Symbolische Erfahrung und Sprache im Werk von Gertrude Stein* [Symbolic Experience and Language in the Work of Gertrude Stein] in 1996. Schiller's approach to Native American cultures is also heavily indebted to American pragmatism, to William James and John Dewey. So far, his papers in this field tend to discuss how Native American aesthetics may be interpreted from a non-native perspective. Other publications focus mainly on body matters and deal with childbirth in public places, shifting body boundaries, and disability (i.e. the body as interface).

Ulf Schulenberg
Ulf Schulenberg is a Visiting Chair of American Studies at the University of Eichstätt-Ingolstadt (Germany). Before that he was a Visiting Professor at the John-F.-Kennedy-Institute for North American Studies (Free University of Berlin). He received his doctorate from the University of Bremen (Germany), where he also wrote his postdoctoral thesis ("Habilitation"). He was a visiting scholar at Cornell University and at the New School for Social Research (Graduate Faculty, Dept. of

Philosophy). His publications include *Zwischen Realismus und Avantgarde: Drei Paradigmen für die Aporien des Entweder-Oder* (2000), *Lovers and Knowers: Moments of the American Cultural Left* (2007), and *Americanization-Globalization-Education* (co-editor, 2003). His current book project, *Romantic Redescribers: Pragmatism, Romanticism, and the Idea of a Poeticized Culture*, discusses the question of a romanticized pragmatism.

Miriam Strube
Miriam Strube is Professor of American Studies at Paderborn University, Germany. She has studied English, American Studies and philosophy at Bochum University and New York University. As part of her Ph.D. studies, she had a scholarship for Columbia University and was a Fulbright scholar in Washington D.C. She is author of *Subjekte des Begehrens: Zur sexuellen Selbstbestimmung der Frau in Literatur, Musik und visueller Kultur* (2009) and has published articles on Gender Studies, feminist philosophy, and on popular culture. She is also editing a textbook on American Philosophy (Lit Verlag). For her book project, *Making Sense of the U.S.A.: Pragmatist Philosophy and Modernist Culture,* she currently is a visiting scholar at Harvard University.

Trygve Throntveit
Trygve Throntveit is lecturer and Assistant Director of Undergraduate Studies in the Department of History at Harvard University, where he received his PhD in 2008. He is the author of several articles and book chapters on the intellectual, cultural, and political history of the United States and its relations with the wider world in the late nineteenth and twentieth centuries. He is currently working on a short book on James's ethics and politics, entitled *William James's Ethical Republic: A Moral and Political Study*; as well as a longer book on the pragmatist origins and popular reception of Woodrow Wilson's domestic and foreign policies, entitled *Power without Victory: Woodrow Wilson and the American Internationalist Experiment*.